P9-DOH-536

Suzy Gershman's

....

BORN TO SHOP

ITALY

....

*The Ultimate Guide for
Travelers Who Love to Shop*

11th Edition

WILEY
Wiley Publishing, Inc.

For Marina, with thanks for a million years of girl talk in English and Italian, and in memory of Egon von Furstenberg, my first prince.

Published by:

Wiley Publishing, Inc.
111 River St.
Hoboken, NJ 07030-5774

Copyright © 2006 Wiley Publishing, Inc., Hoboken, New Jersey. All rights reserved. No part of this publication may be reproduced, stored in a retrieval system or transmitted in any form or by any means, electronic, mechanical, photocopying, recording, scanning or otherwise, except as permitted under Sections 107 or 108 of the 1976 United States Copyright Act, without either the prior written permission of the Publisher, or authorization through payment of the appropriate per-copy fee to the Copyright Clearance Center, 222 Rosewood Drive, Danvers, MA 01923, 978/750-8400, fax 978/646-8600. Requests to the Publisher for permission should be addressed to the Legal Department, Wiley Publishing, Inc., 10475 Crosspoint Blvd., Indianapolis, IN 46256, 317/572-3447, fax 317/572-4355, or online at http://www.wiley.com/go/permissions.

Wiley and the Wiley Publishing logo are trademarks or registered trademarks of John Wiley & Sons, Inc. and/or its affiliates. Frommer's is a trademark or registered trademark of Arthur Frommer. Used under license. All other trademarks are the property of their respective owners. Wiley Publishing, Inc. is not associated with any product or vendor mentioned in this book.

ISBN-13: 978-0-7645-9890-6
ISBN-10: 0-7645-9890-2

Editor: Michael Kelly
Production Editors: Suzanna R. Thompson, Jana M. Stefanciosa
Cartographer: Tim Lohnes
Photo Editor: Richard Fox
Production by Wiley Indianapolis Composition Services

For information on our other products and services or to obtain technical support, please contact our Customer Care Department within the U.S. at 800/762-2974, outside the U.S. at 317/572-3993 or fax 317/572-4002.

Wiley also publishes its books in a variety of electronic formats. Some content that appears in print may not be available in electronic formats.

Manufactured in the United States of America

5   4   3   2

CONTENTS

MAP LIST

Although every effort has been made to ensure the accuracy of this book, please keep in mind that prices—and policies—change. For simplicity's sake, prices quoted in this book have been converted to dollars at the rate of 1€ = $1.25. For Italians, the euro traded in at 1€ to 1,936 lire. Some prices on tags or in stores are still written in lire for the convenience of local shoppers. No prices in this book are quoted in lire. The dollar has fallen significantly since our research—in fact, it's fallen since yesterday. Hold tight.

ABOUT THE AUTHORS

Suzy Gershman is a journalist, author, and global-shopping goddess who has worked in the fashion and fiber industry for more than 25 years. Her essays on retailing have been used by the Harvard School of Business; her reportage on travel and retail has appeared in *Travel + Leisure, Travel Holiday, Travel Weekly,* and most of the major women's magazines. She is translated into French for Condé Nast's *Air France Madame* magazine. The *Born to Shop* series, now over 22 years old, is translated into eight languages.

Gershman is also the author of *C'est La Vie* (Viking and Penguin Paperback), the story of her first year as a widow living in Paris. She divides her time between an apartment on the rue du Faubourg Saint-Honoré (Paris's main shopping street), a small house in Provence, and the airport.

Jenny McCormick is a graduate student and part-time Born to Shop editorial assistant who reports on young women's interests, fashions, and trends. She carries an expensive handbag.

Aaron James is a singer-songwriter who lives and sings in L.A.; he is also a contributing editor for Born to Shop.

TO START WITH

Now that I live in Paris, I am a little more jaded about travel to neighboring Italy—the things that once seemed such good buys are now being reevaluated, either because prices have changed with the arrival of the euro, the fall of the dollar, or the way the world is whirling—or simply because I now live in Europe and have more access to this kind of merchandise, so it doesn't seem so special.

For this reason—and many others—I have two full-time Americans helping me out to give you a different perspective—as well as their version of reality, as seen from the young person's point of view. Okay, okay, they are family; this is Italy—we believe in nepotism. Besides, did I know what Golas were? Not before Aaron and Jenny explained. (See "Sneakers" on p. 61.)

This book has always been different from other titles in the series, because Italy has so many primary shopping cities. This edition is packed with even more destinations—with luck, someday we'll go to two books and even more details. I feel like more and more people are interested in driving around, in renting a summer home, and maybe even in purchasing a second or retirement home.

The fall of the dollar has made me especially sensitive to prices. Besides, with prices as high as they are, I think more and more people are interested in outlets and local sources, which tend to be out of major cities. Besides, I found Florence so filled with tourists (and it wasn't even "in-season") that I can't imagine anyone thinking this would be fun.

I hope some of my extra side trips have inspired you to reach out past the big cities and to slow down, smell the slow food, and buy a little olive oil. There are more factory outlets in this edition, and there's also more information about arranging for someone to drive you into the countryside if you do not want to drive yourself.

In order to make this book as accurate, yet as up to date and fresh as possible, I did a lot of driving around Italy and leaned on many friends, Italian and American-Italian. These pages, and my heart, are totally indebted to Logan Bentley (as always), Maria Teresa Berdonolini, and Marina Maher. At MMC, there was Jerry in the mailroom to constantly keep me on course, I thank him and send him lots of kisses and pizza.

Special thanks to Karen Preston and the guys at Leading Hotels of the World in New York who helped me organize most of my stays. I would also like to thank the general managers and the entire front desk team at the various Baglioni hotels, who helped me with everything from insider information to special Born to Shop rates and map printouts to help me on my way.

Chapter One

....

THE BEST OF ITALY IN AN INSTANT

Italy has more style per square mile than you can shake a *formaggio* at, especially in the northern regions. The south has more *limoncello,* that delectable lemon vodka brew that makes me tipsy after one thimbleful . . . so wherever your travels take you, I know you'll find a lot to buy and a lot more to enjoy. You'll even find a few bargains to be had. If you're on a cruise with little time to shop, you'll still find specialty items to put a smile on your face—and your wallet. Welcome ashore, mates.

If you're in a hurry, I've collected some of the highlights of the whole country, so when you stop by these places, you can worship and shop and feel like you've indulged. By no means is this list comprehensive; it will take years for me to perfect it, so bear with me while I shop, shop, shop.

The Best Store in Italy

10 CORSO COMO
Corso Como 10, Milan.

No, that's not a typo; the store's name is its address.

There's more about this store in chapter 8, but this bazaar is a magic act created by one of Italy's most famous fashion editors and stylists who turned to retail and hasn't looked back.

The store is well bought, but for people who shop a lot, there are no surprises in terms of merchandise. What's yummy is the way it's laid out and presented and served on your platter. You can gawk and enjoy and not buy a thing, but don't

1

miss it. Note the cafe (speaking of served on a platter), the furniture in the garden, the upstairs bookstore, as well as their own outlet store, around the corner.

THE RUNNER-UP STORE IN ITALY

VENETIA STVDIVM, VENICE
Multiple branches.

Fortuny-inspired pleated silks made into wraps, bags, tassels, and treasures . . . a wonderland of fairy tales and dreams in colors that will make you swoon. Two shops in Venice and one in London (go figure).

The Best Mass-Market Store in Italy

OVIESSE
Stores all over Italy.

Maybe it's my large heart that tells you this, perhaps my large bottom—never have I had so much fun in a series of cheapie clothing stores than when I discovered that the fashion-at-a-price chain, Oviesse, carries clothing up to size 52. While some cities have better stores, don't pass up an opportunity to shop here for men's, women's, and kids clothes and accessories.

The Best Grand-Scale Shopping City

Milan may not be adorable or overwhelmingly charming or flashy, but the shopping is divine. Milan offers high-quality goods in many different price ranges. Milan has excellent alternative retail—street markets, jobbers who sell discounted designer clothing, and more—all of which help you to make do with less. Less is always more, as mother used to say.

The Best Small Shopping City

Italy is filled with tiny cities devoted to craftspeople and artists, where shopping has been elevated to an art form. But the best of them is the city of **Deruta,** about an hour from Rome in Umbria, where every store sells hand-painted faience.

The Best Port City for a Quick Spree

Venice is not included on every Mediterranean cruise, but if you can get here, even if only for 1 day, do—it is magic. The shopping isn't bad either.

The Best Factory Town, North

Perhaps because **Como** is ever so much more than a factory town, it wins my vote for the best factory town in Italy. It's about 30 minutes from Milan by train, it's gorgeous, it's upscale, it's got a lake, it's got Switzerland nearby, and it's got silk factories galore. Prices are laughably low on the biggest names in designer fashion fabrics, including French names. Go home with fabric by the yard or ties, scarves, and shawls for at least half their regular retail price. The best factory in town? Ratti, on the Via Cernobbio.

FoxTown, one of the many outlet malls selling designer things at a discount, is located across the Swiss border between Como and Lugano (see chapter 8). Remember though that Switzerland does not use euros, and prices tend to be high.

The Best Factory Area, South

The area between Florence and the sea is filled with factories, whether you go south, toward Arezzo and the Prada outlet, or north, toward Lucca and the Pratesi outlet. Florence is so touristy—and expensive—that you may well want to take in all of Tuscany and enjoy your drive under the Tuscan sun with punctuation marks at various factories and outlet stores. Many are even in real factories, not in fancy malls.

The Best Outlet Mall

THE MALL
Via Europa 8, Reggello, Firenze.

The Mall! We've all seen some outlet malls in our time but, possibly, nothing like this one—a modern architectural structure worthy of Madison Avenue but located a half-hour from Florence. With good reason, this destination is the second-most-popular sightseeing locale in the Florence area, coming in right after the Uffizi. It's home to the best collection of big-name outlets in all of Europe. The Mall has stores representing every big name in design except Viktor & Rolf. Yohji? Did someone whisper Yohji? My all-time favorite, at a real price . . . quick, get me on a train.

THE BEST UP-AND-COMING OUTLET MALL

FIDENZA VILLAGE
Via San Michele Campagna, Fidenza.

Fidenza! Fidenza Village is expanding, and new contenders are opening up daily, but how can you not love a mall that is a village inspired by Verdi's operas? All that's lacking are elephants and music blaring from a loudspeaker system. "Grand March" from *Aida* makes excellent shopping music!

This mall is small, although stage two will be open just about as this book goes to press. What the mall lacks in sprawl it makes up for in location, good eats, and intimacy. There are enough stores for you to have fun, but not so many as to overwhelm you. Fidenza has some big names, but the orientation is on everyday needs.

Note: This mall is an hour's drive north of Bologna and 1½ hours south of Milan. Because it is open on Sundays—not much else in this area is—shop on Sundays, but leave time for the various food stores in the area. In fact, get to those first, and then hit the mall. Parma is also nearby, and that means a lot more than cheese.

The Best Airport Shopping

Rome's Leonardo da Vinci International Airport is virtually a shopping mall, with all major designers represented. Furthermore, a guide to its shops, which lists prices, is made available once a year. Use it to comparison shop. Not everything is a bargain, but you'll have a great time finding out which items are well priced.

The Best Sales

FENDI
Via Fontanella di Borghese 57, Rome.

You haven't lived until you've wandered into the Fendi store in Rome at sale time (twice a year, Jan and July). Mounds of goodies (some of them a few seasons old) sell at a fraction of their regular price. Affordable luxury goods!

While Fendi sales are good at all Fendi shops, the best sale is in this new Rome store. From a design perspective, it is the most fun-to-look-at shop in the Spanish Steps luxury shopping district; to get a sale and an eyeful of glamour at one time is indeed to see the face of bliss.

The Best Department Store

LA RINASCENTE
Piazza del Duomo, Milan.

In response to competition, La Rinascente has redone its image in recent years, and a giant makeover is in the works. The store is a lot like an American department store and may not impress you at first. But wait till you experience its details, where its greatness lies. The store offers non-Italian-passport holders a flat 10% discount on health, beauty, and makeup treatments on the first floor. And there's a tax-free office, a travel agency, a hair salon, and a full-service bank. Its cafe overlooks the Duomo and will drench you with magic and memories.

The Best Historical Shopping Experience

ANTICO SETIFICIO FIORENTINO
Via Bartolini 4, Florence.

You will step back in time when you enter this 18th-century silk factory that was renovated by the Pucci family. It still produces damasks, silks, and cottons on looms that have hummed for hundreds of years.

The Best Street Market

SAN AGOSTINO MARKET
Viale Papiniano, Milan.

Fun? It just doesn't get much better than this! On Tuesday and Saturday, you can enjoy this fabulous street market, which sells fruits and vegetables in one part and designer goods in the other. Arrange your visit to Milan so that you're in town for one of the market days!

The Best Weekly Market (Runner-Up to Best Street Market)

SIENA
In my life, I have been to a fair number of markets in a large number of cities all over the world. When I say this Wednesday market is one of the best, I mean it. It helps if the sky is blue, the sun is shining, the temperature is not too high, and the crowds not too great—but any way you slice it, this is a market for locals, filled to overflowing with everything from shoes to tractors. Thoughtfully organized by category of goods—with foodstuffs to one side and dry goods on the other—this market takes up a half-moon area at the top of town. Sometimes you find factory close-outs with low prices on brand-name goods. But you go for the glory, not the shoes.

The Best Museum Shop

THE VATICAN
Vatican City, Rome.

No cheap pope scopes, but beautiful reproductions of precious treasures, puzzles of the Sistine Chapel ceiling, and more.

The Best Free Postcards

HOTEL EDEN
Via Ludovisi 49, Rome.

Postcards from Il Papiro created in medieval style with a bright blue background, lots of gold stars, flowing borders, detailed insets, and design-school whoop-de-do.

THE RUNNER-UP FREE POSTCARDS

LISA CORTI
Via Conchetta 6, Milan; Via de' Bardi 58, Florence.

This artist is known for her splash of vibrant colors on cotton. Yes, the goods are made in India, but the feel is true south-of-Italy. She gives away free postcards created from several of her prints.

The Best Gifts for $10 or Less

- Designer pasta in fashion colors. Find it in all sorts of brand names, in all Italian cities in grocery stores, *entocas* (wine/food shops), and TTs (tourist traps); 5€ to 8€ ($6–$10) a package. For something extra, team that bag or box of pasta with a wooden pasta measuring spoon.
- Regional pasta. Barilla, which is the largest maker of pasta in Italy, creates "designs" for specific markets. In Venice, I buy Casarecce, a style only available there. Go figure. For less than a couple of bucks, I look like a genius to a foodie.
- Caldo Caldo coffee. Or coffee with grappa, or hot chocolate, all in a "magic" cup that heats itself when you employ

(or deploy) the push-in bottom; about a dollar a cup. *Note:* The best source for these hard-to-find items is the Milan Centrale train station grocery store.

- Chocolate postcards. I wouldn't try mailing these, but they are darn cute gifties. Caffarel, a mass maker of chocolates, does a series of postcards that pictures famous historical sites in what's called Italy's Treasures Collection. I found a selection of "cards" representing five different cities in the main Milan train station.

- Soap. A package of "Weekend Soap" from Santa Maria Novella consists of three bars of soap, one each for Friday, Saturday, and Sunday. It's available at Farmacia Santa Maria Novella stores in Florence and Rome and costs 8€ ($10). The soap maker Rancé has a freestanding store in Rome at Piazza Navona. If Rancé sounds French, the firm started in France 100 years ago but is now Italian, although it specializes in Marseille-process soaps. You can also buy Italian soaps in grocery stores or at any of the *erboristas* (herbalists).

- Limoncello liquor. Sold readily in southern Italy, below Florence, and in most supermarkets and airports, this is a wonderful souvenir. It's like lemon vodka with a pucker; serve chilled.

Jenny's Five Best Buys in Italy

1. Black squid-ink pasta (2.80€/$3.50) at Free Shop, Milan Centrale train station. See p. 219.
2. Caldo Caldo "Magic Coffee" (.95€/$1.20) at Free Shop, Milan Centrale train station. See p. 219.
3. Necklace and other jewelry (15€–38€/$18–$47) at Kalos, Milan. See p. 230.
4. Venetian glass necklace (5.70€/$7.10) throughout Venice. See chapter 7.
5. Pratesi beachwear and shoes (18€–48€/$23–$60) at Pratesi Factory Outlet, in Pistoia near Florence. See p. 155.

Aaron's Five Best Buys in Italy

1. Fedora hat (10€/$13) off the street in Florence. See chapter 6.
2. H&M (14€/$18) and Diesel (38€/$47) jeans at Mercato delle Cascine, Florence. See p. 140.
3. Prada suit (190€/$237) at Space Outlet (the Prada outlet store), near Florence. See p. 145.
4. Ruggeri notebooks (less than 10€/$12) at Free Shop, Milan Centrale train station. See p. 219.
5. Gola sneakers (28€/$35) at Mercato delle Cascine, Florence. See p. 140.

- LUSH gifties. Yes, LUSH is a British firm famous for its bath and beauty products, and yes, there are now nearly 50 LUSH stores in the U.S. and Canada, but the Italian LUSH products are made with local ingredients, so you can buy limoncello soap or shampoo. LUSH stores are all over Italy, often in mainstream tourist areas.
- Cardinal's socks. Sold only in Rome, at about 8€ ($10) a pair. Fine cotton knits; they come only in red. Of course.
- Milk-frothing machine. This battery-operated job looks like a small wand and makes the milk in your cappuccino stand up and smile. I found the old-fashioned ones in a market in Rome for 6€ ($7.80) and in an appliance store in Florence for 8€ ($10), and I found a new and well-designed one in Siena for 13€ ($16).

The Best Extravagant Gifts

- Mantero scarf, in the shawl size. Printed with so many screens of gorgeous color, you will weep for its beauty and finesse. Come to think of it, anything from Mantero will tickle any extravagance bone. Buy yours at the outlet store in Como for savings.

- Important art glass. Venice or Murano.
- Leather handbag. Nothing says you care more than a Birkin-style handbag made in pebble leather. You can get a good-quality bag in any major Italian city for less than 240€ ($300).
- Etro paisleys. Silk or cashmere, in all Etro stores, in most major cities. But then, maybe you can find them at the Etro outlet in beautiful, downtown Milano.

Maria Teresa's Three Best Finds in Italy

Maria Teresa is my secret spy in Italy; she runs Tuscany by Tuscans tour service; I rely on her for news and finds. I often book her tours. It seemed only fair that she should have her own place to tell you about her Tuscan favorites.

BAGNI VOLPI NOEMI
Viale Europa 89, Castelguidi (Pistoia).

This bed linen firm has been in operation since 1925 and is competitive with big-name brands that you have heard about. Fine bed linen, bathrobes, elegant tablecloths—the best quality fabrics. You will pay about 80€ ($100) per sheet here.

BRACCIALINI ACCESSORIES & BAGS
Corso Matteotti 54, Montecatini; Terme and Via Della Vigna Nuova 30r, Florence.

Colorful handbags and styled accessories that are produced near Florence and are so popular that you can often find copies of their distinctive designs in street markets.

GREVI MODE
Via della Spada 11, Florence.

Hat makers established in 1875 making the finest quality hats with the finest materials; this is the only Italian company remaining in the business that uses Italian product and methods.

Chapter Two

....

DETAILS

WELCOME TO ITALY

....

I'm not sure when you were last in Italy, but my heavens, *Madonna mia,* have things changed. Not just the fact that Italy uses euros (€), but also while trying to merge into the whole of Europe—and maybe taking some hints from the U.S.— Italy has all sorts of new ideas.

Get this for a shocker: You can no longer smoke in a public place! That's right; no one smokes inside bars or restaurants.

Also, stores are open on Sundays now, public landmarks have sponsors to help pay for the upkeep, and factory stores and malls are popping up everywhere.

Thank heavens locals aren't on the Atkins Diet, or things would be downright depressing. As it is, you will merely smile at the changes and keep on shopping, looking for bargains and laughing all the way to the gelati.

When lire were converted into euros, the official exchange rate was essentially two to one, but the talk of the town is that prices are now so high, that things cost in euros what they cost in lire, so prices are perceived as being twice as high. The newspapers report that British tourism to Italy dropped 37% in 2004 because of the prices. To survive, people are looking for alternate methods of shopping, so a lot of this book is devoted to three-star hotels and factory-outlet malls. When in Rome . . .

Made in Italy (& Beyond)

Seems like only yesterday—or at least last year—that the Italians suddenly looked up and saw what the Chinese were doing to them in terms of production in textiles, electronics, and more. They have reacted with an incredible marketing plan that now filters into every aspect of shopping in Italy.

Accepting that they can't beat the Chinese manufacturers on price, Italians have banded together to form and promote an organization called "Made in Italy." They are selling the craftsmanship as a marketing tool to make you stop and reconsider what you are buying.

As you shop, you will see much merchandise tagged "made in Italy" or "member made in Italy." To support the marketing plan, a dozen new guidebooks promote artisans and the old-fashioned way of making things. When in Rome . . .

Meanwhile, the French are making a contribution to Italian style. French designers have, for years, produced their clothing in Italy. Karl Lagerfeld (a German Frenchman at that) has designed Fendi furs for decades. Now the French are seriously getting into an Italian mood—French architect cum designer Philippe Starck has created a new-age lion for the gates of Venice; Christian Lacroix has taken over designing Pucci.

Sephora—the French makeup and beauty supermarket now international in scope—has a huge store in the Rome train station and others all over Italy. Sofitel has opened a hotel on a private island in Venice that will surely make you sigh *ooh la la*. In fact, Sofitel has taken several old hotels and turned them around, offering a lot of bang for the euro.

But then, so do many Italian firms. In fact, the new hotels in Italy alone are reason enough to check it out, or just check in and sigh. At last you can afford to give Bulgari your business, if only to spend the night in their new Milan hotel.

The Italian ability to set aside the traditional and adapt to the new is mind-boggling. The new single-currency dynamic and a fluidity of design borders makes shopping a little more expensive than in past years, but more fun than ever.

Giorgio Armani is making chocolates while Gucci is doing custom wares. Bulgari isn't the only luxury-goods firm in the hotel business; there's also Ferragamo. Benetton owns the Autogrill, a series of fast-food restaurants on the highways, but they, too, have now gone into hotels—and not auto-route hotels, but fancy-shmancy hotels. Shopping, seeing, and sleeping in Italy has never been so rewarding.

Italian Contrasts

An Italian wedding ring company has been running an advertisement for platinum wedding bands in all the fashion magazines. The selling image is a bride in traditional white gown and veil, holding not a bouquet of flowers but a bouncy little infant—the latest in wedding accessories. Is this old-fashioned country a place of contrasts or what?

As you shop in Italy, you can appreciate views of hills as old as the ages; peeling palazzi with tile roofs, handmade wrought-iron gates, and window grills; masterful antiques; and then—whammo!—smack in the middle of it all, tables perched precariously on bent triangles, clothes in medieval colors, shoes and bags in styles you've never thought of, and a pride of craftsmanship in absolutely everything.

At the same time, in today's Italy, flea markets and antiques fairs are bigger than ever, and Italians have taken seriously to resale and to outlet shopping—several new outlets and even outlet malls have opened recently.

And most shocking, even though the Italian border hasn't moved, many Italians are going to stores and spas in Slovenia and Croatia. Dubrovnik is just a boat ride away. In fact, Croatia is the newest link to the eastern Riviera. *Venni, venn, ya'll.* I came, I saw, I shopped; now it's your turn.

GETTING THERE

From the U.S.

You'll get the best fares for direct flights from the U.S. to Italy if you latch on to a new gate or promotional rate—or even the launch of a code share (alliances among airlines that expand route options; the increased competition can sometimes lead to lower fares)—so watch local papers closely.

It may even pay to make a domestic hop to a nearby city if direct flights to Italy have just begun to be offered from there. Ask your travel agent. You can always go via New York; explore all options if you are looking for a price break.

You may also want to remember that Italians still have a tendency to declare a strike—or even threaten a strike—every time someone gets PMS. Backup plans (and planes) are a good idea; also, stay away from those carriers that are more prone to strikes than others. Strikes are usually posted in the *International Herald Tribune*. The good thing about Italian strikes is that they are well announced and usually have an on- and off-again pattern so that the world isn't totally crippled.

Alitalia, the Italian national carrier (© 800/223-5730; www.alitalia.com), has various flights and connections from the U.S. to Italy, but doesn't play by the same promotional rules as U.S. carriers. They are also being denationalized in the new century, so they may get competitive in new ways.

I usually fly **Delta Air Lines** (© 800/221-1212; www.delta. com), partly because I can fly into Milan and out of Rome without much ado. Delta also has a great nonstop from New York to Nice, which is only 369km (229 miles) from Milan—a super way to get into Italy. Delta also has a code-share program with Alitalia, so I can get miles and use Alitalia for local connections as needed. Seamless, *uomo,* seamless.

Delta has code shares with several other airlines, which allows me to use Paris as a hub (traveling onward with Air France). Also note that Delta is one of the airlines that did away with regular first class and instead installed something called

Tips for Finding the Best Deals

- Book online. Or at least check it out. Look at regular carriers as well as brokers for discount tickets. I was amazed (maybe because I am unsophisticated in these things) that many airlines have two different sites with different kinds of deals. So, if you check out alitaliausa.com, you get deals created just for the American market. There's another site (in another language) for other deals.
- Book off season. Off-season travel always offers better value; sometimes packages do, too. Use up your miles, buy into promotional rates, and check out websites that offer deals. Consider packages, which may offer the best prices.
- Book specialty tours that include everything and are prepaid in dollars. The way the dollar is going, you don't want any nasty surprises or escalating costs. If the dollar goes back to its previously strong position, buy Italy.

Business First, which is much more first class at a business-class price than any other business-class seat on other airlines. If value is related to your seat size, and you splurge on business-class or upgrade travel, this is the way to go.

American Airlines (© 800/433-7300; www.aa.com) has Chicago–Milan and New York–Rome service, and American still has three classes of service.

From London & Continental Europe

Low-cost airlines have made a huge dent in the Italian tourism business, especially flights from the United Kingdom. **British Airways** (© 0870/850-9850; www.britishairways.com), **Air France** (© 0870/142-4343; www.airfrance.com), and **Alitalia** (© 0870/544-8259; www.alitalia.co.uk) can sometimes get so annoyed at these discounters that they go to war with low, low fares. The big names tend to serve the well-known airports, and the lower-priced airlines use less-popular airports—but in Italy that may work just great. Don't rule out a big-name carrier as too expensive before checking all possibilities. Some low-cost carriers are perceived as offering value but don't really do so.

Note: Low-cost airlines are more likely to go out of business or merge with others, so I can't promise these will be around when you are ready to travel.

ITALIAN LOW-COST CARRIERS

Check out **Volare** (© 070/460-3397; www.volareweb.com), an Italian airline that has some intra-Italian flights. When they have promotional deals, one way of a round-trip ticket can cost as little as 1€ ($1.30), with a 3€ ($3.90) supplement for security. Because this airline is changing a lot as it defines itself, check in online: www.volareweb.com.

Also look at Wind Jet (© 899/809-060; www.volawindjet.it), which serves Catania, Palermo, Rome, Milan, Venice, and several cities within Europe. Before you book to Monaco, note that *Monaco* is *Munich* in Italian, not the home of Monte Carlo.

EURO BRANDS/LOW-COST CARRIERS

Sometimes you'll save money by flying into a European city and getting a low-cost flight from there. Some thoughts:

- Air Berlin (www.airberlin.com) flies to Milan, Rome, and Naples from cities throughout Germany (not just Berlin), as well as London, Vienna, Zurich, and Budapest.
- RyanAir (www.ryanair.com) flies to Milan, Genoa, Florence, Venice, Bologna, and Rome from cities throughout Europe.
- Transavia (www.transavia.com) occasionally has fares from Amsterdam to Genoa for 50 bucks each way in a special promotional deal.
- SNBrussels Airlines (www.flySN.it) flies to six cities in Italy from Brussels, which happens to be an easy city to reach from the U.S.

Ask about new destinations or airport changes. Low-cost carriers are now even using Rome's second airport, Ciompi.

Low-Cost Trains

There's no such thing as a low-cost train. Still, there are train passes that give you a break or specialty cards related to your age that may offer discounts. Sometimes it pays to go directly to the train websites and order from there, using your hotel address for a local address and printing out your own tickets. Try www.trenitalia.com to get into the Italian rail system.

Online Consolidators

I booked some of my last research trip with www.expedia.it. I can't say it was hard, but it was time-consuming as I cross-checked various sites and deals and hotels, often calling hotels after I saw an offer online to verify the price or explore the deal. In one case, the assistant general manager of a hotel told me that Expedia had a block of rooms, and he couldn't give me a press rate that was as good as what Expedia was offering. If you prefer to work in English, try www.expedia.com.

Hidden Travel Values

If you are coming from another European country via train, try combining your U.S.-bought train passes. A complete Eurailpass may be a wasted value, especially if you are just visiting two countries (say, France and Italy). Nowadays there are so many different types of rail passes that it pays to figure out which kind is best for you.

If you are flying between connecting European cities, price your tickets carefully. I needed to go to Rome and priced the airfare from Zurich and from Nice and found Nice offered me a $500 savings. If I had had the Swissair pass program, it would have been less money, but since I didn't, I could just call my travel agent and pray. French prayers were answered.

For Americans, the various air-pass systems offered by different carriers can be, if not a lifesaver, surely a fare saver. But they do have restrictions and must be bought in the U.S. before you depart.

Also note, the city of Nice (France) is only 369km (229 miles) from Milan. If you are a Delta customer, as I am, you can fly into Italy through Nice, Milan, or Rome—the Nice International Airport is only about an hour's drive from the Italian border. If you are driving around northern Italy, or combining the two Rivieras (Italian and French), this is even better—as you're in Torino in no time at all. To depart from Italy through Nice, you can take the train from Milan to Nice, or even from Venice to Nice (this is an overnight journey and saves on a hotel room), or you can hop on the 1-hour flight.

SPECIALTY SHOPPING TOURS

A couple of companies that offer trips to various Euro cities, with airfare, hotel, and an antiques dealer to help you, include Antiques Abroad Ltd. (✆ 704/332-5577; www.antiqueslimited. com), which offers Italian antiques shopping packages for about $2,500; their expert goes with you to help with shipping and shopping, and you are with like-minded people who are intent on serious shopping.

I now lead a Hidden Italy Born to Shop tour each year with Women's Travel Club (✆ 800/480-4448; www.womenstravel club.com).

GETTING AROUND IN ITALY

By Plane

Most intra-European flights are outrageously expensive. However, as European skies deregulate, new local services are popping up. There are now air wars over business travelers flying between Rome and Milan, a 20-minute flight. **Alitalia** flies this corridor, of course, but so do some upstarts, and now **Lufthansa** is in the action by going into partnership with **Air One** (www.fly airone.it). Check with your travel agent.

Note that prices may vary based on the time of day. Usually, flights between 11am and 3pm are 40% cheaper than early-morning and late-afternoon flights. Alitalia also has a deal where if you buy your tickets 7 days in advance you get a 40% discount; 14 days, 50%; and 21 days, 55% off. Not bad.

By Train

I just can't imagine driving around Italy when you can take a train to the big cities and then rent a car to explore the countryside for a day or two. While train fares from city to city are not expensive (especially in second class), your best buy is an Italian Rail Pass, which you can buy from a travel agent, from Rail Europe in the U.S., or online (© **800/361-RAIL** or 888/382-7245; www.raileurope.com).

This pass, which comes in a variety of flavors, provides travel for a certain number of days, and its price depends on many factors, including the class you choose and the number of days you actually want to travel within a given 2-month period. Kids can buy passes for those ages 12 to 26, which offer second-class travel at a low rate.

On my first trips to Italy, I purchased first-class passes; thereafter, I switched to second class. I usually pay about $150 for a 5-day second-class pass, and it's good for unlimited travel on all trains, including the luxury Eurostar, the faster IC (Inter-City) trains, and the *rapido*.

I recently bought a three-country Eurailpass and splurged on first-class seats. I flew into Milan and out of Nice, and used the Eurailpass to connect me to Venice, Geneva, and Monte Carlo before returning to Nice. I got five train rides for about $300, which I thought was a fabulous bargain.

If you have a first-class ticket and a reservation, which are two completely different things (and are even purchased separately), you will not have to worry about finding a seat on a crowded train—which can be hairy, especially if you are schlepping some luggage with you. Even with the train pass, you do not have a specific reservation—so plan ahead and book one if you will need it. Note that reservations in Italy are one of the items that have gone sky high, price-wise. They cost 8€

($10) each, which for me was enough of a reason to not book one and to take my chances.

There are extra *supplementos* for some trains, and reservations are required—even with the train pass—for others. I suggested that Aaron and Jenny save the cost of reservations, but they ended up paying a fine (32€/$42 each) when they got onboard. *Mea culpa!*

By Car

If you want to drive around Italy, reserve your car in the U.S. before departure, using a prepaid plan. It'll be half the price you'll be charged in Italy—even if you reserve through an American rental agency, such as **Avis** (℃ 800/331-1084) or **Hertz** (℃ 800/654-3001). **Thrifty By Car,** the Italian division of Thrifty, has beefed up promotions with fair daily rates and special 2-day weekend rates. Other options include **Kemwel** (℃ 800/678-0678; www.kemwel.com) and **AutoEurope** (℃ 888/223-5555; www.autoeurope.com).

European rental rates are usually more expensive than those offered in the U.S. for use in Europe, although a package plan will always be less expensive than a daily rate. Avis offers a 3-day, winter promotional package for 153€ ($191) and a 7-day package for 325€ ($406), both including unlimited mileage. If you can read Italian, go online to www.avis autonoleggio.it. Depending on the route you plan to drive, you may want to rent your car in France or Switzerland.

Curious You

Note that some trains are called **Eurostar Italia.** These trains do not go through the Chunnel, but they are new, fast, and deluxe. And expensive. They even come with a cute little boxed snack. Such trains are marked "ES" on the schedule or the big board.

I Have Gas

The cost of gas in Europe is four times what you are paying in the U.S.; you will also pay high fees for the use of highways. Both highways and gas stations do take credit cards. Gas in Italy is slightly less expensive than in France. Go figure.

Fly-drive packages may offer the best prices; check to see if your airline has a fly-drive affiliation with a car-rental agency.

The crime rate in Italy makes car rentals there more expensive than in other European countries, and various insurance plans are mandatory. Furthermore, American Express and credit- and bank-card firms that offer car insurance automatically with your membership have now waived coverage in Italy. *Do not assume you are covered by your credit card.*

Shopper's trick: If you want a car at the last minute and you are already in Italy, you can reserve by making a long-distance call to the U.S. and pay by phone, receiving a faxed prepaid voucher with U.S. prices.

DRIVING AROUND

I bought the Michelin spiral-bound map book to Italy (18€/$23) for my driving trip. This book also has a handy mileage chart, so you can plan just how far you want to drive.

CAR & DRIVER

If you can afford it, or you want to splurge, hiring a car and driver is a wonderful way to do a day trip or to connect to other parts of Italy. I certainly wouldn't want to be driving the Amalfi Pass on my own. And sometimes I have so much luggage that going through a train station could be a nightmare.

However, make sure your driving company knows where they are going. I recently used a service to drive me to Como and to outlets along the way. Not only did the driver not know where anything was, but he also didn't speak English, refused to call the factories for directions, and wouldn't cross the border into Switzerland to get to FoxTown. *Urrrrrgggh.*

To avoid problems like this, consider taking a train to your destination, and then hire a local taxi driver for a flat rate.

SLEEPING IN ITALY

Hotel Chains

While each city chapter in this book has specific hotel information, if you like to make all or most of your reservations with one hotel chain or one phone call, a few firms can help you out. Ask each about promotional deals.

- **Baglioni:** This is a small chain, still owned by a real family and offering up four and five star hotels in major cities. The top of the line is their hotel in Milan (member of the Leading Hotels of the World), but my fave is in Verona. Check online at www.baglionihotels.com.
- **Boscolo:** Be still my heart! The Exedra Hotel is part of my love affair with Rome, but the Aleph Hotel ain't bad either. I first met this chain when it took over one of my regular hotels in Nice. They do have a handful of hotels in France, although there are over a dozen properties in Italy. Some of the hotels are normal four stars that are good finds; a few are to-die-for places worthy of a spread in *Architectural Digest.* Call © 888/626-7265 or look online at www.boscolohotels.com.
- **InterContinental:** This chain is changing its image and renovating many hotels. While their showcase hotels are in Hong Kong, London, and Paris, the InterContinental in Rome is in a great location and has very grand style and excellent prices and promotions. I found a deal at 288€ ($360) per night in summer! Call © 888/303-1758 or check out www.intercontinental.com.

- **Jolly Hotels:** This leading four-star hotel chain in Italy also has hotels in other European cities and some spas too. Some hotels are rehabbed grande dames. Many are modern and may look like they are stuck in the 1960s from the outside, but inside they are great. They have special weekend promotions—you can luck into a very good hotel for 66€ ($82) per night per person. Trust me on this: it's a great find and you can make all your Italian bookings with one chain. In the U.S., call © **800/221-2626** or 800/247-1277, or look online at www.jollyhotels.com.

- **Leading Hotels of the World:** Also represents Leading Small Hotels of the World, with a wide selection of the fanciest hotels in the world, and sometimes multiple choices in the same city (three hotels in Florence, three in Milan, and five in Rome; © **800/745-8883**). Note that most of the hotels have their own websites, posted in the annual Leading Hotels directory, which you can order at www.lhw.com. Also check out www.luxury-alliance.com, which is the combined website for Leading Hotels and Relais & Châteaux.

- **Meridien:** There are two branches of Meridien Hotels (www.lemeridien.com): Art + Tech, which are artsy boutique hotels, and plain old Le Meridien, an excellent business and leisure hotel chain. When both are on the same property, as in Lingotto (Turin), it can get confusing.

- **Rocco Forte Hotels:** Sir Rocco Forte has reclaimed several luxury hotels around Europe (www.roccofortehotels.com), including the over-the-top Savoy in Florence and De La Russie in Rome. You can book into a weekend promotional deal at a fancy hotel for 207€ ($259) a night.

- **Relais & Châteaux:** With some 30 properties all over Italy, you'll rest in a luxury property and eat awfully well (© **800/735-2478**; www.relaischateaux.com); note a newish partnership with Leading Hotels of the World called Luxury Alliance (www.luxury-alliance.com).

- **Sofitel:** There are hotels in Venice, Bologna, Florence, and Rome; it's part of France's Accor Group (© **800/763-4835**; www.sofitel.com). The Isola in Venice is a knockout, more like a resort than a hotel, a destination unto itself. Most of the other hotels (worldwide) are less extravagant. The company has a weekend promotional deal that takes 30% off the room rate and includes complimentary breakfast in most of their European hotels.

- **Space Hotels:** This association of independent Italian hotels has an easy-to-use bible of their properties and a booking service (© 06/44-57-346; www.spacehotels.it). The printed catalogue is in English and Italian; the group serves 50 Italian destinations with mostly four-star properties.
- **Westin:** Westin ended up with some of the old CIGA hotels through Starwood, so they do have several luxury hotels in key cities and can take care of your needs with one swift phone call (© 888/625-5144; www.westin.com). For Starwood's Luxury Collection hotels and resorts, call © 888/625-4988 or go online to www.starwood.com/luxury.

Sleeping Promotions

When business is slow, promotional rates get better. Airlines do 'em, hotels do 'em, and even credit-card companies play ball. Check with the travel service division of all the cards you hold to find out what's on offer; also go online to hotel and airline sites—very often, special deals are offered only online.

I recently found a deal through Visa that offered 2 nights for the price of 1 at Le Meridien Hotels. To get the deal, you had to know the code word (in this case, "2 pour 1"). There were also restrictions, such as length of stay. Still it's worth checking out: in the U.S., call © 800/543-4300 or go online to www.lemeridien.com. You may also want to look at www.visadestinations.com for all their deals.

If you have an American Express Platinum Card, you can buy two-for-one airline tickets and get various hotel amenities. I also found a free-night offer at the Hotel Eden in Rome.

Most hotel chains also have deals, either with partners or just to sell rooms during odd seasons or on weekends. Jolly Hotels, in partnership with Sixt Car Rental and Lufthansa, also has promotions; go online to www.jollyhotels.com.

Electronically Yours

The Internet is a great source for tourism information. Here are unusual addresses you may want to check out before you begin your Italian adventures:

- The Vatican (www.vatican.va)   Dial a prayer.
- Italian National (www.italiantourism.com)   This is the Italian National Tourist Board's official online source for information—find a hotel or look up a train schedule.
- Charming Italy (www.charmingitaly.net)   Specializes in small towns, great three- and four-star hotels, and shopping tours.
- Italian furniture (www.italydesign.com)   California firm that can help you learn about and price Italian furniture and design, which may be cheaper in the U.S.
- Made in Italy (www.made-in-italy.com)   Logan Bentley's fashion- and design-related site has information on wine and food, travel, and shopping; can also arrange Roman shopping tours with Barbara Lessona.
- Faith Heller Willinger (www.faithwillinger.com)   All sorts of info—not just for foodies, though internationally famous for her food, restaurant and recipe info; offers cooking classes in her home.
- Tuscany by Tuscans (www.tuscanybytuscans.it)   This is Maria Teresa Berdondini's site—she arranges shopping and cooking tours and tastings—I book my car and driver through her and often take her tours.

Don't be shy about calling a hotel directly and making a deal. Just don't be rude or pushy. Sometimes a nice fax to the hotel's general manager can get you a good rate and added perks. Write to the effect of, "I love your hotel, have stayed there for years, but prices are too high now—can you cut a deal for me?"

Home Suite Home

If you'd rather rent an apartment, or even a villa, several services can help you. If you are looking for something very high

end, there's a rental division of tour masters **Abercrombie &
Kent** (© 800/323-7308; www.abercrombiekent.com), but a castle will cost you from $5,300 to $66,000 a week. **Best In Italy**
(www.thebestinitaly.com) handles properties that begin around
8,000€ ($10,000) a week. If your budget is far below that, try
Custom Italy (www.customitaly.com); prices begin around
3,200€ ($4,000) per week.

PROFESSIONAL HELP

If you are looking for guidance in making travel plans, a few
organizations specialize in showing you the insider's Italy. The
good ones are usually regional. They charge by the day or half-
day, but sometimes you have to spend money to save money.
Try contacting these people, whom I know, trust, and, in most
cases, have worked with. What you get is a personal touch,
hands-on attention, expertise with shopping, bargaining, insider
tips and connections, and help with reservations.

In Venice:
Samantha Durrell
Fax 041/523-23-79

In Tuscany:
Maria Teresa Berdondini, Tuscany by Tuscans
Villa L. Galvani 13B, 51016 Montecatini Terme, Italy
©/fax 0572/70-467; www.tuscanybytuscans.it

In Rome:
Barbara Lessona
© 348/450-3655 (cellphone); www.personalshoppersinitaly.com

In Rome and Florence:
Elisa Rossi, With Style

2 Via Monte Santo, 00195 Rome, Italy
© 06/481-90-91

PHONE HOME

....

Getting the Best Deal

Here are a few cost considerations to remember when using
the phone in Italy:

- Phone cards offer the best deal in terms of price when calling around, especially on international calls. The best card
  is called an **Edi Card** (600 min. for 10€/$13) and is a tad
  hard to find; you need to go to a bar that also has a bet-
  ting office. The good news is that all news dealers sell other
  phone cards that offer adequate savings.
- International phone calls made from the U.S. to Europe are
  far less expensive than those made from Europe to the U.S.
  If you are in Italy and want to talk to the U.S., your easiest solution is to call home on the hotel phone and ask family or friends to call you back.
- An international call from Italy to the U.S. on your cellphone
  may be less expensive than calling from a hotel. Check it
  out. This may be especially advantageous if you have a U.S.
  cellphone with an international calling plan. Various phone
  companies and travel agents provide you with a cellphone
  that works in Europe.
- Hotels usually charge a flat rate for a fax—it often comes
  to 8€ to 13€ ($10–$16) per page. Though still outrageous,
  this rate is often less expensive than a phone call, so consider communicating with home via fax. Ask about rates
  so you can compare.
- Text messaging costs less than phone calls; consider send-
  ing them to friends back home, if your phone is working
  in Italy or you have a rental phone.
- USA Direct is a marvelous gimmick and is often a lifesaver,
  but it doesn't necessarily give the best rate possible. If you

prefer to use your American long-distance carrier, the access codes for the major carriers in Italy are: **USA Direct** (AT&T), ✆ **800/172-444; MCI Direct** (MCI), ✆ **800/172-1022;** and **Sprint,** ✆ **800/825-8745.** Each carrier charges a flat fee for providing this service; it appears on your monthly phone bill.

If you are using your laptop computer to connect to e-mail, work with your hotel front desk or business center directly. I have had great difficulty with AOL in Italy and end up using my hotel business center or finding an Internet cafe. There are Internet cafes all over Italy. My favorite is easyInternet Café, at Piazza Barberini in Rome, right next to the cinema.

Understanding Country Codes

For calling Italy from abroad, the **country code** is **39.** The access codes (area codes) for the major cities are: **Florence,** 055; **Milan,** 02; **Venice,** 041; **Rome,** 06; and **Naples,** 081. For example, to call Rome from the U.S., you would dial 011 + 39 + 06 (the access code for Rome) + the number. All calls, local and long-distance calls, include the "0" in the access code.

SHOPPING HOURS

Shops open at 9 or 9:30am and usually close at 1:30pm for lunch. They reopen at 3 or 3:30pm (or even 4pm) and stay open until 7:30pm.

Some stores close on Saturday from 1 to 4pm. Stores are open on Saturday afternoon in winter and are closed Saturday afternoon in summer.

Some stores do whatever they please. The notion of staying open all day is catching on in big cities, but not the countryside. You never find shops open all day in the south, where it is too hot to think in the afternoon, let alone shop.

Stores that do not close for lunch write their hours as "nonstop" or "continual hours," usually spelled out in Italian. In all cities, major department stores stay open at lunchtime. Unless it's Monday, which has its own rules (see below).

Surviving Monday

Monday mornings are a total write-off for most retail shopping in Italy. With the rare exception, most stores open at 3:30pm on Monday.

But wait, that's why God invented factories. Because factories are open on Monday mornings, most factory stores are also open. Not all, just most. Call and ask, or have your hotel's concierge call. If you are in Milan on a Monday, fret no more, my lady—you are off to Como (see chapter 8). Also note that food shops are open.

Sunday Shopping

Laws have changed, and most of Italy's big cities have some Sunday shopping now; often, big department stores are open even if mom-and-pop stores are not. If you want to shop on a Sunday in a town that has no regular retail, try a flea market.

- Venice is wide, wide, wide open on Sunday.
- Milan is far deader on Sunday than other communities, but you can get lucky—at certain times of the year, things are popping on Sunday. During fashion weeks, for example, stores in the Montenapo district often open on Sunday; beginning in October and going on until Christmas, they also have specific Sundays when they open. Some stores in the Navigli area are also open on Sunday. The regular Sunday stores are **Corso Como 10** and **Virgin Megastore**. Sunday hours are most often noon to 5pm.
- Florence has a lot of street action on Sundays, and department stores and chains are usually open.
- Rome has special Sundays when stores are open.
- Verona is wide open.

Sale Shopping

Each city in Italy has the right to decide when the twice a year official sales will begin—and it does vary from city to city by as much as a week. Good luck.

Exceptional Hours

Summer hours   Summers in Italy have two problems: It can be too hot to shop, and stores can be closed.

Summer hours begin in the middle of July for many retail businesses. August, the official summer vacation season, especially in northern Italy, is a total loss from a shopping point of view because most stores are closed in major cities. Sophisticated people wouldn't be caught dead in Milan in August, so shoppers beware: Most shops in Milan, and many in Rome, close between August 1 and September 1. Shockingly, some stores close for a longer time.

When stores are open in August, they close at lunch on Saturday and do not reopen until 3:30 or 4pm on Monday.

In southern climates, especially in summer, expect stores to close from 1 until 5pm, during the heat of the day, but to reopen until late in the evening.

Holiday hours   The period between Christmas and New Year's Day can be tricky. Stores will close early a few days before a major holiday and use any excuse to stay closed during a holiday. Sales begin in the first week of January (usually after Epiphany), but store hours are erratic before then. But then, the first half of January can also be erratic (see below). There are weekend candy markets around the Duomo in the weeks before Lent.

Keep track of local holidays because shops will close then. When you check into a hotel, ask the concierge about any approaching holidays and how they will affect the banks and stores. Cities celebrate religious holidays with differing amounts of piety. Shops that are closed in Rome may be open in Milan. (Dec 8 is a big holiday in some towns, not so big in others.) August 15 is a big religious holiday (one of the feasts of the Virgin), and all stores are closed.

Early January   The first week to 10 days of January are slow to slower—all factories are closed until after Epiphany, as are many stores. Others decide to close for inventory. Do not assume that shopping life returns to normal on the first day of business after New Year's Day.

Night hours   Stores usually close between 7:30 and 8pm. Should you need an all-night pharmacy, there is usually one at the train station in a large city.

SCAMS

....

Despite the arrival of the euro, or maybe because of it, there are still plenty of locals and immigrants who are ready to take advantage of tourists, and they especially consider Americans as fair game. Most are small-time shopping scams, but they are annoying nonetheless, and can be expensive if you get taken. Scams exist in stores, on the streets, and especially in taxis, which are the most difficult to nail when you don't know your way around or there are one-way streets.

One reader told me about a really sophisticated scam. A store in Venice changed its name. The store next door had someone standing out in front saying the "new" store had been bought and was closed. Guess what? It was bought, thus the name change, but it was open.

Reputable shops (and hotels) are usually safe. But even in classy establishments, be careful when you talk to strangers. I've met some wonderful people in hotels and on airplanes around the world, but there is a rather well-known scam in which the con artist pretends to be just the kind of person you'd like to know and then—whammo—takes you for a ride.

Here are a few things to remember that may help you spot a scammer:

- Merchandise, especially name-brand merchandise, selling at a price that is too good to be true, is usually too fake to be true. I don't care how fancy the store; I don't care how good the sob story is about why they are taking a loss.
- If a person volunteers to go shopping with you, to steer you to some real "finds," to help you find some long-lost family

members, or whatever, don't trust him or her! There are more tourist scams of this nature in Italy than anyplace else, except maybe Hong Kong. Be safe—not sorry.

- No matter how well dressed the person is, no matter how friendly the person is, no matter how helpful and endearing, the answer is still "No." If such a person is following you or becomes a real nuisance, call the police, duck into a prestigious hotel and ask the concierge for help, or walk right into the American embassy.

- Likewise, if a person volunteers to take your money and buy an item for you cheaper than you could get it because you are an "Ugly American," forget it. If you want the concierge of a reputable hotel to handle some shopping for you and you know the hotel well enough to trust the concierge, by all means, do so. (Don't forget to tip for such a favor.) Otherwise you are taking a risk.

- Always check your purchases while they are being packed by the store, and when you return to your hotel, unwrap them to make sure you got what you thought you were getting. Mistakes occur, but occasionally someone will switch merchandise on you. Return to the shop the next day with your sales slip if an error has been made. If you anticipate a language problem, have the concierge call the shop and explain the situation, and then have him tell the shop when you will be in for the proper merchandise.

- Don't forget the old newspaper scam. A street person (or two or three) spots you with an attractive shopping bag. He or she is reading or holding a newspaper as he passes you on a crowded street—or worse, on a bridge. The newspaper passes over your shopping bag while the thief's hand goes into your bag for the goodies. The person reading the newspaper may or may not be the thief—this scam is worked by mothers with three or four children in tow. We've also heard it worked so that the person reading the newspaper passes you, grabs your glasses, and then runs off while several children pounce on you, take your shopping bags and handbag, and dash away while you are left wondering what hit you.

- Watch out for the old subway trick. You know the one, where some "boys" pick a fight among themselves between subway stops, and your pocket is picked, and they are out the door before you know what has happened.

- There is a variation of this one that I call the "Ice-Cream Trick." Someone bumps into you and knocks his ice cream cone all over you. He's very apologetic and helps clean you up. He also cleans you out.

- And then, there's the old *O sole mio* scam. You are involved in a transaction being conducted in Italian, which you barely speak. If you question the mathematics, the vendor rolls his eyes, waves his arms, and screams at you. You feel like an idiot and leave, not wanting to cause a scene. You have just been cheated out of $50 in correct change. (This actually happened to me.)

- And then, there's the mail trick, which is a hotel scam. You ask the front desk to mail postcards or letters. You are charged a mark-up on the stamps—or are even charged the U.S. rate for mail within the E.U.

- My favorite (this also happened to me): You give the taxi driver an address that is slightly off the beaten track. He pulls up to a door and says something to the effect of "here you go." You disagree because you know this isn't it. He insists on getting out of the cab, going to the front door, and verifying that this is not the place you want. Meanwhile, the meter is running . . . and running.

It's a Crime

I don't want to put a damper on your shopping spree before you even start out, but I do feel compelled to point out that the hard times in Italy have brought more and more criminal elements to the fore. They are in front of, and behind, your handbag. And your rental car.

I was accosted not once but several times by thieving bands in Milan. Two incidents occurred on different days, but in full daylight, in the area immediately surrounding the Duomo. In one case, it was a Saturday, and I was surrounded by a throng of shoppers. When I screamed out, none of the other shoppers even gazed in my direction.

Keep handbags close to your body and under your coat or sweater. Don't put valuables in a backpack or fanny pack that is beyond your watchful eye. Don't sling shopping bags across a shoulder and away from your body so that their contents can be lifted from the rear. Leave nothing in your rented car, and be careful where you park it. Last time I rented a car in Italy, I was told which cities, such as Naples, were considered unsafe for parking a car on the street or in an unattended lot. If you're given a similar warning, heed it.

BUYING FROM DUTY-FREES

While intra-European duty-free has been outlawed, this does not affect travelers leaving the E.U. through Italy and may not affect those traveling within the E.U., depending on airport policy. On a recent departure from Paris to Milan, one of the French duty-free shops was allowing the discount for E.U. travel, and the other one was not. Go figure.

It's easier upon departure from Italy, especially if you are indeed flying back to the U.S. or out of the E.U. The Rome airport is virtually one giant shopping mall once you pass through Immigration. While there are tons of stores and the selection can be huge, the savings are not a sure bet. Perfume and cosmetics may be cheaper at the duty-free you left behind in the U.S. or London, or in the in-flight magazine. Not every shop in an airport selling area is duty-free (or, more accurately, tax-free; you may pay duty on what you buy in a "duty-free" shop when you take it home). Many of the designer shops are not duty-free. Ask! Not every shop offers a bargain—many are outrageously expensive; some just charge the going rate.

You may get a flat 19% discount off regular Italian retail on Trussardi, Enrico Coveri, and Ferragamo shoes as well as many other things. The catch is that the Italian retail price may be so inflated that a discount of 19% is meaningless. If you buy at the Ferragamo sale, you'll do better than at the airport.

Don't forget that whatever you buy at the duty-free shop must be declared when you return to the United States. Unless you eat it on the plane. And never forget that duty-free shopping no longer ends when you leave the airport. All airlines now have duty-free shopping on the plane. The price list should be inside the in-flight magazine. *Buon viaggio.*

MAILING & SHIPPING FROM ITALY

Shipping anything from Italy begins before you get there. If you are smart, or serious, you will do some homework before you leave and have your shipping arrangements partly made before you even arrive. You'll complete the transaction once you arrive in Italy with a pre-selected and guaranteed broker.

Contact a shipper in your hometown, or in New York, London, or your chosen port of entry for your goods, and work with them to make sure all your shipping days are pleasant ones. The shipper should be able to act as your agent—the buying game will be much less tense once you have someone to take care of you.

Find out if you need a customhouse broker to meet your goods and clear them, or if the shipping agent does this, and if so, is it included in the shipping cost or is there an additional fee? Likewise, make sure you pay for adequate insurance, and do not assume that it is included in the freight price.

Small items should be shipped via FedEx, DHL, or another courier service you know and trust. Italy does have a service called "express mail," but don't trust it.

Before I totally pooh-pooh the Italian mail system, I want you to know that all the postcards I've ever sent from Italy have been delivered home and abroad, sometimes in less than a week. I've also noticed that concierges have charged differing rates for a simple postcard stamp. Actual postal rates are posted at the post office. I have mailed items in Jiffy Bags from large city post offices, and gifts have arrived—always mark an item sent to the U.S. as "Unsolicited gift, under $50."

THE MOSCOW RULE OF SHOPPING

....

The Moscow Rule of Shopping is one of my most basic shopping rules and has nothing to do with shopping in Moscow, so please pay attention. Average shoppers, in pursuit of the ideal bargain, do not buy an item they want when they first see it, because they're not convinced that they won't find it elsewhere for less money. They want to see everything available, and then return for the purchase of choice. This is a rather normal thought process. However, if you live in Russia, for instance, you know that you must buy something the minute you see it, because if you hesitate, it will be gone. Hence this international law: the Moscow Rule of Shopping.

When you are on a trip, you probably will not have the time to compare prices and then return to a certain shop. You will never be able to backtrack to cities, and even if you can, the item might be gone by the time you get back, anyway. What to do? The same thing they do in Moscow: Buy it when you see it, understanding that you may never see it again. But because you are not shopping in Moscow, and you *may* see it again, weigh these questions carefully before you go ahead:

- Is this a touristy type of item that I am bound to find all over town?
- Is this an item I can't live without, even if I am overpaying?
- Is this a reputable shop, and can I trust what they tell me about the availability of such items?
- Is the quality of this particular item so spectacular that it is unlikely it could be matched at this price?

If you have good reason to buy it when you see it, do so.

Now hear my tale of warning. I bought a pair of trousers at Marina Rinaldi in Rome that turned out to be great for me. They were also available in navy in Rome, but by then, it was Sunday, and I couldn't go back to the store. When I got to Florence, I went to the Marina Rinaldi store, wearing the trousers and asked for them in navy. The saleswoman swore they weren't from Marina Rinaldi. Then she swaggered that they came from Marina Rinaldi in the U.S., a different kettle of pants. When I told her they came from Rome, she simply shrugged. Buy it when you see it, and don't expect the same brand to have the same stock.

Caveat: The Moscow Rule of Shopping breaks down if you are an antiques or bric-a-brac shopper or if you are shopping in a factory outlet. You never know if you can find another such item, or if it will be in the same condition, or if the price will be higher or lower. It's very hard to price collectibles and bargains, so consider doing a lot of shopping for an item before you buy anything.

ITALIAN CITY PLANNING

If you are going to a variety of Italian cities, you probably are wondering which one offers the best price, the best selection, and the best value. There are no firm rules—the Moscow Rule of Shopping really applies—but I do have a couple of loose rules to guide you.

The City of Origin Axiom   An item usually is cheapest in the city where it's made or where the firm's headquarters are. That's because the trucking and distribution costs are less. Following this rule, **Pratesi** linens should be bought at the factory store in Pistoia; **Fendi** goodies should come from the mother store in Rome; and **Etro** should come from the factory near Como, or, at least, Milan.

The Milan Rule of Supply and Demand   If you don't know the city of origin for an item, or want to be safe, use the Milan Rule of Supply and Demand. Because Milan is the center of the fashion and furnishings business, it should have the best selection of big-name merchandise. If you are only shopping in one city or creating a schedule that allows only a 1-day spree, Milan is the city for you.

Milan is far more industrial than the other big cities. Its entire psychology is one of moving and selling goods and services. Furthermore, while in Milan, you have the opportunity to shop at factories that are just outside of town, or at flea markets that sell leftovers from factories (you mean those ties didn't just fall off a truck?), or you can luck into very good sales that are created to move merchandise.

The Roman Holiday Rule of Shopping   If you just want designer merchandise and a good time, forget about the rest of Italy, and just do Rome. You won't get the faience, the souvenirs, or the gilt-wood trays, but you will find all the big names in one easy-to-shop neighborhood.

Venice and Florence are crammed with tourists, especially in the spring and summer months, and the shopkeepers know you are a tourist. Prices in Venice are high to begin with and soar in season. Florence has changed dramatically in the last couple of years: The merchandise in the streets and stalls has gotten junkier and junkier, but prices here for clothing are often less than in nearby cities because of the turnover.

If you're going on a cruise of Italy, please note that chapter 9 in this book has information on shopping in various Italian port cities. Unless you have a pre- or post-cruise layover in Rome or Venice, you will not have an opportunity to do much traditional Italian-designer shopping.

The Coca-Cola Price Index   To find out how prices fare in any destination, ask for the price of a Coca-Cola. Just so you know, the price of a single can of Coke in a grocery store is .52¢). A six-pack is about 2.35€ ($2.94). The average Coke on the street costs 2€ ($2.50); it is expensive if it costs 3€, and it is a crime if it costs 7.50€ ($9.34).

SHOPPING FOR FAKES

In years gone by, some of the best buys in Italy were on fake designer leather goods and scarves. These items are harder to find and, once found, are often so inferior to the real thing that the game is no fun to play at all. Although there is that pesky little rumor that Prada makes its own fakes . . .

The bigger question is, why buy a fake when you can have the real thing through an outlet store or a sale? Fendi key chains were going for 13€ ($16) at the sale in Rome. I mean, *really.* Get real, buy real.

IN THE BAG

Shopping bags are freely given out at boutiques and department stores when you make a purchase. Not so in grocery stores. Either bring your own or expect to pay about .50€ (63¢) per plastic sack. The large can of olive oil that you came to buy comes with a handle, so you may not need a bag.

If you score at a sale in a designer shop, you can ask for gift wrap and a designer bag, but you may not get them. Pucci gave me tons of attention and free wrap; Fendi settled on tissue and Fendi bags—no wrap or ribbon. Best of all was Armani; all I bought was a blush, but they gave me a canvas tote bag.

BAR NONE

This is not strictly a shopping secret, but is nonetheless a strategy: Next time you belly up to the bar, consider how much money you've just saved. That's right—eating at the bar (while standing) is a money-saving tactic.

If you see a bar you'd like to wander into for a coffee or a snack, remember that all bars in Italy have two systems: Either you order at the bar and stand and drink at the bar, or you order at the bar or a table and then sit down. To eat at a table will cost just about double the price of a meal at the bar. It is rude to order at the bar, pay at the bar, and then wander to a chair with your snack and sit down.

TO MARKET, TO MARKET

One of the difficulties of shopping in Italy is deciding which markets to visit and which to pass up. Italy is crawling with good markets, for food and for fleas. There are dozens of them, and it's impossible to get to them all unless you spend a month doing little else. Maybe a year or two. Here are some tips:

- Dress simply: The richer you look, the higher the price. If you have an engagement ring or one of those wedding bands that spells out "Rich American" in diamonds, leave it in the hotel safe. Do not carry a $700 designer handbag.
- Check with your hotel's concierge about the neighborhood where the market is located. It may not be considered safe to go there alone, or after dark. Beware Rome. Beware the ides of March.
- Have a lot of change with you. It's difficult to bargain and then offer a large bill and ask for change. As a bargaining point, be able to say you have only so much cash on hand.
- You do not need to speak any specific language to make a good deal. Bargaining is an international language of emotion, hand signs, facial expressions, and so on. If you feel like you are being taken, walk away.
- Branded merchandise sold on the street may be hot or counterfeit. If the deal seems an exceptionally fine one, suspect fraud.
- Go early if you expect the best selection. Go late if you want to make the best deals price-wise.
- Never trust anyone (except a qualified shipping agent) to mail anything for you.
- In Florence and Rome, most market areas are so famous that they have no specific street address. Usually it's enough to give the cabbie the name of the market: Ask your concierge if you need more in the way of directions. Usually buses service market areas. Expect markets to be closed on Monday morning.

OUTLET SHOPPING

....

Italian factories have had outlet shops for their employees or the local community for years; these addresses used to be secrets. Not anymore. They say the second most visited sight in Florence, after the Uffizi, is the Prada outlet store.

Outlets are so popular to locals and tourists alike that there are locally published guides to them. I often use a book called *Lo Scoprioccasioni (Bargain Hunting in Italy)*, written in Italian, which, according to the cover, lists over 1,400 outlets. This book costs 16.80€ ($21). The competition is named *L'Italia delle Occasioni* and comes from the Touring Club Italiano— it's easier to read than *Lo Scopriaoccasioni* but not as jam-packed. It, too, costs 21€ ($26). Here are a few more thoughts about outlet guidebooks:

- There is another edition of *Lo Scoprioccasioni* in English (titled *Designer Bargains in Italy*). It costs as much as the Italian edition, but isn't revised as often or isn't as comprehensive. Beware.
- Check the copyright page before you buy. I once grabbed the display copy only to find I had mistakenly bought the previous edition.
- Finally, may I say that I don't agree with a number of the listings of the books I've checked out, which is a small portion of the total. I've also found listings for stores that had been closed for 5 years. Call ahead if you are driving out of your way or trusting solely this book.

Italy has three new, American-style factory outlet villages. The outlet malls are in the middle of nowhere, but not far from big cities. Outlet stores are open on Sundays, making them a popular shopping destination for a normally dead day.

- **Serravalle Scrivia,** an enormous fake village, is located between Turin, Genoa, and Milan, and usually listed in Milan shopping resources. (For more on this outlet, see p. 258.)

- Between Milan and Bologna, **Fidenza Village** is also in the village format, and the village is meant to be inspired by *Aida,* because Verdi is from nearby.
- Just 20km (12 miles) from Bologna, going toward the sea in the east, is **Castel Guelfo Outlet Centre.** This is actually a small mall, but there's enough other stuff to do nearby that it can be worth the trip.
- Florence and its outskirts, all the way to Arezzo, are filled with outlets, malls, factories, and other chances to buy wholesale. **The Mall** has become so famous that it's simply called The Mall and is the number-two tourist destination in Italy. A new mall is coming to the edge of Florence in 2006. Watch this space.
- South of Rome, the Pontina outlets are owned by the same firm that has Serravale Scrivia (MacArthur Glen) and are built like an antique-Roman village, officially named **Castel Romano.**
- **Fashion District** is a somewhat new outlet mall south of Rome on the road toward Naples.

One of the older outlet malls, **FoxTown,** is, technically, in Switzerland—it's 5km (3 miles) from the Italian border and right near Como. Because it's in Switzerland, and Switzerland does not use the euro, you must change money to CF (Swiss Francs), which may not be worth it to you. Prices in Switzerland tend to be high, even on bargains.

Italy also has a system of jobbers (usually called *stochistas*) and also of freestanding outlet stores, often in the heart of a big city and easily on the tourist path. Some are as fancy as regular boutiques—wait 'til you shop at Max Mara and Etro outlets in Milan; you won't believe they are outlets until you see the price tags.

Mills & Thrills

Outlets can offer truly great bargains—if they are the real thing. Sometimes outlet villages are so upscale that their prices are actually between regular retail and true discount—this limbo-land is confusing for the shopper and provides the raison d'être for a big brand to actually go into an outlet mall in the first place—the prices are not seriously discounted and do not therefore hurt the brand's image.

Sometimes, the merchandise they sell is specifically made for sale at outlets; true stock is almost always from a previous season. There is a small business in hustling big-city locals through warehouses in industrial suburbs that sell fakes; sometimes they are just normal businesses that market themselves as outlets. Know your stuff, know your regular retail prices, and know a few other rules of the road:

- Most outlets in factories close for lunch.
- Salespeople in out-of-the-way, small communities may not speak English. It's not a bad idea to bring an Italian-English dictionary with you.
- Be sure you have a size conversion chart, or know the sizes you want in the continental sizing system. There is a size conversion chart at the back of this book.
- Many mills are open Monday morning but close in the afternoon; others are closed the entire day. Remember the Monday rule of shopping—anything goes. Call first, especially on a Monday.
- Mills are never open on Sunday; not all are open on Saturday. Most fancy factory outlets are open on Sunday, however. In fact, in outlet malls, stores may be open 7 days a week. Welcome to the new Italy.
- Few mills will take credit cards, although Pratesi does. Outlets will take credit cards.
- If you have chosen a day trip with specific outlets and/or mills in mind, do yourself (and me) a favor—call first. Actually, have your hotel concierge call in case your Italian isn't as good as his. Get hours, credit-card information, and confirmation of directions.

There is more information about specific outlets (all flavors) and discount shopping ops in the individual city chapters that follow.

RETURNING TO THE U.S.

Note that the per-person duty-free allowance for returning U.S. residents has been increased to $800. See p. 49 for more.

To paraphrase my fellow Texan, Lance Armstrong, please remember that your trip to Italy is not about the handbag. I had this realization while I was online at AOL the other day and clicked on "Deal of the Day," which offered many Italian-designer handbags, from the biggest brands, at half-price. On eBay, you can find these brands for less than U.S. retail.

We travel to see another world and taste another lifestyle. If you get a good deal, that's extra luck.

Chapter Three

·····················

MONEY MATTERS

EUROS "R" THEM

···

Italy, like most of continental Europe, adopted the euro (€) and has successfully switched from lire. Surely they did it for you, to make shopping all of Europe so much easier.

That was the good news. The bad news is that the euro has gained enormous strength against the U.S. dollar. Since switching to euros, all of Europe has become more expensive, and with a weak dollar in your wallet, you may feel somewhat crippled. Don't worry too much—this book is dedicated to finding you real values. Read on, read on. *Andiamo*.

Don't forget that the euro is a transterritorial currency serving the member nations; bills are Pan-European in design but the coins are created on a local basis. One side of each coin conforms with the E.U. master; the other side is created by individual countries. Thus, you will encounter Italian- and also Vatican City–euro coins, some of which are considered collectible depending on which pope is pictured.

ATMs "R" Us

The single best way to exchange money is to simply withdraw it from a wall—via an ATM. Bring along your bank card: All Italian cities have banks with ATMs. Still, there are a few caveats here:

- You will see similar looking machines that have a different function, such as exchanging dollars for local currency. Don't be fooled by them; they'll cheat you. Only an ATM (usually marked *bancomat*) will give you a good rate.
- Most banks (though not all—ask about yours) charge a fee for using a foreign ATM, but you do get a good exchange rate. If your bank charges a high fee, you don't want to keep going to the wall for 100€—do it all at once.
- Most ATMs operate 24 hours. Call your bank and find out if the PIN you have will work in foreign locations, or if you need a new number. I have never had any trouble using my same old PIN with my Cirrus card.

If you need cash for a big purchase in a specific store, ask the sales clerk where the nearest ATM is located. Very often, a small store will give you a sizable discount if you pay cash and are willing to forego your VAT refund (see "Taxing Matters," later in this chapter). Of course, they do this because they have another set of books that Brussels knows nothing about, but what else is new?

Currency Exchange

Currency rates and exchange rates (from dollars to euros) vary tremendously. The rate announced in the newspaper is the official bank-exchange rate and does not apply to tourists. Even by trading your money at a bank, you will not get the official rate. The best way to change dollars to euros is at an ATM. To exchange at a bank or hotel, consider the following:

- While hotels give a less-favorable exchange rate than banks, they don't charge a fee to guests, they are convenient, and they rarely make you wait. Your time may be worth the difference.
- If you want to change euros back into dollars when you leave, remember that you will pay a higher rate for them. You are

now "buying" dollars rather than "selling" them. There-fore, never change more money than you think you will need, unless you plan to stockpile for another trip.

Other Options

- Check, mates: Never travel without your checkbook. You just never know.
- Wired money: You can have money sent to you from home; it usually takes 2 days, but allow for a week. Money can be wired using Western Union (whoever is wiring you money must bring cash or a certified check, and Western Union does the rest) or an international money order, which is cleared by telex through the bank where you cash it. Money can be wired from bank to bank, but this is a simple process only with major big-city banks that have European branches or sister banks. Banks usually charge a nice fat fee for doing you this favor. In an emergency, the American consulate may lend you money, which you must repay.

TIPPING

With the arrival of the euro, tipping becomes an even more murky matter because it's a lot more expensive to be a good sport, and the low dollar doesn't make it the same alternative it was when the local currency was in lire. These days, no one wants a tip in U.S. dollars. Figure on paying a euro per suit-case at a moderately priced hotel and two per suitcase at a lux-ury hotel; leave a euro for calling a taxi. For taxi drivers, round up the fare, but don't tip if you feel you were cheated.

TAXING MATTERS

Let's start at the beginning so you understand the system, then I'll explain the tricky parts.

Refunds 101: The Easy Part

In the U.S., when you pay for an item, sales tax is added at the time of purchase. In Europe, the taxes have already been added, so you pay the price on the ticket.

European Union (E.U.) countries have a system that allows foreign shoppers who buy goods and take them out of the country to receive a tax refund on these added taxes. In France, the tax is called TVA. In England, it's called VAT (value-added tax). In Italy, it's called IVA.

- You only claim the refund when you depart the E.U.—this means the E.U.—not when you depart Italy. So, if you are driving from Italy into France, you are still in the E.U. and, therefore, can't claim the refund until you leave the E.U. for the U.S. If you go into Croatia, a non-E.U. country, you get the paperwork stamped at the border.
- When you are at the airport, but before you check your luggage, go see the Customs officer.
- Mail the papers from the airport if you want a credit-card refund.
- If you want an immediate refund in cash, find the cash-refund desk. Look for the desk bearing a red, white, and green logo and the TAX FREE FOR TOURISTS sign.

Refund Me, You Fool

Please note that there are several ways for you to receive a refund, and this is where it begins to get complicated.

There's the tax-free check, which you can cash or deposit at any bank; or a voucher, which can only be redeemed in currency. The voucher can be tricky because you will lose money on the conversion and have no chance to get a credit-card refund. Whenever possible, have the refund applied to your credit card, as you won't pay two exchange rates.

The new cash-in-town methods still mean that you have to show the goods at customs when you depart the E.U. (an imprint is made for the tax refund; if they don't get the paperwork back, you are charged the difference).

If you are leaving Italy via train or car, there are refund desks at the borders. Remember that you only do tax-free declarations at your final point of exit from the E.U.

If you plan to visit another E.U. country, you don't need to worry about Italian tax-free plans. *Ciao*, baby.

ITALIAN TAX-FREE

If you spend 154.94€ (which comes to a little more than $194) or more in the same shop on the same day, you are entitled to a tax refund. You must apply for this refund at the store and then follow through with the proper steps (outlined above) at the airport or when you depart the E.U. on your last stop within the union. This must be done within 3 months of the purchase time, and goods must be for export purposes.

DETAX SCAM

Many designer shops say to you, after you inquire as to the price of a high-ticket item, "but you get a 19% discount from the tax." The implication is that the item will automatically be about 20% less—and this fact is meant to tip your judgment in favor of the sale.

There's just one problem: You don't get 19% back. You don't even get 15%. Because of the various fees involved, you probably get 13%. You may get less.

U.S. CUSTOMS & DUTIES TIPS

- You are currently allowed to bring in $800 worth of duty-free merchandise per person. Each member of the family is entitled to the deduction; this includes infants.
- You pay a flat 10% duty on the next $1,000 worth of merchandise. It's worth doing—we're talking about the very small sum of $100.
- Duties thereafter are based on the type of product. They vary tremendously per item, so ask storekeepers about U.S.

duties. They will know, especially in specialty stores. Note that the duty on leather goods is only 8%.

- The head of the family can make a joint declaration for all family members and should take responsibility for answering any questions that the Customs officers may ask. Have receipts ready, and make sure they match the information on the landing card. If you tell a little lie, you'll be labeled as a fibber, and they'll tear your luggage apart.

- You count into your $800 per person everything you obtain while abroad—this includes toothpaste (if you bring the unfinished tube back with you), items bought in duty-free shops, gifts for others, the items that other people asked you to bring home, and—get this—even alterations to clothing.

- Have the Customs' registration slips, for things you already own, in your wallet or someplace easily accessible. If you wear a Cartier watch, you should be able to produce the registration slip. If you cannot prove that you took a foreign-made item out of the country with you, you may be forced to pay duty on it!

- The unsolicited gifts you mailed from abroad do not count in the $800-per-person rate. If the value of the gift is more than $50, you pay duty when the package comes into the U.S. Remember, only one unsolicited gift per person.

- Do not attempt to bring in any illegal foodstuffs—dairy products, meats, fruits, or vegetables (coffee is okay). Generally speaking, if it's alive, it's verboten. Dried mushrooms happen to be okay.

- Antiques must be at least 100 years old to be duty-free. Provenance papers will help (so will permission to actually export the antiquity, since it could be an item of national cultural significance). Any bona fide work of art is duty-free, whether it was painted 50 years ago or just yesterday.

- Thinking of "running" one of those new Italian handbags? Forget it. New handbags shout to Customs officers.

Chapter Four

....

ITALIAN STYLE

TOGA, TOGA, TOGA

Italian style goes back, well, centuries—even before there was an Italy. It was the city-state system back then, and even up until the mid-1800s, where part of what we today know as Italy was in France. What you're thinking about, when you think of chic, is indeed, half French. But not the sheets.

I sympathize with the politicos who say that modern Italy is actually two countries—north and south—as I see it in fashions and trends. But with a weaker dollar, you need not worry your pretty little head over politics—it's what's worth buying that is the real question. The answer lies within your own closet and your own lifestyle. Don't buy anything that makes sense in Italy but does not translate to your own world. At these prices, you want classics that will last 20 years.

Northern Fashion

Fashionistas in Milan are known to wear black—as they usually do in New York. To save themselves from going nuts with boredom, their black clothes have to have a style detail that makes them unique. This, then, is the epitome of northern Italian style—hard-edged and clever details. Often the fresh approach revolves around technology and fabrics. New fabrics make the price of the garment go up.

In complete contrast to this style is a style that is worn by real people, not fashion victims—it looks like English-country style and is prevalent as far south as Florence. While Italy now sells clothes from all over the world, you will find that certain brands—Italian or global—have not ventured into the southern regions, even as far down as Florence—which, where the south is concerned, is still north. Likewise, if you are looking to buy killer style, don't waste much time outside of Milan.

Buying Boutique Lines

If you crave a designer name, but don't want to blow too much money, consider one of the lesser lines by the designer—most of the designers have at least one, if not several, mass-market line of clothing and possibly accessories. These lines are often created to be more young-at-heart (and light of price tag) so that the designer can woo the younger market and then trade them up when they are into the big euros. Newest member of the clan: T, from Trussardi.

The tricky part? Big-name designers have boutique lines that may not have their names on them. You'll often find these lesser lines in department stores, such as La Rinascente, or even in the duty-free shops at the airport. In some cases, these lines end up with their own stores—such as Armani Jeans and D&G (from Dolce & Gabbana). In many cases, the less expensive lines come and go and no one can even remember them or their stores—does anyone miss Oaks or Versus?

If you see a name you don't know, ask about it. Flexa is the young-style division of Fratelli Rossetti. The Marina Rinaldi line is the large-size version of Max Mara. A. Testoni is a rather traditional line, but the Duckling line is anything but.

DICTIONARY OF TASTE & DESIGN

The following lists some of the big names in Italian design. Most of the brands and concepts are Italian, but a few are French or British or global brands. If the brand is not well known in the U.S., but you have an opportunity to discover it in Italy, I have included it in this section.

Anna Molinari   The name you'll remember is not Anna's, but that of her label—Blumarine—which has been making waves with hot-cha-cha fashions for hot-cha-cha women for over a decade. There are now a few Blumarine boutiques. The lesser line is called Blu Girl; very sultry and sexy.

Beauty Point   The very poor man's Sephora. This Italian chain of *profumeria* is stocked with makeup and beauty treatments but lacks the same edge as Sephora.

Benetton   Benetton can only be described as a phenomenon, hanging in there and continuing to reinvent, perhaps not the wheel, but at least the sweater and maybe the future. Check out some of the Benetton superstores in Italian capital cities; they even have play areas for kids.

Bottega Veneta   Tomas Maier (formerly of Hermès) came on board 2 years ago and now everything is revitalized. There's still plenty of woven leather (in throw pillows!) and 800€ ($1,000) handbags, but you'll also find more shoes and clothes and cashmeres.

Braccialini   Well-loved cult brand of handbag that hits the niche market of novelty handbags. Bags may be in the shape of Cinderella's coach, a VW bug, a train engine, and more. Stores are in most major Italian cities.

Brioni   A name and a brand synonymous with men's style and elegance. James Bond (Pierce Brosnan) wears Brioni suits. There are stores—and stores that sell the brand—all over the world, but the Milan shop is the temple for service, and Rome is the original flagship. The factories are in Penne.

Carpisa   From Naples with love—this chain has stores all over Italy and several stores in most large cities. The brand makes handbags and totes, mostly in brightly printed canvas with a sort of Lilly Pulitzer kind of resort feel. Prices are in the 20€ ($25) range, making this the find of your next trip.

Jenny's Turn: I Love Pocket Coffee

Ferrero (the makers of Nutella and other goodies) have the answer you are looking for to satisfy your caffeine addiction. Pocket Coffees are small, individually wrapped chocolate candies with real liquid espresso inside.

These chocolates are available in most grocery stores, and a box of five costs about a euro (about $1.25) each. Aaron wants to point out that these candies are for extreme coffee enthusiasts only! The bitterness of the coffee combined with the dark chocolate is not for the faint of heart.

One piece of advice: Put the whole chocolate into your mouth at once, lest you want espresso squirting from your lips and dripping on your new *camiseta*.

Chocolate   Although most people don't associate Italian taste with chocolate, some of the world's most famous chocolate brands do come from Italy (see "Nutella," below). Perugina, the best-known mass-market brand, sells not only chocolate candy but also chocolate cooking supplies; I buy their tiny chocolate chips in the grocery store.

Coccinelle   Mass-market firm that makes jazzy handbags at affordable prices; free-standing stores in most large Italian cities. Not considered a status line, but who cares?

Coffee   The best-known brands make coffee for all kinds of coffee machines, not just espresso. My favorite is what I call "magic coffee"—a plastic self-heating container with a brand name of Caldo Caldo. If you want to bring home a bag or two of coffee, try any supermarket; the best-known brands are Segafredo, Illy, and Lavazza. The grind is different for espresso. If you get hooked, fret not—Illy has a home-delivery program in the U.S. (© 877/ILLY-DIR; www.illyusa.com/casa).

Consuelo Castiglioni   Designs the Marni line, a whimsical line of men's and women's clothing with five boutiques around the world.

C.P. Company   Casual but elegant line of mostly men's sportswear and some outdoors wear designed by Carlo Rivetti, best known for his choice of textiles.

Diego Della Valle   The man who created Tod's and Hogan (shoes) and is also responsible for Acqua di Parma fragrance.

Diesel   Has nothing to do with cars or trains but may inflame the engine of any teen or 'tween—clothing and jeans that are pricey, tight, and very hot. Stores all over the world especially in all major Italian cities; check out the Style Lab line too. The designer is Renzo Rosso.

Dolce & Gabbana   Bad boys with reputations on the cutting edge of fashion, and highly influenced by their southern Italian roots.

Emilio Pucci   Being dead doesn't mean much when you have a name brand in Italy, or children who can carry on the business. Count Pucci's children sold to LVMH so that the Pucci brand could be revived and expanded. LVMH then did a smart thing—assigning their resident genius, Christian Lacroix, to also design this line. New shops and styles are popping up, and the public is Pucci-crazed all over again.

Etro   Gimmo Etro's family has been in the paisley business with some of Italy's most famous mills in the Lake Como area for centuries. The "new" Etro line is composed of fashions so chic you could swoon.

Fabriano   Paper-goods firm with excellent graphic design and format; free-standing stores opening in all major Italian cities. Fabulous gift items for less than 89€ ($10).

Fendi   Fendi is a sisterhood of five women who run various aspects of the family business, which includes leather goods, ready-to-wear, and furs; now their children are in the business. If you just want to gawk—check out the brand-new Palazzo Fendi in Rome, their "global store." There is also a new home-style line.

Ferragamo   Most famous for the shoes, then the silks, then the clothes, and now the hotel—ask at one of the stores for a free booklet on how to tie a silk scarf. The flagship store is in Florence, which has expanded to take up a full city block. Sizes are American; note that large sizes are often more readily available in the U.S. than in Italy.

Fiorucci   While there are still a few free-standing Fiorucci stores in Italy, many of them have merged with H&M, which has Fiorucci clothes and accessories sold within its stores.

FNAC   This French multimedia chain has expanded into Italy—good for books, CDs and DVDs, and small electronics.

Frette   Italian bed- and table-linen line with consumer and professional (that is, hotel) lines. The somewhat new home-style line includes pajamas and robes. This brand actually began in the French Alps, moving into Italy in the late 19th century. It has rejuvenated its look and expanded into home collections (and stores) in recent years.

Gianfranco Ferré   This former architect's work is identifiable by its construction and architectural lines. The flagship store in Milan is gorgeous, and from an architectural point of view, is of course, stunning. The clothes are divine but are crafted more for the tall woman.

Gianni Versace   The line survives under Donatella's watchful eye. Despite Gianni's death, Versace defines shape and color, flair, drape, and humor. In most Italian cities, the men's, women's, and home-design stores are separate boutiques.

Giorgio Armani   Giorgio Armani has been called one of the top designers in the world; if you listen to *garmento* whispers, you can hear the clucking of wonder as to what will happen to his empire when he moves to the great minimalism in the sky. Meanwhile, his business just keeps growing; he opened headquarters in a renovated chocolate factory in Milan and then even began making (and selling) chocolates.

Gucci   Tom Ford is long gone but the beat goes on. Savings in Italy are minimal (about 48€/$60 on a 480€/$600 hand-bag), but the cachet is high. The new Gucci means status and a whole new look—if you haven't been keeping up, you should check it out. Besides shoes and leather goods, there's clothing, scarves, jewelry, and more. Outlet prices offer handbags in the 240€ ($300) range.

Jil Sander This German line was sold to Italians but was just rebought by Frau Sander herself. The sleek and well-cut men's and women's clothing used to be worth their high price tags. Watch this space.

Kiton Trade name for Ciro Paone, Neapolitan men's tailor, although he himself is not the tailor. In fact, more than 200 tailors work for this menswear brand.

Krizia No, Krizia isn't the designer's name—it's the name of a character created by Plato. The designer behind it all is Mariuccia Mandelli, who has several licensees and creates many Krizia lines, including several fragrance lines. Imaginative, with a good sense of humor, Mandelli still manages to produce those drop-dead elegant clothes that rich women wear.

Laura Biagiotti Although she shows couture and ready-to-wear, Biagiotti is best known for her cashmere knits and her new passion: golf. In her cut-and-sew work, Biagiotti has been known to show a sense of humor. Many of her styles are loose (they make stunning maternity dresses!) and fit nicely on women with imperfect figures. Her cashmeres are expensive but sought after. She has just announced plans to open shops in China!

Les Copains Despite the Frenchified name, this firm is an Italian sportswear company, something on the order of an American bridge designer. They are pretty well known and pretty pricey, but not quite in the same league as Armani. The line is now designed by two young men from southern Italy—one from Sardinia and the other from Naples. This southern slant makes the line hot.

Loro Piana Although most people associate this name with cashmere, the truth is that the factories also make technologically advanced wools for men's suits and produce fabrics of all kinds. Their cashmere is considered unique because it is Italian, not foreign. They also use their fascination for technology in outerwear products and make Storm System, cashmere sweaters that are water repellent.

LUSH British brand but slightly re-created for the Italian market, making bath and beauty products with locally made ingredients, so you get things such as limoncello soap or shampoo. These stores are popping up all over Italy; there are nearly 50 stores in the U.S. and Canada, but none of its branches have the Italian mode except the dozen or so in Italy.

Luciano Barbera A brand so fancy that most people have never heard of it, this men's haberdashery line is carried in Bergdorf Goodman and Neiman Marcus in the U.S. Expect to pay over 800€ ($1,000) for a cashmere sweater. The reason everything costs so much is related to the quality, created in the family mills near Biella. In Italy, there is also a women's line and a golf line.

Madina This makeup line is created by Madina Ferrari, the makeup artist for La Scala opera house in Milan. Her husband happens to own the chemical company that produces most of the world's designer-color cosmetics. Free-standing stores are slowly opening all over the world.

Marni Based in Forte dei Marmi, the Palm Beach of Florence, the Marni family (actually named Castiglioni) has become well known in the U.S. only recently, partly because of the backing of a handful of New York specialty stores. Marni does a cross between whimsy and silly, and provides clothes that people talk about; not your average, bland garments—that's for sure. Lotsa flowers and bold prints.

Missoni A family venture, the Missoni firm is famous for its use of knits and colors. They have become affiliated with architect-designer Saporitti, who has designed many of their boutiques, including one in Milan. The architecture of the Milan shop is worth seeing and is an incredible example of new Italian style. Prices are high. Missoni bed linens are sold in T&J Vestor boutiques around Europe (and Italy).

MiuMiu This is the childhood nickname of Mariucci Prada and the name of the designer bridge line with three stores in Italy: Milan, Florence, and Capri.

Moschino The most successful ghost in Italy, Franco Moschino is actually dead, but his spirit lives on and thrives. If you believe that fashion should be fun, you'll love the work inspired by bad boy Franco Moschino, who was what the French call a *créateur* (a big-name designer who doesn't create couture). The line is designed by Rosella Jardini, who shares Moschino's innate sense of humor and keeps the edge for which the line has always been known.

Nutella The chocolate/hazelnut spread is a personal favorite and one of Italy's best inventions. You can usually find it in grocery stores in the U.S. but in Italy, you can't (and shouldn't) avoid it. I've put the stuff on just about everything. It's best on crepes, fruit, and bread, but in Italy, if you can find it, Nutella-flavored gelato is a truly legendary experience.

Few gelato shops carry this amazing flavor; many will have chocolate/hazelnut gelato, but the real Nutella flavor . . . now that's the good stuff. Since Italy is the home of Nutella and its makers, Ferrero, there is a certain freshness to it that you can't find anywhere else, especially in America where it sits on grocery shelves for almost as long as Twinkies.

Patrizia Pepe This clothing line from Prato (just north of Florence) has become so successful recently that there are now freestanding stores in the best shopping areas of all major Italian cities. This is a bridge line; somewhat hip without being totally over the top.

Pompea Dime-store/mass-market brand of underwear for men and women, knit and seamless. I have given up my La Perla look-alikes in favor of a bandeau bra and string made by this firm—very comfortable. I buy at Upim; the factory outlet store I visited was disappointing.

Pratesi The family name of a small Italian bedding firm on whose sheets most of the crowned heads of Europe were conceived; they also makes sheets for the Pope. Stores are in Boston, New York, and Beverly Hills, as well as major Italian cities, Harrods in London, and Lane Crawford in Hong Kong.

Founded in 1904, and now run by the fourth generation of the family, the sheets are considered the most luxurious in Italy.

Rene Caovilla   This shoemaker from the Veneto makes many designer lines, and now has his own line and a series of small shops in major Italian cities—catch-me-if-you-can heels that cost about 400€ ($500) a pair. Stores are in Venice, Milan, and Rome.

Renzo Piano   Italian architect known for buildings all over the world, but especially talked about now because of his part in revitalizing Rome. He's designed a new music auditorium (has a gift shop and cafe) as well as the art gallery built into the Fiat factory in Turin. The name of the restaurant inside the music hall in Rome is ReD; not Red, like the color. It means *ristorante e design*.

Roberto Cavalli   A legendary talent in Italy, Roberto Cavalli made it into the global scene when movie stars and rock artists adopted his wild jeans. Then he segued into sexy chic with the lingerie look. Now he makes actual lingerie. In the 1970s, his flower-power position was hip; more recently, the clothes were featured on *Sex and the City,* and people in the street say he is the "new" Versace. Check out its boutique line, Just Cavalli. He also has his own restaurant in Milan.

Roberta di Camerino   This Venetian handbag designer offered cult luxury products in the 1970s. Giuliana Camerino, the daughter, now reissues old styles in fabrics that are hard to find and very "in." Also popular in vintage versions.

Ruffo   Officially named Ruffo Research, this firm is famous for cutting-edge leather clothing; the star designer is actually a young Greek woman who went to school in London. (Go figure.) Headquarters are outside Florence, although the best-known store is in Milan.

Sephora   A French chain with an international series of stores created in the style of supermarket beauty products and fragrances—Italian branches have a large selection of French and Italian brands. While there are over 100 stores in Italy alone, they are often in real-people districts and not in tourist areas.

Sneakers

Just like the inception of "designer" jeans, the last 2 years have seen more and more sneakers get fancy Italian makeovers. The big designer brands now make their own, with Prada leading the pack. Many of these designer shoes are incorporating leather into the sneaker for the fancy/casual look; some are still nylon and canvas.

Finding a nice pair in Italy for under 80€ ($100) is almost impossible. Even Puma and Adidas have become status symbols, and likewise, are selling for anywhere from 83€ to 135€ ($104–$169). If you really want to find some cool sneakers without going broke, I strongly recommend going to Florence's outdoor market at Cascine on Tuesday mornings. Granted, you will find your share of the worst fake sneakers here: Adidas with four stripes, and Pumas with an upside-down logo that resembles the Nike "Swoosh" (I like to call these "Pu-kees"). Don't be discouraged; the bargains are here.

For me, cool sneakers are mostly about cool colors and good contrast. In Florence, I saw a very small, no-name brand called "Cric-Ups" that were well built and very cool: best yet, they were 10€ ($13) a pair.

At the same market, I found 30 boxes of Golas at 21€ ($26) per pair. Gola is a brand that was once thought of as an Adidas imposter but has really established itself in the last year as its own shoe. Before leaving New York for Italy, I was able to find Golas for 26€/$32—a definite bargain—but after returning to the U.S., I have seen a few stores selling the new models for 58€/$72—and I was only gone for a week.

Perhaps the easiest one to shop is in the Rome central train station (downstairs).

Shoes Italian shoes, gloves, and handbags have been world famous for centuries. If you are looking for a fun spree without the usual tromping around stores and malls, drive the area between Padua and Venice, where zillions of shoe factories dot

Jenny's Turn: Vintage Clothing

The two best vintage stores on Porta Ticinese are *Spazio 29* and *Lo Specchio di Alice*. Lo Specchio di Alice has recently expanded into two adjacent stores and has a bigger selection, but I liked the feel of Spazio 29 a bit better. Both have clothes from the '60s and '70s, with a few styles from the '80s.

the back roads. The most famous factory is Caovilla, where most designer shoes are made.

Tzemis Despite this difficult-to-remember name, this is a brand to remember; it's the low-cost division of Golden Point and a purveyor of underwear, pajamas, and knits for the young at heart. There are tons of colored wares (I find these pretty boring), but the prints are sensational. I have inspected several of these stores, and not all of them are impressive. Keep shopping the brand; you won't be sorry.

Valentino The famous designer Valentino, known for his work in beige, is legally named Valentino Garavani. In some countries, licensed goods are registered in his legal name. These are not necessarily the man's own designs. If you want true Valentino, you must buy it in Italy—either through Valentino couture, or ready-to-wear.

Vintage clothing Wearing vintage clothes seems to be the trend that just won't end. That's fine with me; I like clothes with a history . . . just not underwear with a history. Vintage in Italy seems to be a northern thing, and Milan is its capital.

Yamamay Despite the Asian-sounding name, this is an Italian underwear and bathing suit manufacturer with stores in every trading district. It appeals to the teens and 'tweens set.

Chapter Five

....

ROME

WELCOME TO ROME

....

I don't know how to be coy about this, so I will just blurt it out: I think the best shopping you can do in Rome is the wander-around-and-enjoy-what-you-find kind of shopping. In short, this is not the best place for a deal, or for much more than wandering and window shopping, unless you get lucky.

Rome has always had a great-designer, upscale-shopping neighborhood, but the arrival of the euro has brought new high prices, and the arrival of eBay has brought new opportunities to shop without travel. So what is truly spiritual about the place—aside from the Vatican, of course—is to wander little streets and alleys, munch on ice cream, look through store windows, and pop into the places that really interest you. Another pair of shoes? Sure, why not!

Now, you shop Rome for selection, or for the big brands at discount stores, or for really cheapie fun clothes that will be over in a season but will give you no end of pleasure until then. Part of the glory that is Rome is that while there are heaps of designer shops, there are also heaps of everything else, too. Even the magazine stands are fabulous to drool over.

And let me tell you about **Oviesse**; oh my, did I score at this Italian version of a fashion-based Target store for locals.

Truth be told, aside from the new Fendi store, I'm not that knocked out with the so-called luxury Spanish Steps district.

About Oviesse

Once upon a time, in Italian-shopping history, there were lots of stores in a chain called Standa, which was much like Upim, a dime store that sells fashion. Standa was sold off; most of their properties have become Oviesse stores—all over Italy, not just in Rome.

I mention the Rome store that I went to because I have spent a lot of time shopping this brand and visiting stores in every Italian city. Had I first shopped in Florence, I would not be raving to you right now. That I jumped in at a Rome store and was wowed by the designs, prices, and large sizes has a lot to do with my love affair with this brand.

While Upim remains a dime store/general store, Oviesse sells just clothing—for men, women, and children with emphasis on a range of sizes for women. There are plus sizes and petites, junior styles, and everyday styles. The fabrics are good; clothes are undoubtedly stitched in some third-world country far away. There are also accessories and some shoes and even pieces of luggage, which you will need if you buy as much as I did.

The average price of a total outfit at Oviesse is under 80€ ($100); a linen dress costs about 32€ ($40). Are you running with me, team? The styles are the latest fashions, so you can be chic and glam for small amounts of bread. And the large-size fashions are so good looking that you can continue to eat bread—or pizza.

About their size system: Tags usually have two sizes printed on them—one is the Italian size (these tend to run small, so you probably wear a larger-than-average numbered size—don't freak) and the other is the continental size, usually marked with a D (for Deutschland—Germany) or CH (for Switzerland).

The stores in Rome are not in a tourist shopping district—stores in other Italian cities are, but not in Rome. There are eight stores in Rome, including the one at Viale Trastevere 62/64 (© 06/5833-3633; www.oviesse.it).

I'm not saying ignore it; I am saying that if your dollars are dear, and if you are not a first-timer, you may have more fun on side streets and in back alleys and away from the slick brands.

I prefer to buy alternative retail, funky designs, vintage clothes, and soap. I prefer to prowl the Campo dei Fiori, to get lost in the medieval warren of streets behind the Piazza Navonna. I prefer to shop at Oviesse; but, I repeat myself.

ARRIVING IN ROME

By Plane

Thankfully, you can fly into Rome's airport from anyplace in the world. Just allow yourself plenty of time before you are actually in the stores and shopping.

The airport (Leonardo da Vinci) is quite a bit out of town, and a taxi will easily set you back 50€ to 70€ ($65–$91). A private car and driver cost about the same as a taxi, by the way (or a little more, but usually not much). As a result, many people book a car and driver to meet them or ask their hotel to provide this service. When I stay at the Hotel Exedra in Rome, I ask them to pick me up—their airport service is 52€ ($65).

I also use one of the many shuttle services from the airport, which generally cost 42 € to 52€ ($52–$65).

If you can manage your luggage on your own, you may want to take the shuttle train (Leonardo Express) from the airport right to the central train station (written as Roma Termini) in beautiful downtown Roma. It costs about 10€ ($13) and is a total breeze.

If you arrive in Rome's airport from another E.U. country, there are no formalities. The color of your luggage tag is coded so that you don't even go through Immigration or Customs. You suddenly end up in the luggage retrieval area, watching fashion shows and car videos on large-screen TV monitors while waiting for your bags.

Trolleys are free. There's both a *cambio,* for changing money, and a bank machine (better rates than the *cambio*), although the lines can be long. Still, since you have to wait for your bags to arrive, you may as well stock up on cash and be ready for the spree to come.

You can connect to the train from within the arrivals terminal (it is well marked), but you must forfeit your trolley to use the escalator, so again, make sure you can handle your luggage on your own or with your travel companion.

If you are headed to the taxi line, be aware that you may be assaulted by taxi drivers: gypsy drivers who may even have official taxis with medallions and may convince you that they are legit. Watch out!

There is an official taxi stand, but you must find it, which I happened to have had trouble doing over a period of many years (slow learner). If you end up on the curb wondering what to do—look right and then walk right, you will find the taxi stand. I promise.

By Rail

All rail tracks do indeed lead to Rome, be it intra-Italian trains or any of the fancy intra-European trains, including Eurostar (Italian Eurostar, not the Chunnel version). Termini—the main station in Rome—has been spiffed up and is looking far better than you may remember it. The fact that it has a giant **Nike** shop in the front and a huge **Upim** with fancy vaulted ceilings to one side helps. A series of electronic kiosks for e-tickets should give you a hint that this is the *new* Italy.

As you emerge from the main train station, you'll see taxis everywhere; you may even be approached by some drivers who offer their services. Again, there is an official taxi stand with a very long line right in front of the train station. You wonder why you don't just hop into one of the waiting cabs, defying the queue. Why does everyone stand in line for up to 20 minutes? Because they don't want to overpay, be cheated, or come to blows with aggressive taxi drivers. I was offered rides to a friend's house for 40€ and 50€ ($510 and $62.50); the legitimate cab fare was 8€ ($10). When I didn't accept the hustlers' offers, they were very insulting in a variety of languages.

Tip: A good reason to stay at the Exedra (see "Sleeping in Rome," later in this chapter): Borrow a trolley from the train station and walk to the hotel.

By Ship

If by chance you are coming to Rome via ship, the port is Civitavecchia (say "Cheat-a-*veck*-ee-ahhhh"); it lies along the coast north and west of Rome. It can take up to 2 hours to get into downtown Rome from here, although 1 hour is the no-traffic estimate. If you are going directly from your ship to the Rome airport, it will take 1 hour on a superhighway, and you will not actually go into Rome at all. *(Arrivederci, Roma.)*

And one final ship-to-shore report: On Saturdays during summer, most stores close for the day at 1:30pm. This isn't really a problem for you, however, because you arrive in port at 7am and make it to Rome by 9:30am, when the stores open. You have the whole morning to shop.

You go to lunch at 1:30pm, when the stores close, and slowly eat a glorious Roman midday feast. Head back to the ship around 4pm and arrive in time for cocktails. Or stop off in Tarquinia, a sneeze away from the port, with its cutie-pie retail and—I thought you'd never ask—a few pottery shops.

There is a train station at the port, but you have to get from the boat to the train in order to connect (you can walk, but it can be a hike, depending on your ship's berth). And, as part of the 2000 Jubilee, there was a major renovation and improvement of the port area. They even added on some shopping venues.

GETTING AROUND

The Lay of the Land

The city of Rome is divided into 33 zones, working in circular rounds, much like the *arrondissements* of Paris. The oldest part of the city is 1, *Centro Storico*. I have instead divided

Rome & Its Shopping Neighborhoods

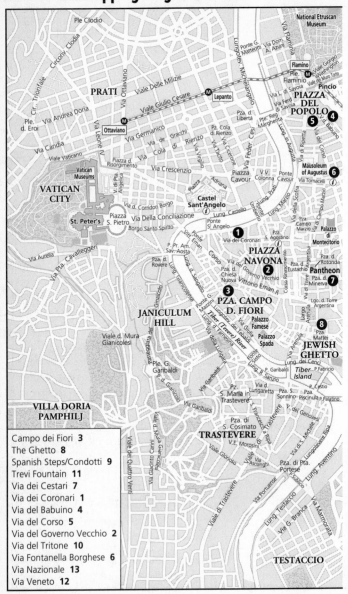

Campo dei Fiori **3**
The Ghetto **8**
Spanish Steps/Condotti **9**
Trevi Fountain **11**
Via dei Cestari **7**
Via dei Coronari **1**
Via del Babuino **4**
Via del Corso **5**
Via del Governo Vecchio **2**
Via del Tritone **10**
Via Fontanella Borghese **6**
Via Nazionale **13**
Via Veneto **12**

Rome into my own areas or neighborhoods (see "Shopping Neighborhoods," later in this chapter).

Technically speaking, Vatican City is a different city than Rome; that's why it has its own guards (who are Swiss), and its own postal service and euro coins.

Traversing the City

Walk as much as possible.

Okay, so it's too hot to walk that much, and the city's too spread out.

So, the best time investment you can make is to organize your days so that you can do lots of walking; this keeps you out of crazy Roman traffic and on the streets where you can count the fountains.

When you must resort to transport, these are your options:

Taxi   Roman taxi drivers are known to be difficult, especially to tourists, especially to Americans who can't speak Italian, and most especially to women traveling without men. Be prepared to occasionally argue with the driver; be aware of when you should pay a supplement (for extra baggage and for rides after 9pm and on Sunday and holidays). I continue to have unpleasant situations with drivers, enough so that I think the difference between Italy and France can be summed up in the way you are treated by taxi drivers. But enough about me.

Legitimate taxis carry a shield with a number. Cars for hire are black with a shield. Taking any other car can be dangerous.

Metro   There is a metro, the Metropolitana. It's nice and gets you to most tourist attractions, but it does not blanket the city. You may find the walk from your hotel to the nearest stop (look for the big red M sign) worthy of a taxi in itself. One reason I switched hotels to the Exedra is that it is 50m (164 ft.) from the Repubblica stop. These days, these things count.

To ride the metro, have change to put into the ticket machine, or look around for a machine that produces change. You must get your ticket from one of the machines; there is no booth selling tickets. (The newsstand will not give you change without a purchase.) Because the metro is not too involved, it is easy to ride and safe. A Metrobus card, which costs about 2.40€ ($3) per day, allows you unlimited use of the metro and buses. It's sold in train stations and at newsstands.

Bus I love to take the bus in Rome, although many people will tell you that buses are slow and not dependable, especially in the rain. But buses are air-conditioned, give you a nice view of this gorgeous city, and get you easily to the main attractions.

To find out which bus to take, you can buy a bus map at a newsstand, you can ask your concierge, or you can read the sign at the bus stop that lists all the stops. Also, check inside the telephone book in your hotel room, which may have a bus and metro map.

I once took the right bus in the wrong direction—a typical mistake for those who don't speak the language or know their way around the city very well—but I had a great time and saw a lot of sights.

Rome has many bus islands that act as little stations where buses congregate. There's one such island in front of the Vittorio Emanuele monument in the old city, and another called San Silvestro, which is in the heart of the shopping district at the base of the Via Veneto and halfway to the Spanish Steps.

The bus system in Rome is similar to those in other Italian cities: You must purchase your ticket at a tobacco stand or newsstand ahead of time (they do not sell tickets on the bus or take money); you enter from the rear and cancel your own ticket in the box; and you exit from the center of the bus. Instructions in English and Italian are inside the bus. Bus tickets will cost you a euro ($1.25).

My favorite bus is the no. 80, which you get at the beginning of the line at the bus island at San Silvestro. You can take this bus directly to a very good Oviesse store and enjoy air-conditioning, being off your feet, door-to-door service for a euro ($1.25), and my favorite cheapie store. Your stop is Trieste, about a half-hour from San Silvestro, but verify with the driver, and he will get you to the door of the store. Remember, to head back toward San Silvestro, you must cross the street

About Addresses

Addresses seem to bounce around from street to street; some alternate in a sensible way and some make no sense at all. Frequently, all the stores in a block have the same street number and are designated by letters. It's not unusual for a store to be listed according to its piazza or its street corner.

and catch the bus in the other direction. If you have been gone only 75 minutes (this is unlikely), you do not need a new bus ticket.

SLEEPING IN ROME

American Hotel Chains

The American hotel chains have made a comfortable dent in the Roman scene; they often offer deals (in dollars, no less) that are too good to be true. While there are several chains (see below), note that with the addition of a spa, the Hilton has reached icon status. While it has a slightly screwy location, it has become a major, major player.

ROME CAVALIERI HILTON
Via A. Cadlolo 101 (no metro but free shuttle bus service).

We all know to trust the Hilton brand, but few of us know that this is one of the most famous, and different, Hilton hotels in the system. Yes, it is out of the downtown area—but the benefits overcome that disadvantage.

The hotel has a fabulous, and famous, rooftop restaurant, La Pergola. But it gets better: Always famous for its swimming pool and parklike grounds, this Hilton now has a spa. Not just any old spa, as is the rage among all hotels, but a spa of such grand proportions that it was possibly created to make Cleopatra roll over in her grave. This spa has become so important in the local landscape that now zillions of celebs stay here. The buzz on the hotel has changed from that of insider's secret to bastion of hip.

Lest you forget, summer in Rome is so hot that you can rarely shop for more than half a day, and it's great to have a pool and a spa to repair in.

Last time I called Hilton to book, they had a deal that had to be booked in the U.S., for 119€/$149 per room per night. I don't need to tell you that 119€/$149 per night is about the least-expensive five-star room you can get in Rome. To try for your own great rate, call ✆ **800/HILTONS** in the U.S. and Canada, or 06/3509-2031. www.cavalieri-hilton.it.

INTERCONTINENTAL DE LA VILLE ROMA
Via Sistina 67–69 (metro: Spagna).

The InterContinental De la Ville Roma has the best location of any of the U.S. chains for shopping, as well as some rather good deals. Last time I checked, the Hotel de la Ville was booking at 199€ ($249) per night. Note that you get breakfast with this rate, as well as 500 frequent-flier miles. The Hotel de la Ville is at the top of the Spanish Steps and is divinely swank, as well as service oriented. Call ✆ **888/303-1758** or 06/67-331 for reservations. http://rome.intercontinental.com.

WESTIN EXCELSIOR
Via Vittorio Veneto 125 (metro: Veneto).

In Rome, it's the Excelsior—grande dame hotel right on the Via Veneto just up the block from the American Embassy. This is one of the fanciest hotels in town and is particularly prized when it does a tie-in with cruise ships. Call ✆ **800/325-2525** or 06/47-081 for reservations. www.starwoodhotels.com.

Dream Hotels

EXEDRA
Piazza della Repubblica 47 (metro: Repubblica).

This hotel changed my vision of Rome. It's new inside, old outside, and built over ruins that you can see through glass floors
on the lower level (head for the business center).

The restaurant is designed by my hero, Adam Tihany. The
hotel location right above a metro station makes transportation a breeze. The staff is dressed in very chic black on black,
everyone is friendly and helpful, and because the hotel is so
new, you have the feeling of having made a great discovery.

There's a cooking school, sumptuous rooms, and, get this,
a McDonald's next door. Any luxury hotel with a McDonald's
is my kind of place, although I hear they are trying to ease out
the fast food. There's also a movie theater (with some selections in English), a rooftop pool and spa, and more chic than
the average person can begin to absorb. *Note:* Do not confuse
this hotel with the trendy Es Hotel.

Rooms begin at 260€ ($325); I found a room online for
250€ ($313)—more or less the same price at current exchange
rates. Call © **800/337-4685** or 06/489-381. www.exedra.
boscolohotels.com.

ALEPH HOTEL
Via di San Basilio 15 (metro: Barberini).

Considering that my heartthrob, Adam Tihany, designed this
hotel, it's a pity I had to stare at it without sleeping in it. Indeed,
this is the small, cozy, artsy boutique hotel for those who want
luxury on the sly. There's a spa, a Moroccan-style restaurant,
and a location nestled not too far from the Spanish Steps and
Via Veneto. This hotel is so hot it has been photographed for
various design magazines, guide books, and books on Roman
style. Don't miss it, even if you just come by for a drink. Call
© **800/337-4685** or 06/422-901. www.aleph.boscolohotels.com.

Snack & Shop

LA CARBONARA
Piazza Campo dei Fiori 23 (no nearby metro).

This is one of the few places in Rome where it is as pleasant to eat inside as outside, where your experience is as special in winter as in spring. Located right on the Campo dei Fiori, this seems to be the nicest of the surrounding cafes. The interior is done in a rustic country style, with some tables overlooking the piazza. The daily fruit and flower market adds to the charm of the location and makes this restaurant a must. This is one of the few restaurants in the area that is open on Sunday (although it's closed on Tues). However, the flower market is closed on Sunday. For reservations, call © 06/686-47-83.

MCDONALD'S
Piazza di Spagna, near the Spanish Steps (metro: Spagna).

Stop laughing. I love this McDonald's, and not just because my son does. The architecture (it's in a fake villa) is astounding, the location is sublime, and the food is inexpensive for Rome, if not by U.S. standards. You can get the usual burgers and McNuggets, or load up at the salad bar, where you can get tomatoes and mozzarella. You have to see this place. The crowd it gets is amazing. It's a good place to rest between stores. Logan, my Roman insider source, says to sit downstairs where it's less noisy; Baci (the chocolates) is sold, and there's an ice-cream counter.

NINO
Via Borgognona 11 (metro: Spagna).

My favorite restaurant in Rome, Nino is a small bistro with dark, wood walls, and it's located right in the heart of the Spanish Steps shopping area. It attracts a nice, fashionable crowd without being chichi.

Prices are moderate by Rome standards, which to me is incredibly inexpensive, especially for this location and style.

I just got my Visa bill: My last lunch at Nino, an admittedly simple affair consisting of bottled water, one Coca-Cola, spaghetti, and a coffee, was under 16€ ($20). Tip included.

The waiters are friendly; I often eat here solo and feel comfortable doing so. If you get here early (by local standards) for lunch, you don't need a reservation. Closed Sunday. © 06/ 679-56-76.

Ristorante Girarrosto Toscano
Via Campania 29 (metro: Veneto).

This country-style place is at the top of the Via Veneto (across the street from the Jolly Hotel, around the corner from the Westin Excelsior). Sit down and feast on the antipasti, for which there is a flat charge per person no matter how much you eat. After you've eaten more than you thought possible, they bring dinner. The cooking style is Florentine; the wine is Chianti (although there are plenty of others); the atmosphere is adorable (covered in tiles and charm); the crowd is well heeled (although there are some tourists); and the prices are moderate. Book a reservation, especially after 8pm, as the place does fill up. Closed Wednesday. © 06/482-18-99.

THE SHOPPING SCENE

Shopping is something you do in Rome while you are doing Rome—or in between meals. Aside from a frontal attack on Via Condotti and the fancy stores in that area, you will find shopping opportunities as you explore Rome, not vice versa.

Roman style is still a little bit old couture, but Roman fashion mostly reflects Rome's geographic location, which is philosophically—and fashion-wise—the south of Italy. As such, Rome is rather like the Beverly Hills of Italy, and the clothes for sale here have a glitz and gleam to them that you won't find up north. Even the Milanese, who have moved on down here, don't wear black.

Colors are hot in Rome. Women are not flat-chested in Rome. Skirts are shorter in Rome. Nailheads, studs, bugle beads, and sequins with, yes, truly, little bits of fur or feathers—faux and/or real—can be found sewn to clothing and . . . hmm . . . even shoes and tote bags.

The globalization of money and designer franchises means that Italian designers sell their lines all over their own country, most certainly in Rome, and in just about every other country as well. The line may be most fully shown in stores in Milan, but you can find an excellent selection of these designer clothes in Rome. In a few cases, the Rome store is better than the Milan store.

Best Buys

Rome doesn't have any cheap best buys, unless you shop at Upim or Oviesse. Oops, I lied. You can get lucky.

Designer Fashions   You won't find too many designer bargains unless you hit a sale, but if you do, things can really go your way. If you are bargain conscious, the best deals in Rome are at a few outlet shops (see "Outlets," later in this chapter) or in the airport, which has a gigantic duty-free shopping area. If you are status conscious, the best buys are due to the fact that there is a selection of styles in any given designer brand that goes beyond other cities in the world.

Note that items imported to Italy for sale at the duty-free shops at the airport (English sweaters, for example) are 19% cheaper than they are in a regular Italian store, but they are still outrageously expensive. Buy Italian when in Italy; forget everything else. Also note that, even though it may look like one, not every store in the Rome airport is a duty-free shop.

Handbags   Although I usually buy my handbags in Hong Kong and have long ago sworn off $1,000 handbags, I found a store in Rome that not only tickled my fancy (I bought three bags) but also seems to be very popular with visitors. In my week of work in Rome on my last research trip, every woman I passed in the Spanish Steps shopping district seemed to have a glossy shopping bag from **Francesco Rogani** (Via Condotti 17; ℂ 06/ 678-7737) on her arm. See the listings section of this chapter for the lowdown.

Home Style   From Tad's to Lisa Corti, the hot Mediterranean colors and the mix of imported looks with Italian chic have arrived. This is mondo home style, from Asia to the subcontinent and beyond, shaken up with the Italian touch. Lisa Corti is sold at Saks Fifth Avenue, but the Italy prices—even in euros—are better than the U.S. prices. If you can't stand the colors, back into beige or monotones in bed linen, from Frette or Pratesi.

Ties   I got caught up in the number of status ties for sale in various shops in Rome. Prices are less expensive than in the U.S. and the U.K. In fact, prices can be so low you may giggle. The average price of a power tie in New York, without New York state sales tax, is 76€ to 108€ ($95 to $135). The same ties in Rome cost 52€ to 88€ ($65–$110). You can even buy a power tie in Rome for 28€ ($35). I kid you knot.

Shopping Hours

Hours in Rome are the same as in all of Italy, but Sundays are really loosening up. In fact, the department store La Rinascente is open on Sunday from noon to 5pm. Wonders never cease. Furthermore, there's a new mall, **Piazza Colonna,** which is not only open on Sundays, but is even open until 10pm. Note that stores open for Sunday shopping may close for lunch and then reopen from 4 to 7 pm.

For normal retail days (Tues–Fri), shops open at 9:30am and close at 1 or 1:30pm for lunch. They reopen at 3:30pm in winter and at 4pm in summer. In the summer, stores stay open until 8pm. Because Romans (as do all Europeans) dine late, many people are out shopping until midnight. Do not let any hotel concierge or signpost lead you to believe that stores in Rome open at 9am—even if it says so on the door. This is Rome, remember?

If you don't like to give up shopping for lunch, the department stores and mass merchandisers stay open during these hours, and a growing number of high-end merchants are following suit. Fendi is open through lunch, as are many other stores on Via Borgognona and in the Spanish Steps area.

The odd days are Monday, Saturday, and Sunday. Some stores are closed Monday morning; in summer, they are often also closed Saturday afternoon. But that's not a rule. On my last Monday in Rome, I found that mass-market stores and chains were open by 10am that day. Designer shops open at 3:30pm on Monday.

Finally, watch out for those August closures—some stores call it curtains totally. Only madmen go to Rome in August. The sales are in July.

Special-Event Retailing

If you happen to be in Rome any time between December 15 and January 6, get yourself (and your kids) over to the Piazza Navona, where there is an annual Christmas fair. Stalls surround the large square and offer food, candies, and crafts. You can buy tree ornaments and crèches. *Warning:* Much of the Hong Kong–made merchandise is less expensive in the U.S. Stick to locally crafted items at the fair, and you won't get ripped off.

Because Easter in Rome is also a big deal, there are more vendors in Vatican City at this time.

Personal Needs

You will find neither grocery stores nor real-people department stores in the middle of the usual tourist shopping haunts, although there are branches of **La Rinascente** and of **Upim** just near San Silvestro, close to the main tourist areas, such as the Trevi Fountain and the Spanish Steps.

Rome has dozens of all-night pharmacies, including one at the airport. The pharmacy at the Termini train station is open until 11:30pm daily. The station also has a fabulous mall that can meet most needs; stores are open on Sundays.

Rome is more spread out than some other cities you may visit; you may need to take a walk around your hotel to find a local minimart for buying water, snack foods, and all those things that cost too much from your minibar.

Ask your concierge where to find the nearest pharmacy or grocery. Condoms are sold from machines in public places, as well as at pharmacies and grocery stores.

Shopping Neighborhoods

Spanish Steps/Via Condotti   No matter what season of the year, the Spanish Steps are so gorgeous that you can't help but be drawn to them. They are particularly magical because they lead to all the best big-name stores. Don't forget that there's an **American Express** office at the Steps, so when you run out of money on a shopping spree, you can get more without missing a beat, and then get right back to spending it.

The **Via Condotti** is the leading shopping street of the high-rent Spanish Steps neighborhood—but it is not the only game in town, or even in the block. The area between the Spanish Steps and the Via del Corso is a grid system of streets, all packed with designer shops. Via Condotti has the most famous big names and is the equivalent of Rodeo Drive, but you'll miss a lot of great stuff if you don't do the side streets.

Note: There is one street that leads away from the Spanish Steps, the Via del Babuino (yes, it's the baboon street), which appears to be an equal spoke from the Steps but actually has a very different neighborhood feel to it; so, I have separated it from the rest (see below).

If you have only a few hours to shop in Rome and you are seriously interested in designer fashion, your assignment, should you accept it or not, is to shop the Spanish Steps/Condotti area and to get to some—or all—of the Via del Babuino and a block or two of the Via del Corso down at the Condotti end. By all means, make it into the recently built **Palazzo Fendi**

Boncompagni, which is like an art gallery of creativity. Even the handles on the front door are works of art.

Via Fontanella Borghese   Right now, this area is still coming into its own as an extension of the Via Condotti on the other side of the Via del Corso. This street is quiet, unvisited by tourists, and home to several new branches of big-name designer shops, such as **Fendi** with its new palazzo, which just about takes up a city block. In this same quiet area is the new **Lisa Corti** store.

Via del Babuino   Remember when I told you that Spanish Steps/Condotti had another part to it that was the same but different? Well, this is it. This is one of the antiques neighborhoods of Rome, and boasts some snazzy designer shops, too. It's a fun neighborhood, especially if you're just looking for furniture, paintings, or the hottest items in Europe these days: Art-Deco tabletop accessories. I take it back—this is more than a fun neighborhood. This is a must-do.

Via Veneto   I know that every American in Rome has heard of the Via Veneto, if only from the movies. While I invariably stay at a hotel in this area, the shopping here is nothing to write home about or to go out of your way to visit.

The large bookstalls on the street corners are handy for a vast selection of magazines (all languages) and supplies from postcards to videos (yes, even dirty movies) to paperback best-sellers in English. There are some shoe shops and several glitzy cafes. It's a pleasant street to wander, but not exceptional. If you are staying in the area, you will probably enjoy the side streets more.

Via Nazionale   This is a very long street, but its best parts are between Repubblica and Termini, where there are a slew of fashion shops for young women and a few big names. More and more big names are opening here, and you can now find Max Mara, Frette, and a few others. Watch this space.

Trevi & Tritone   From the Spanish Steps, you can walk to the Trevi Fountain and segue into several "real-people" Rome neighborhoods. Of course you want to throw three coins in the fountain, and then have an ice cream.

The shopping is touristy but the atmosphere is real. Be sure to hit **Via del Tritone,** which is on the way to or from Trevi; both sides of the street have good offerings. You will also find that this niche of shopping and ice cream heaven is located right near the San Silvestro bus terminal, so you can travel onward to other shopping destinations from here.

Via del Tritone   This big, real-people shopping street connects the Via del Corso and Spanish Steps areas to the Via Veneto and Piazza Barberini areas; it is also an extension of the Trevi neighborhood. At the top is the **Piazza Barberini,** with the Bernini Bristol Hotel and a metro stop. If you are looking for an Internet cafe, easyInternetcafé, one of the best in Rome, is right there next to the cinema (Via Barberini 2/16), and it's open 24/7.

Downhill, the street dead-ends into Via del Corso, where you have a lot of regular shops with more moderate prices than the big-name designer shops 3 blocks away. A large **La Rinascente** department store is on the corner.

Via del Corso   Via del Corso is a very long street; the part that you will be most interested in begins where Via del Tritone intersects it and extends all the way to Piazza del Popolo. Both sides of the street are lined with stores; many are branches of famous names, such as Frette or even Benetton, and many are stores that I just like for local color. A lot of the stores in this stretch are devoted to younger shoppers, teens, 'tweens, and 20-somethings.

The really hot part of Via del Corso is right below the Spanish Steps, in the area from Via Condotti to Piazza del Popolo, where you'll find all the fancy designer shops, a zillion teen shops (rock music blaring), and the cheapie fashion stores such as **Onyx.** While you are here, don't miss **Tezemis** (Via del Corso 148), which is a branch of Calzedonna. This particular branch is not as great as others, but if this is your first chance to discover this unheralded brand of underwear and sleepwear for girls of all ages, go for it.

Via dei Cestari If you're looking for a unique shopping experience, a unique gift, or just something special and different after you visit the Pantheon (bad gift stalls), check out the Via dei Cestari, which is filled with ecclesiastical shops selling ribbons, robes, socks, and all sorts of fascinating supplies. Start at **De Ritis** (no. 48) and check out the surrounding stores. Many also sell chalices and religious souvenirs.

Via dei Coronari You say you like to stroll down medieval streets and look at antiques shops? Hmm. Well, have I got a street for you. This particular street takes you back to a previous century, and has the best antiques stores in Rome. Located right around the corner from the Piazza Navona, the Via dei Coronari is very small; study your map first.

Walk down one side of the street and back up the other, an area of maybe 2 or 3 blocks. Some shops are extremely fancy salons with priceless pieces; others are a little funkier. Almost all the dealers take credit cards. Those who don't speak English may speak French if your Italian isn't too sharp. The shop numbers will go to the middle 200s before you've seen it all; there are possibly 100 dealers here.

The dealers are very community minded and have their own block association that has various parties and promotions for the public. They've organized a few nights in May when the stores stay open late, and a party in October, also for late-night strolling and shopping (officially called the local **Antiques Fair**). Candles and torches light the way.

If you are looking for some place super to eat in the midst of the antiques stores, try **Osteria dell'Antiquario**, Piazzetta di San Simeone (☎ **06/687-96-94**). You can eat outdoors or in at this simple but elegant place that's also quite "in." Lunch for two costs about 64€ ($80). Don't let the address throw you; it's right on the Via dei Coronari. If you want to spend less for lunch, try **Le Streghe**, vicolo del Curato 13 (☎ **06/687-81-82**). I eat there—often outside—for about 20€ ($25).

Campo dei Fiori Campo dei Fiori is one of those neighborhoods that is beginning to attract tourists and will certainly be ruined in no time at all; right now it is a genuine daily fruit and flower market that packs up by about 1pm. Get there mid-morning, browse the stalls and photograph the fruits, and then plop down at any of the dozen or so cafes nearby. There are also pizza places, if you don't want a 48€ ($60) lunch.

Aside from the market, you are in the midst of an old Roman neighborhood, where rents are lower and fun shops are opening up. There is a number of food and cookware stores surrounding the Campo dei Fiori; the Piazza Navona is just a few blocks away, which gets you to the **Rancé** soap shop and a stroll around the piazza, of course. Note that there is no market at Campo dei Fiori on Sunday.

Via del Governo Vecchio   This is sort of a hidden street, between the Piazza Navona and the Campo dei Fiori. Before you attempt to find it on foot, first try to locate it on a map. The street is dark, narrow, medieval, and blessed with a few vintage clothing shops. Some are the army-navy type; others sell serious vintage. Aside from the vintage stores, there are some cutting-edge fashion boutiques. I like **Morgana** (no. 27) and **Arsenale;** both are hot and happening. This neighborhood is easy to reach, is fun to shop, and gives you a less touristy perspective on Rome.

The Ghetto   This is a far cry from the Grand Hotel, but for those of you who want to stay in a fabulous hotel but then travel to the grittier parts of the city, you are off on a crazy adventure. Take a bus from the train station to the Vittorio Emanuele monument and walk, or just taxi, right to the oldest part of Rome, where the ghetto was.

Take the **Via delle Botteghe Oscure** for 2 short blocks, note all the fabric jobbers (wholesalers), then turn left at the **Piazza Paganica.** You'll now enter a small neighborhood that seems very residential. Wander the weaving streets looking for the shops that interest you. This is the kind of adventure that is welcomed by a true *garmento,* someone who likes to see bolts of fabric piled up in store windows and doesn't care about fancy architecture or salespeople in matching uniforms. The area is charming, crumbling, and undiscovered by tourists. All of

Via dei Coronari

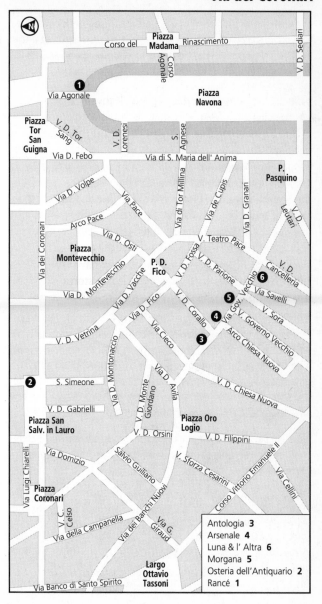

Antologia **3**
Arsenale **4**
Luna & l' Altra **6**
Morgana **5**
Osteria dell'Antiquario **2**
Rancé **1**

these stores are jobbers; you'll find jeans and underwear and sweats and even a few jewelry stores. *Don't miss:* **Leone Limentani,** Via Portico d'Ottavia 47, a discounter with mounds of dishes and china—even Richard Ginori patterns.

The Five Best Stores of Rome

LISA CORTI HOME TEXTILE EMPORIUM
Via di Pallacorda 14 (metro: Spagna).

I am a huge Lisa Corti fan, so I send you here with delight. It's right near the Piazza Fontanella Borghese, not too far from the Spanish Steps. The Lisa Corti collection includes home style, tabletop, and home fashions. Look for the merchandise in any Saks Fifth Avenue catalog, and then compare prices in person. Call ✆ **06/6819-3216.** www.lisacorti.com.

LUNA & L'ALTRA
Via del Governo Vecchio 105 (no nearby metro).

This store isn't much bigger than a walk-in closet, but it carries an international cadre of funky-chic names, such as Issey Miyake and Dries Van Noten, and puts it all together in a look that is comfortable and fabulous. Call ✆ **06/6880-4995.**

SOLE
Via Gregoriana 34 (metro: Spagna).

This isn't technically a store; it's an atelier and should be visited only by serious shoppers who call ahead for an appointment. The studio is on the top floor of a residential building near the top of the Spanish Steps. If you love creative clothes and an artistic look, you'll find it worth the walk.

Sole is the child of Soledad Twombly, an artist and the daughter-in-law of the famous artist Sy Twombly. Her husband, Alessandro, is also a well-known artist. Her studio features clothes, along with shoes, jewelry, sweaters, knits, and all the pieces you need for a complete look. She does only two seasons; the fabrics all work together, so you can add on pieces and change around the outfits.

Prices are dear, but less than in stores when you buy directly from the designer. You can order by your size or have items made to your measurements. © 06/6992-4512. www.soledad twombly.com.

TAD'S
Via del Babuino 155a (metro: Spagna).

Home style by the mile, even though it's not that hard-line Italian look. In fact, the look is somewhat international in scope, with imports galore and items from India with beads and hand-painting and glitter and tassels. If you like Anthropologie stores in the U.S., you will love Tad's in Rome. Ask them for the address of the stock shop that was around the corner when I visited; it may have moved. There is a cafe, too. © 06/3269-5131. www.taditaly.com.

TERMINI ROMA MALL
Rome central train station (metro: Termini).

Perhaps you can never take the love of a mall out of the American heart. This is truly an American-style mall located underneath the main train station, but it has French and Italian stores—and places to eat—and it is great fun. There's a shop devoted to merchandise for race-car drivers and wannabes. There's a Sephora (the beauty supermarket). There is a real supermarket. Aboveground, on the main level, there's a tease of what's below—a Nike shop, a Benetton, a bookstore, even a large Upim. If you haven't seen the brand Bottega Verde, this is a place to check it out—sort of the local version of The Body Shop. Note the barrel vaulted ceilings, the ochre colors, and the attempt at a lush-hush historical Roman feel.

ROME RESOURCES A TO Z

....

Antiques

While I can't go so far as to suggest you actually buy antiques here, Rome is the Italian center of fancy antiques shops. There are several streets where stores abound, including **Via del Babuino** and **Via dei Coronari** (see above). If you're shopping for serious antiques and looking for a dealer to trust, look for the gold seal representing the Associazione Romana Antiquari. Note that the shops on Via dei Coronari are usually open at night, and each fall, for 1 week; there's an antiques market at Pala Parioli.

Beauty

AVEDA
Rampa Mignanelli 9 (metro: Spagna).

Although this address sounds screwy, actually *rampa* very well describes the fact that the shop is on a ramp to the Spanish Steps. This is an American brand, and prices are slightly higher in Rome than in the U.S., but it's a high-quality brand and good for travel sizes if you need products. © **06/6992-4257.** www.aveda.com.

BEAUTY PLANET
Grand Hotel Palace, Via Veneto 66–70 (metro: Veneto).

A full-service spa and beauty center, this is not one of the new, low-rent rip-offs of Sephora, but a very fancy, high-end shop with expensive brands and some expensive accessories, such as hair clips and bands. You need not be a guest at the hotel to shop here. Closed Sunday. Call © **06/481-71-49.**

Books

The large news kiosks on the Via Veneto sell paperback books in many languages, including English.

FELTRINELLI
79–87 via VE Orlando (metro: Repubblica).

This famous chain has stores here and there in busy shopping districts. This location is divided into a few stores in a row; the international shop, with books in English, is no. 87. There's also a ton of guide books and a wide selection of videos and DVDs of famous Italian movies. They are open on Sundays, 10am to 1:30pm and 4 to 7pm. Call © **06/482-78-78.**

RIZZOLI ROMA
Largo Chigi 15; Via Tomacelli 156 (metro: Spagna).

Tomacelli is the larger of the two shops; both are open on Sunday at 10:30am until 1:30pm and then 4 to 8pm. During the week, hours are nonstop. Italy's best bookstore with books in all languages. To reach the Largo Chigi location, call © **06/679-66-41.** The Tomacelli location is at © **06/6882-8513.**

Cashmere

AMINA RUBINACCI
Via Bocca di Leone 51 (metro: Spagna).

Visitors to Capri will know the name of this famed Neopolitan source that has recently opened a small shop in Rome specializing in cashmeres, but there are also cottons and cashmere blends. To die for. © **06/679-53-54.** www.aminarubinacci.it.

MALO
Via Borgognona 5 (metro: Spagna).

This flagship of the famed brand has home style, gift items, accessories, and more cashmere than you can dream of. Malo even has an outlet store outside of Florence; see p. 145. Call © **06/679-13-31.** www.malo.it.

Costume Jewelry

CASTELLI
Via Condotti 22 and 61; Via Frattina 18 and 54 (metro: Spagna).

This small, wood-paneled shop is crammed with perfume, beauty supplies, and a wonderful collection of costume jewelry. Don't miss the variety of evening bags. I once saw this fabulous hair contraption in chenille (sort of a chignon catcher), but it cost 80€ ($100)—and that was with the stronger dollar. The store at Via Condotti 22 is open nonstop (through lunch, that is); you can reach that store by calling © 06/679-09-98. For other locations, check out the Castelli website at www.castelli-it.com.

Department Stores

Italy doesn't have great department stores, and I don't suggest you go out of your way to shop in one. In Rome, two are somewhat convenient to mainstream tourist shopping: a branch of **La Rinascente** at Via del Corso 189; and a branch of **Coin** at Piazzale Appio, which is across the street from the Via Sannio market, and may be on your itinerary (if you can't stand to look at another fountain).

Upim, the dime-store version of an Italian department store (which may be a contradiction in terms), has stores at Via del Tritone 172 and Via Nazionale 211. The **Standa** on Viale Trastevere 60 has a supermarket downstairs.

Designer Boutiques

The best metro stop for all these addresses is Spagna. For more detail on many of these well-known brand names, check out my "Dictionary of Taste & Design" in chapter 4.

CONTINENTAL BIG NAMES

BURBERRY
Via Condotti 60.

CARTIER
Via Condotti 83.

CELINE
Via Condotti 20.

CHANEL
Via del Babuino 98/100.

DIOR
Via Condotti 3.

ESCADA
Salita San Sebasstianello 8.

FOGAL
Via Condotti 55.

HERMÈS
Via Condotti 67.

KENZO
Via del Babuino 124.

LOUIS VUITTON
Via Condotti 15.

SWATCH
Via Condotti 33.

YVES SAINT LAURENT RIVE GAUCHE
Via Condotti 3.

ITALIAN BIG NAMES

ALBERTA FERRETTI
Via Condotti 34.

BENETTON
Piazza di Spagna 67–69.

BOTTEGA VENETA
Piazza San Lorenzo 9.

BRIONI
Via Condotti 21a.

DOLCE & GABBANA
Piazza di Spagna 82–83; Via Borgognona 7d.

EMPORIO ARMANI
Via del Babuino 140.

ETRO
Via del Babuino 102.

FENDI
Via Fontanella di Borghese 57.

FERRAGAMO
Via Condotti 73.

GIANFRANCO FERRÉ
Via Borgognona 42.

GIORGIO ARMANI
Via Condotti 77.

GUCCI
Via Condotti 8.

HOGAN
46 via Borgognona.

LA PERLA
Via Condotti 79.

LAURA BIAGIOTTI
Via Borgognona 43.

LES COPAINS
Piazza di Spagna 32–35.

MAX & CO.
Via Condotti 46.

MAX MARA
Via Condotti 17–19; Via Frattina 28.

MISSONI
Piazza di Spagna 78.

PRADA
Via Condotti 92/95.

ROBERTO CAVALLI (JUST CAVALLI)
Piazza Espagna 82.

TRUSSARDI
Via Condotti 49.

VALENTINO
Via Condotti 13.

ZEGNA
Via Borgognona 7.

Discounters

DISCOUNT SYSTEM
Via Viminale 35 (metro: Repubblica).

This store is possibly owned by the same people who own Il Discount Dell Alta Moda (see below), or else it is just patterned after it. They have a very similar brochure and the same pricing system, which means that, to get the accurate price, you must deduct 50% from the marked price on the tag; so, don't let the price tags throw you.

In terms of selection, Discount System is a larger store and has a much, much, much greater selection. I spent an hour here touching everything and trying to buy something but left empty-handed. There's menswear, women's wear, shoes, handbags, luggage, belts, ties, dressy dresses, and every big-name Italian designer. The clothes are at least a year old.

The location is convenient enough to make this a thought-provoking choice for bargain shoppers. It's around the corner from the Grand Hotel and down the street from the main train station; you can take the metro to Repubblica and walk. The same metro will also take you to Piazza di Spagna and the Spanish Steps. © 06/474-65-45.

IL DISCOUNT DELL ALTA MODA
Via di Gesù e Maria 16 and 14 (men's store) (metro: Spagna).

I'm leaving this store in the book for now, but my last visits have been very disappointing. The problem is lack of range, lack of sizes, and sometimes high prices (even at a discount, some of these prices will make you wince). *Important note:* The price is one-half of the price marked on the ticket. So if you are going to wince, do so accurately. The staff may not speak English.

Now for the good news: There are plenty of big names, and the store is easy to shop because it is arranged by color group. The handbags are probably the best deal.

The best news is the men's store, two doors down, at no. 14. This store is huge and well stocked, and has many things that will fit women. While Armani jeans at 96€ ($125) weren't my idea of a bargain, I wanted everything. The style, colors, and sophistication of their men's suits are beyond compare. © 06/361-37-96.

Gloves

MEROLA
Largo Goldoni 47, off Via del Corso (metro: Spagna).

This is the oldest glove shop in Rome and a far cry from much of the rest of the fare on Via del Corso, which nowadays seems to cater to teens. Yes, Audrey Hepburn's gloves in *Roman Holiday* came from here. © 06/679-19-61. www.merolagloves.it.

Gifts

FABRIANO
Via del Babuino 173 (metro: Spagna).

Another find from Milan, this store sells pens, writing goods, bound notebooks, and papers. There are some great gifts with tons of style for not much money. © 06/686-42-68.

Handbags

What's a trip to Italy without a touchy-feely session with 1,001 handbags? There may be better buys north of Rome, but Rome is a good place to start to look.

CARPISA
Via del Corso 164, via Belsiana 59 (metro: Spagna).

This is a chain begun in Naples with stores all over Rome and most of Italy—they are newly arrived, are hugely popular due to low prices and lots of great colors, and appeal more to the younger set. Most of the summer bags are canvas; fabrics are also used in fall and winter—this, of course, helps keep prices down. Indeed, where else can you find a great bag for 20€ ($25)? ✆ 800/777-155 (toll free within Italy). www.carpisa.it.

FRANCESCO BIASIA
Via di Torre Argentina 7 (bus: Largo Argentina); via Due Macelli 62 (metro: Spagna).

This brand is well known for its *ooh la la* interpretation of southern Italy and is often sold in department stores throughout Italy. The brand is also often sought at discount sources because it tends to be a little pricey. The Largo Argentina location, by the way, is walking distance from Trevi Fountain and the area around San Silvestro. ✆ 0444/360-500. www.biasia.com.

FRANCESCO ROGANI
Via Condotti 17 (metro: Spagna).

This is a very fancy tourist trap (TT) and may not be your cup of Hermès copy, with many versions of both Kelly and Birkin styles and even a Bugatti or two. The store locks the doors when they think there are too many shoppers, they do not have a very service-oriented attitude, and they offer sales that may or may not be real. I found great stuff and am thrilled with my buys, but I don't know if I believe that the marked-down price isn't the price the goods originally sold for. The bags I bought were great because of the ratio of quality to price; at twice the price (as marked on the tags), I would not have pounced.

They use a pebble grain leather, which is good for travel because it doesn't mark up that easily and wears well. At 135€ ($169) per bag, they're worth loading up on. There is a mock-croc version for 218€ ($273) that I also think is a winner. © 06/678-40-36.

FURLA
Piazza di Spagna 22 (metro: Spagna).

This is an Italian chain with stores all over the world—including a dozen in Rome—and is known to offer high style and some glamour at realistic prices. Sort of the poor man's Prada, with bags that sell for under 160€ ($200). There are outlet stores in various malls covered in this book. © 06/6920-0363. www.furla.com.

Home Style

Tad's is another great location for home-style shopping (see "The Five Best Stores of Rome," earlier in this chapter).

C.U.C.I.N.A.
Via Mario de'Fiori 65 (metro: Spagna).

This store is actually similar to Pottery Barn or Crate & Barrel in the U.S., or even Conran's in London, but this is the Italian version. It's a must for foodies and those seeking gifts for cooks and gourmands—lots of little doodads. For those who have visited the store before, yes, this is a new address. © 06/679-12-75.

FRETTE
Piazza di Spagna 11 (metro: Spagna).

This is a branch of the famous Italian linen house that sells both luxury linen and a hotel line, which is high quality but less expensive. © 06/679-06-73. www.frette.com.

Malls

Especially if you arrive by train, your first mall stop may just be the very fine Forum Termini, in the Roma Termini train station (see "The Five Best Stores of Rome," earlier in this chapter).

PIAZZA COLONNA
Galleria Alberto Sordi (metro: Spagna).

This mall is V-shaped, is open on Sundays—and until 10pm most nights—and has cafes and some fun stores. What's not to like? The anchor is a large **Zara** store, but the location near the Spanish Steps and the San Silvestro bus stop make it ideal. The bookstore, Feltrinelli, has books in English.

Markets

Although Rome's main flea market at Porta Portese is famous, I've never found it that good—except when I needed to buy extra luggage because I'd gone wild at Fendi. The biggie is held on Sunday from 6am to 2pm. You can get there at 8am and do fine; this is not like the Bermondsey Market in London, where you must be there, in the dark, with a flashlight in your hand. In fact, in Rome, go to flea markets only in daylight.

The big flea market is officially called the **Mercato di Porta Portese;** it stretches for about a mile along the Tiber River, where about 1,000 vendors are selling everything imaginable—a lot of which is fake or hot (or both). Enter the market about halfway down Viale Trastevere, where the old clothes are. This way you avoid miles of auto accessories, which, as far as I am concerned, you can give a miss.

The big news in Rome, though, is that "private" flea markets are popping up—real people just rent a table and sell off last year's fashions or whatever turns up in Grandma's palazzo. Often the sellers are aristos or celebs. Check the Friday edition of the local newspaper, *La Repubblica,* for the weekend market schedule, listed under a heading called *Mercatini* (Markets) on the weekend "what's happening" page.

Typically, these events are held on Sunday, may cost 3€ to 9€ ($3.90–$10) to attend, and have a few hundred vendors. They do not open super early, but struggle to open around 10am, and are hottest from noon to 1pm; most are in areas off the beaten track and may require a bit of a taxi ride.

The newest flea market is held monthly, beginning on Saturday afternoons (3–7pm), and running all day on Sundays, starting at 9am on the banks of the Tiber between Ponte Milvio and Ponte Duca d'Aosta. Most people call it the **Ponte Milvio Market.**

Via Sannio is a busy "real people" market area with all kinds of fabulous junk. Everything is cheap in price and quality. The goods are all new, no antiques. Many of the vendors who sell on Sunday at Porta Portese end up here during the week, so if you miss Sunday in Rome, don't fret. Just c'mon over here. Pickpockets seem fewer during the week, also. There's a **Coin** department store on the corner. You can get here by bus or metro (stop is Sannio); because it's in a corner of central Rome, the taxi fare can be steep.

Piazza Fontanella Borghese, not far from the Spanish Steps, has 24 stalls selling prints, maps, books, coins, and some antiques. Good fun; a class act. Open Monday to Saturday 9am to 6pm, possibly later on summer evenings.

Outlets

MacArthur Glen Outlets
Via del Ponte di Piscina Cupa 51, Castel Romano (no nearby metro).

Also called Castel Romano (for its location) or Pontina (for a nearby location), this is the Rome area's grandmother outlet mall. More and more outlets are coming on board, although outlets to the north are still larger. This mall is owned by the same family that built Serravalle Scrivia (between Milan and Genoa) but is not nearly as large, with fewer than 100 stores. It's located some 12 miles south of Rome, and various tours can get you here. Of the two malls south of Rome (see below

Papal Shopping

Merchandise ranges from the serious to the kitsch. Papal shopping falls into three categories: There are a number of gift stands and shops scattered throughout the Vatican; there is a string of stores in Vatican City; and there are vendors who sell from card tables on the sidewalks as you walk from the entrance/exit of the Vatican Museum (this way to the Sistine Chapel) to the front of St. Peter's.

If you are on a quest for religious items (non-antique variety), a dozen shops surrounding St. Peter's Square offer everything you've been looking for. Bottle openers with a bas-relief portrait of the pope, anyone?

Most of the shops will send out your purchase to be blessed by the pope. Allow 24 hours for this service. Some of the stores will then deliver the items to your hotel; others ask you to return for them. If you are having items blessed, find out how you will be getting your merchandise back.

for the second), McArthur Glen has more upscale names. ☎ 06/505-00-50. www.mcarthurglen.it.

FASHION DISTRICT
Via della Pace, localita Pascolaro, Valmontone.

The good news about this mall is that you pass right by it while on the highway that connects Rome and Naples. There really isn't any bad news, although the mall is not a great one. It's worth a stop and should improve in years to come as the mall is built to handle more than 200 stores. ☎ 06/959-94-91. www.fashiondistrict.it.

Pharmacies & Soap Sellers

RANCÉ
Piazza Navona 53 (no nearby metro).

This firm was from the south of France, where its ingredients originate, but is now Italian. They are most famous for their soap, although now there is a full line of bath and beauty products as well as scents. The brand is sold mostly through catalogs in the U.S. but costs half the U.S. price when bought in the boutiques in Rome and Milan. You'll have a wonderful time with the assortment and with making up gift baskets and packs. There is a booklet in English that explains the French origins of the goodies as well as all the properties of the line. Check out some of the product line at www.ranceusa.com.

Santa Maria Novella
Corso Rinascimento 47 (no nearby metro).

Yes, this is a branch of the famous Florentine address (p. 149). They have expanded enormously in recent years with stores in many European capital cities. This one, small and new, is a block from Piazza Navona. The salespeople do not speak English, but if you give it some time and some mime, you'll sample everything and figure it all out. Weekend soap, for 9€ ($10), is one of my favorite gifts. © 06/687-24-46.

Plus Sizes

Elena Mirò
Via Frattina 11 (metro: Spagna).

This Italian line begins at size 46 (about a size 14). The store is a chain with stores popping up all over Europe selling chic and stylish work and play fashions for less money than Marina Rinaldi. They also have outlet stores in many of the new outlet malls around Italy. © 06/678-43-67. www.elenamiro.com.

Marina Rinaldi
Largo Goldoni 43 (metro: Spagna).

A division of the design firm Max Mara, Marina Rinaldi is now a global brand with chic fashions for the large-sized woman. Their sizing system is strange, so please try on before you buy. Even if you use their chart that compares the sizes to American sizes, you may be in for a surprise. I wear a size 16 in American sizes but, according to them, I wear a 12, which in their system is a "21." ✆ **06/6920-0487.**

Shoes

There are scads of little shops selling leather goods all over Rome, and all over every other major Italian city, for that matter. Note there is also a section of this chapter called "Handbags," although most shoe stores also sell handbags.

Bottega Veneta
Piazza San Lorenzo 9 (metro: Spagna).

This gorgeous Bottega shop is across the way from the newer Louis Vuitton that has since become luxe headquarters off of the Spanish Steps shopping district; it is hard to find unless you know where to look.

Is the store worth finding? Well, yes. Prices are less than in the U.S., but there are no bargains here. That won't shock anyone, as Bottega has never had inexpensive merchandise. The store has two levels, many collections, and is to drool for. The prices are so high you could drool, and then faint. ✆ **06/6821-0024.** www.bottegaveneta.com.

Fratelli Rossetti
Via Borgognona 5a (metro: Spagna).

The Rossetti brothers are at it again—shoes, shoes, shoes, and now at somewhat-affordable prices. There are men's and women's shoes, as well as belts and even some clothes. ✆ **06/678-26-76.** www.rossetti.it.

Hogan
Via Borgognona 45 (metro: Spagna).

Tod's moved out and here we have the Hogan line of sports shoes, high heels in the Tod's line, and very fancy (and expensive) leather handbags. Shoes begin at around 160€ ($200). ℂ 06/ 678-68-28.

TOD'S
Via Condotti (metro: Spagna).

The original driving shoe, Tod's has become part of an international uniform of casual chic, and is even knocked off by the makers of fake brands. It carries men's and women's casual shoes, as well as some heels and handbags for women. ℂ 06/ 678-68-28.

Teens

DIESEL
Via del Corso 186 (metro: Spagna).

The Italian firm with jeans and other casual clothing items is a must-do for the local scene and the perfect gift for any blue-jeans snob. The Style Lab is upstairs. ℂ 06/678-39-33. www. diesel.com.

ONYX
Via del Corso 132 (metro: Spagna).

There's another Onyx on the Via Frattina and stores all over the world; this Roman flagship is a block deep and lined with video screens, blue neon lights, teenage girls, and copies of the latest looks re-created into inexpensive clothing and trends. Even if you buy nothing and know no teens, come by just to wander around and marvel at what has happened to civilization. ℂ 06/699-321. www.onyx.it.

Chapter Six

·················

FLORENCE

WELCOME TO FLORENCE

···

Love him, hate her? Love the outskirts, love the area, hate the crowds? That's my problem, totally mixed up—crazy in love and made crazy too.

I love Florence and its treasures (including stores, of course, and even a few supermarkets), but I hate the tourist crowds, the prices, and the atmosphere in which local shopkeepers know that you will buy or eat or favor their firms, and so provide little as they laugh all the way to the *bancomat*.

If you haven't been to this part of Italy recently, note that Florence has changed enormously—even Siena has changed. In the old days, we used to go to Siena to find what we all used to go to Florence to find (charm). Now Siena is so popular that smart visitors are headed for Lucca. More on Lucca in "Beyond Florence," later in this chapter.

I'm not bad-mouthing Florence—or Siena—I'm just warning you. And asking you to note that I am reporting in these pages on several different faces of Florence, as I search for hidden values and hidden finds. There is much in Florence to enjoy, so step this way.

The Shopping Scene

Florence does not offer as much of the classic, big-name, big-ticket Italian designer stores as Rome or Milan, although Florence does have a street of dream shops and a side street of fashionable big names. You won't go naked if you hit Florence without a garment to your name, but you won't find Chanel either. Not to worry, Zara has arrived.

In many ways, you must expect your shopping finds to reflect the geopolitical situation. Florence is in many ways the unofficial beginning of the south of Italy. Few people here wear black; there is no hard-edged fashion. In fact, you are more likely to find that the locals with money and pedigree wear English-influenced country styles.

This is not a case of keeping Italy for Italians or keeping out northern, big-city style. It's cultural. Strangely enough, you will find many French chains have invaded not only the tourist shopping areas but also the real-world parts of town. There's also Blockbuster DVD/video stores in residential areas—an American contribution—and a LUSH bath and beauty store—from London—in the heart of tourist land (though I do love that limoncello soap). Even French superchef Alain Ducasse has opened a restaurant in Tuscany as the area becomes more international and less related to Milan.

Best of all, Florence serves as the gateway to some superlative factory outlets and the wonders of everything else under the Tuscan sun. The bargains and buys are just outside Florence; the city is a good jumping-off point for many adventures.

Florentine Choices

Because Florence has so many faces and opportunities, you will have to make choices in terms of what kind of sights you want to see and stores you want to shop. And because prices are so high, you may want to change your orientation a bit to get the best experience for your euro.

- Choose a hotel on the edge of town if you want to get away and onto the road or into real-people parts. If you want to be in the thick of it all, choose a hotel well located in city center. Make a list of your priorities in terms of having a real experience, not just mingling with the tours behind the red umbrella.
- Choose the one great handbag you promised yourself based on its quality, not its label.
- Take home an experience as a souvenir instead of a handbag. Book a day with Faith Heller Willinger, the famous American food maven living in Florence, who now takes on visitors (p. 132) or Maria Teresa Berdondini (see chapter 2), who can book other cooking classes.
- Think foodstuffs in terms of shopping and gifts to bring home; think tastings in terms of sightseeing. Get back to the land.
- Shop at outlets. Window-shop in Florence if you want, but get a car—or a car and driver—and take a day trip to the nearby outlets for serious savings. You can even take a bus, a free shuttle, or an official tour to outlets; outlets are the number-two most-visited Italian cultural sight these days. When you see all the new stuff happenin' at The Mall, you won't want to shop elsewhere anyway.
- Look beneath the surface, head to the fringes of the tourist districts. Find the hidden gems. You may want to book a day with Maria Teresa Berdondini (see chapter 2), who does a Hidden Florence tour that will touch your soul and show you artisans and craftspeople behind closed doors that will turn shopping into a religious experience.

ARRIVING IN FLORENCE

By Train

If you are coming to town by train, do pay attention: you want the **Santa Maria Novella** (often written as S.M.N.) rail station.

The train may stop at another local station; do not panic. Wait until you get to S.M.N.

The Florence train station is smaller than the one in Milan and less intimidating. To get a taxi, follow signs to the left side of the station (left, that is, if you are arriving and walking toward the front of the station). There are a few stores in the arrivals area (and a McDonald's); there's a small mall beneath the station. Yes, you can check your e-mail while at the station at an Internet cafe downstairs.

The train ride from Rome takes about 2 hours; from Milan about 4 hours. Bologna is slightly more than an hour away.

Note that there are Eurostar trains and IC (InterCity) trains; the IC to Rome is a half-hour longer but may be less expensive or included without a supplement in your travel pass.

By Plane

Before small intra-European airlines were fashionable, you had to fly into Pisa to fly to Florence. While you still have that option and the Pisa airport is larger, you can now fly directly into Florence. Pisa is now served by some low-cost carriers as well as by the major E.U. airlines.

The Florence airport is lovely (good shopping for such a small airport) and only about 15 minutes by taxi from the heart of town; but, there are often weather problems. You can't count on a timely arrival or departure.

Many still use the Rome airport because you get your long-haul flights there and can easily connect to Florence by train from Rome, although there is no longer a train from the Rome airport straight to Florence. Still, you can connect through Rome's Central station quite easily.

The real trick is to take one of the many low-cost carriers into Bologna, and then catch one of the hour-long trains to Florence.

GETTING AROUND

It's a good thing you can walk just about everywhere in central Florence, because more and more bans are being put on vehicular traffic. This is true not only in Florence but also in Siena and other nearby towns. To enter the historical parts of town, a car must have a specific sticker on the windshield. Rental cars do not come with these stickers.

Taxis

You can get a taxi at the train station; taxis have stickers. There are no free-roaming taxis driving around town—you don't just hail a taxi. You must call ahead. If you need a taxi to pick you up somewhere, call © 055/43-90 or 055/42-42. Your hotel probably has a button or direct hotline that summons taxis in a matter of minutes.

Bus

For your day trip to Siena or Lucca (see "Beyond Florence," later in this chapter), you may want to take the **SITA bus**. The SITA station (© 055/214-721) is across the street from the Santa Maria Novella train station, and it's an easy walk from most hotels.

For your day trip to **Forte dei Marmi** (also see "Beyond Florence," later in this chapter), you'll need the **LAZZI line** (© 055/215-154), also located near the Santa Maria Novella station. Note that if you are going on to the new Ducasse restaurant nearby, you will want a car or a taxi to connect you from Forte dei Marmi.

Car Service

Most hotels will offer you car service, but it's rather pricey. I prefer to book through Maria Teresa Berdondini because she has better rates and most of her drivers speak English: Tuscany by Tuscans (Tuscany@italway.it). All legit car service has the proper license to enter city streets forbidden to regular traffic.

SLEEPING IN FLORENCE

GRAND HOTEL VILLA MEDICI
Via il Prato 42.

I have been hanging out at this hotel for years, and while the location at first seems slightly off, it's actually great—you are within walking distance to the train station, the bus station, and city center, and, importantly, not far from the *autostrada*. *Note:* Do not confuse this hotel with the Grand Hotel.

This is the hotel you pick if you want to visit outside of Florence, if you are headed to the outlets or to the countryside. It's also near the Tuesday open-air market and a 10-minute taxi ride from the airport. Traffic problems in Florence cannot be underestimated, and location becomes one of this hotel's major selling points.

On my last visit I had what they call an apartment, which is sort of a suite, but it has two bathrooms, and the living room has a sofa bed—great for those traveling with kids. It has numerous rates and promotions based on the season; doubles are about 240€ ($300) without a promotion.

You can book through the Leading Hotels of the World (© 800/233-6800; www.lhw.com/ghvmedici), of which this hotel is a member, or call locally © 055/277-171.

HOTEL BERNINI PALACE
Piazza San Firenze 29.

Oh my! A visit to this hotel explains exactly why I revise this book every other year. The hotel has gone from a shabby chic dump with great bones and true soul to a palace worthy of grand opera or 1,001 nights and a harem of Arabian princes.

Totally redecorated in Asian modern chic, the hotel is the poshest thing in town; not too big, not too small, and very dark

Florence

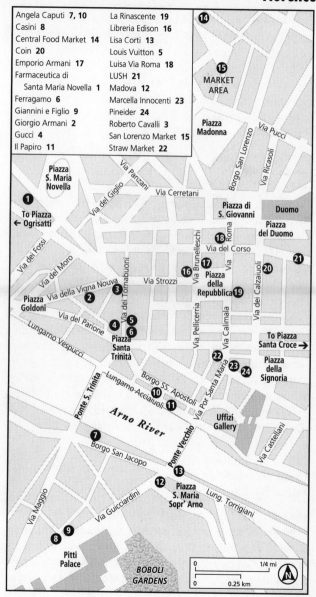

Angela Caputi **7, 10**
Casini **8**
Central Food Market **14**
Coin **20**
Emporio Armani **17**
Farmaceutica di
  Santa Maria Novella **1**
Ferragamo **6**
Giannini e Figlio **9**
Giorgio Armani **2**
Gucci **4**
Il Papiro **11**

La Rinascente **19**
Libreria Edison **16**
Lisa Corti **13**
Louis Vuitton **5**
Luisa Via Roma **18**
LUSH **21**
Madova **12**
Marcella Innocenti **23**
Pineider **24**
Roberto Cavalli **3**
San Lorenzo Market **15**
Straw Market **22**

MARKET
AREA

Piazza
Madonna

Piazza
S. Maria
Novella

Via Panzani

Via del Giglio

Via Cerretani

Piazza di
S. Giovanni

Duomo

Piazza
del Duomo

To Piazza
← Ogrisatti

Via dei Fossi

Via del Moro

Via della Vigna Nuova

Via del Corso

Via Strozzi

Piazza
Goldoni

Via del Parione

Via del Tornabuoni

Piazza
della
Repubblica

Via dei Calzaiuoli

Piazza
Santa
Trinità

Via Pellicceria

Via Calimala

To Piazza
Santa Croce →

Piazza
della
Signoria

Lungarno Vespucci

Borgo SS. Apostoli

Via Por Santa Maria

Ponte S. Trinità

Lungarno Acciaiuoli

Arno River

Uffizi
Gallery

Via Castellani

Borgo San Jacopo

Ponte Vecchio

Via Maggio

Via Guicciardini

Piazza
S. Maria
Sopr' Arno

Lung. Torrigiani

Pitti
Palace

BOBOLI
GARDENS

Borgo San Lorenzo

Via Pucci

Via Ricasoli

Via Roma

Via Brunelleschi

0   1/4 mi
0   0.25 km

and Venetian and dramatic and bold. If you want a hotel in the historical center of town, you cannot find one with a better location or more you-ain't-seen-nuthin'-yet style.

Rates vary between 160€ and 240€ ($200–$300) per night depending on the season; there are various promotional offers and online deals. *Note:* Born to Shop readers may write ahead or show their book at check-in for an availability upgrade. © 055/288-621. www.baglionihotels.com.

J. K. PLACE
Piazza Santa Maria Novella 7.

New hotels continue to pop up in Florence—or rather, new old hotels—they are new, but put into old buildings! This hotel is ready for its close-up in any international design magazine—a slew of small salons on the ground floor welcome you, there's a restaurant that's already the talk of the town, and bedrooms (some are apartments) are modern and luxe and cozy. This is a boutique hotel in every sense of the concept.

The location is a block from the train station, so you are near everything, but isolated by the famed medieval church of the same name as the piazza. The clientele is so glam that you will want to stop by for a meal if you don't stay here.

Low-season rates are 260€ ($325) for a double superior; that same room costs 320€ ($400) in high season. Rates include breakfast, online services, coffee, tea, soft drinks, and other extras. © 055/26-45-181. www.jkplace.com.

JOLLY HOTEL FIRENZE
Piazza Vittorio Veneto 4a.

Jolly is a chain that I frequent because they cover Italy and have good four-star hotels you can depend on. This hotel, on the edge of Florence, is modern and ugly from outside, but great inside and well priced. Being on the edge of town is a blessing due to some of the traffic problems—you can walk or bus into the historical center, but you can also get out of town quickly.

E-Mail Home

Florence is crammed with Internet cafes and inexpensive ways to communicate with the folks back home. While your hotel probably has a business center, it may not be free; find a low-cost Internet cafe—they abound in the main tourist parts of the city, especially between the Duomo and the Straw Market.

I spend a lot of time at **intotheweb, The Cyber Café** (Via de Conti 23r; ℭ **055/264-5628**; www.intotheweb.it), which has student prices, phone cards, drinks and snacks, printing services, and photo services. They are wired for Wi-Fi and take credit cards. You get 2 hours of time for 10€ ($13). To get the student discount, show your STA card. This is on a small street near the Duomo, but very convenient. Open daily 10:30am to 11pm.

They do have a shuttle that will take you to town, and for public transportation, you can buy bus tickets at the front desk.

The hotel is also directly across the street from the Tuesday open-air market I love so much. If you're into supermarkets, you can take a 20-minute walk across the Arno and into real-people Florence and shop at a big grocery store.

Prices vary with season, but a double can still be yours for under 160€ ($200). I booked a room on my last visit by using Expedia.com and sprang for the highest quality room available, which was 207€ ($259) for two including full buffet breakfast for two. The room was large, had a terrace, and was decorated in a nice English-country style. ℭ **800/247-1277** or 055/27-70. www.jollyhotels.it.

THE SHOPPING SCENE

If you're in Florence for the first time, you may be overwhelmed—or just plain faint. It's the heat! It's the crowds! It's the handbags! If you are combining art, culture, and shopping on a short time schedule, you will most certainly be dizzy.

If this is a repeat trip, and you have a discerning eye, you may want to take shortcuts. Certainly the shopping scene is changing quickly, and sophisticated travelers may not be pleased. Fret not, follow me. And remember, we don't buy junk anymore—those days are gone. We're counting our dollars, our euros, and the number of shoes in the closet.

Comparison Shopping

Many designer big names keep coming to town to stake a share of the crowds; existing stores are constantly renovating. Best plan: Do your serious fashion shopping in other cities and save Florence for specialty shopping, unique items, and shopping experiences you simply can't get elsewhere.

- Rome and Milan have more designer stores.
- Florence and its surrounding area are good destinations for buying $5 to $10 gifts that don't look junky, see below.
- Museums all have gift shops, most of which offer unique gift items at reasonable prices. Crowds may be thinner.
- The Straw Market and the San Lorenzo market are both wonderful fun, but they have very, very similar merchandise, and, let's face it, it's mostly junky and touristy. If time is truly limited, choose one. It won't hurt you to miss them both. Foodies should pick San Lorenzo; in fact, I'd pick San Lorenzo no matter what.

The Best Buys in Florence

Junk   I love junk; I love $5 to $25 gift items. But we don't want it to look cheap or tacky or end up at someone's yard sale next summer.

Junk that doesn't look like junk? How about those silk ties I found in San Lorenzo for 5.60€ ($7) each? Not only are the same ties sold elsewhere in Italy for 20€ to 28€ ($25–$35), but these ties also compete with 40€ ($50) ties. And yes, I do tie my hair back with a men's tie—so don't think these are just for those who wear suits or haven't found dress-down days. The fashionable ties are textured solids in gelati colors.

Smalls   This is what I call small stylish items with low prices that are easy to pack. The markets are a good source if you have a discerning eye. Grocery stores are filled with choices. Even LUSH, the British store for bath and beauty, has Italian-influenced product. Florence provides better quality, easier-to-get-to smalls than any other major Italian city.

Olive oil   Olive oil is much like wine, with olives very much like grapes. Often, vineyards that make wine also make olive oil, and have wine shops *(entoca)* that sell it. The airport in Florence has an excellent selection; otherwise you can try a wine shop, a grocery store, or even some of the specialty sources directly. There are many tours and tastings that help educate your palate (see "Out-of-Town Touring," later in this chapter).

  Remember, the good stuff isn't cheap; it usually comes in a glass bottle and is heavy and fragile. Expect to pay 16€ ($20) per bottle. The selection at **Baroni** at the Central Market (near San Lorenzo) is excellent; check them out online at www.baroni alimentari.it.

Ceramics and faience   If you get into the hill towns and pottery towns, you will save off Florence prices. If you don't have the opportunity to get out of town, you'll find plenty to choose from in Florence—from the huge jardinières to the little rooster jugs. I am horrified at how expensive these items have become—I can't fall in love with a plate to hang on the wall for 40€ ($50) and up. But you can get a salad serving set for 4€ to 6€ ($5.20–$7.80). Some items are sold in the two town markets; better-quality items are sold in specialty shops around town. But prices for ceramics are even lower in Siena, just an hour away. They are even better in Deruta, 2 hours away (p. 158).

Paper   If you didn't get your fill of Italian-style papers in Venice, you can buy more in Florence. The assorted merchandise is so classy looking that it makes a marvelous gift; pencils cost less than $1 each. There are about a half-dozen stores in central Florence that specialize in Florentine paper works; items of lesser quality are sold at souvenir stands and in the markets. *Note:* I am seeing less marble paper here and more engineered prints.

Cheap handbags   I am only slightly ashamed to tell you this: The triumph of one trip to Florence was a faux, reptile-printed plastic Birkin-style handbag for 24€ ($30) that is so stunning you could faint. Because it is textured, it's harder to detect that it's plastic, and it's absolutely fabulous with gray flannel. It's also great for travel because it's not too fragile.

Designer brands at nearby outlets   It takes some time and trouble, but it's worth it. Buy clothes, shoes, cashmeres, handbags, and bed linen from a variety of nearby sources.

Secret Dealings

To compensate for lack of sales in off periods, many store owners, especially those outside the deluxe brands, will make deals. I saved about 80€ ($100) on a handbag once because I was able to go down the street to the cash machine to retrieve and pay in cash and was equally willing to waive the tax refund paperwork.

HIDDEN FINDS IN FLORENCE

If you are offended by all the tourist junk in Florence, fear not. There are a handful of hidden places that are yummy and worth the slight trouble it takes to find them.

ALESSANDRO DARI
Via San Niccolo, 115R.

I found my visit to this shop to be a religious experience—or at least a very spiritual one. I don't mean because it carries religious merchandise, but I felt myself surrounded by the work of a master, perhaps the Michelangelo of our time; I felt as if Dari's work was straight from the angels or even God.

This is basically a jewelry shop with a workshop, so you can commission a piece or buy from the display cases. Works start at 416€ ($520) and go up; but, for less than 1,040€ ($1,300) you can have some serious work. There are rings that are buildings, rings that do tricks, and pieces with hidden mechanisms and secrets.

The shop is away from central Florence, but within easy walking distance from the Ponte Vecchio. ℂ 055/244-747. www. alessandrodari.com.

Antico Setificio Fiorentino
Via Bartolini 4.

Within easy walking distance of the center of downtown, this factory is truly hidden in an industrial neighborhood, behind a high fence. Once through the gate, you will step back in time to the 18th century. The compound includes a private house, a factory (hear the hum of the shuttles?), and a showroom laden with fabric and ribbons. The showroom is organized by price and by types of silk and cotton: Prices are not low. To visit this factory is an experience all its own. If you don't intend to buy 80€- ($100-) per-yard (or more) goods, don't worry. You can afford a small bag of potpourri. You may want your concierge to phone ahead, as you need an appointment; you may be asked to pay for the right to visit. ℂ 055/21-38-61. www.setificio fiorentino.it.

Chianti Cashmere Company
Siena.

American Nora Kravis breeds cashmere goats in the hills outside Florence; she uses the milk from these goats to make soap and skin-care products. Check it out on her website and arrange ahead of time to visit. ℂ 0577/738-080. www.chianti cashmere.com.

Farmaceutica di Santa Maria Novella
Via della Scala 16r.

This is by no means a new source or much of a secret, but it is a little hard to find and fits with the mood of most of the other shops in this list—it is a step back in time as you enter a former convent that looks like a museum. The usual soaps and skin creams are sold in the front rooms; in the rear, a newly opened room sells herbal cures. ✆ **055/216-276.** www.mnovella.it.

GREVI
Via della Spada 11/13r.

This centuries-old family business makes hats outside of Florence and sells from a small shop in the heart of town. There are a wide variety of styles with some exotics and many plain-old useful styles. They do make a packable hat good for travel. Expect to pay about 80€ ($100). ✆ **055/264-139.** www.grevi.com.

LORENZO VILLORESI
Via dei Bardi 14.

This place is as hidden and private as they get, and you must telephone for an appointment at least a day in advance. Mr. Villoresi has a nose for some big-time scents, and he's created them for some big-time firms, but he will allow you a private workshop with him. It costs 260€ ($325) and takes as long as it takes, because the two of you are creating your own fragrance from scratch. Heaven scent. ✆ **055/234-11-87.**

About Phones & Addresses

Florence is stricter about its numbering system than many other Italian cities; stores (to differentiate them from residences) are zoned red, or *rosa,* and therefore usually have an "r" after their street number. The same number in black (to depict a residence) is somewhere else entirely on the street. Go figure.

Some local phone numbers have six digits, some have seven. Don't freak.

Shoppers Beware

Be careful when buying the following items:

Leather goods   I know, I know, Italy, especially Florence, is famous for its leather goods. I'm not telling you to refrain from a leather purchase. I merely ask that you purchase slowly and carefully. There are so many fake leather factories in Florence and so many handbags for sale, in markets and on the street, that you will lose your mind in short order. More important, leather goods in Italy are well made but expensive. If it's not expensive, it might not have been made in Italy.

For real value in leather goods, you'll do far better spending a little more money and buying from a big-name leather-goods house with a reputation to back up the goods. And forget about those so-called outlets.

Do note that there is a huge territory of no-man's land: no-name, no-brand handbags and leather goods that are not inexpensive (200€/$250 and up) but offer great value if bought properly. Buying and bargaining for them is tricky.

Gold   There are plenty of jewelers on the Ponte Vecchio, but I can't give you one good reason why you should buy from them unless you have romance in mind and are willing to pay for it. Despite the hype, this is not the place that you must buy. If you are looking for a Nomination bracelet—gold or silver—try jewelers on the side streets.

Silk   Avoid fake designer scarves; instead, check out the ties. *Warning:* While you associate silk with this part of Italy (as well as to the north), most of the market stock comes from Asia. Check edges to see if they are hand-stitched; make sure it's silk and not polyester—unless you want polyester, which is less expensive.

Shopping Hours

Like all Italy, Florence is celebrating a new world in shopping hours. The two big department stores are open on Sunday, and there's a lot going on that didn't used to happen. Many stores still close at lunchtime during the week, but Florence doesn't close tight for lunch. You can find some life if you look for it.

Shops are basically closed Sunday and Monday, or at least on Monday until 3:30pm. In summer, they also close on Saturday afternoon at 1pm. Sunday is now livelier than Monday morning (even Sun morning), so don't stay home making false assumptions—get out there and shop.

Sunday hours for those stores that are open are 10am to 4pm or 11am to 5pm.

Also note that the last Sunday of the month is a special day in retail, so more stores are open than on the first Sunday of the month (there's also a cute flea market that day); the suburban American-style shopping mall is open. Most of the big factory outlets are also open on Sunday, but check before you make the trek.

Markets always close for holidays but do not necessarily close for lunch. The San Lorenzo market is closed on Sunday and Monday, but is open during lunch on other days. The Straw Market is open but not in full bloom on Monday; it is open during lunch every day—except Sunday.

Food stores are open Monday morning. In winter, food stores are also open on Saturday afternoon but are closed on Wednesday afternoon. In June, the pattern switches, and the food stores close on Saturday afternoon and stay open on Wednesday afternoon.

Speaking of summer hours, everything, except major tourist traps (TTs), is closed from mid-August through the rest of the month.

Sunday Shopping

While Sunday isn't a big shopping day in most of Italy, if the weather is nice, or if the tourists are in season, you'd be surprised at just how much business goes on.

The Straw Market has sellers who open up their carts. It's not as hot and happening as Venice, but Sunday is beginning to catch on. The last Sunday of each month, stores do open.

Every Sunday, there's a big bookstore open (see "Florence Resources A to Z," later in this chapter).

In town, there is action on the **Ponte Vecchio.** The usual shops are indeed shuttered, but on the walkway over the bridge, standing shoulder to shoulder on both sides of the walk, is an incredible array of vendors—from boys with imitation Louis Vuitton tote bags, to hippies with poorly made jewelry, to real artisans with craft pieces. Much of what you will see here is delightful junk—the exact kind of thing you want to see on a Sunday. But there are a few buys.

There's also a vast amount of Sunday shopping available in the so-called in-town factory outlets and TTs that stretch from the Duomo to Santa Croce. I think the single-best store for Sunday shopping (if you have to pick one) is a dressed-up version of a TT, that's more like an art gallery, called **Ducci** (Lungarno Corsini 24r).

But the real factory outlets—outside of town—are also open, afternoons only. Some open at 2pm, others at 3pm, so check before you drive or hire car service. Don't be surprised if there are lines out front before the outlets open. At Prada, you take a number, but the cafe is open before the shop, so you can queue or sip a coffee.

If you like upscale, tony shopping rather than touristy stuff, there's magnificent shopping in **Forte dei Marmi** on Sunday. It's just an hour from Florence.

Alternatively, you can go to **Montecatini** where stores are also open; this is a town famous for its spa, but it is adorable and real and very lush Italian; it's also about an hour away and easily reached by train.

Sending It Home

If you don't feel like schlepping your purchases with you, a giant post office in the heart of town—right near the Straw Market—offers what's called **Express Mail.** Italian mail makes me nervous; you can use FedEx if you prefer or if cost is no object.

A branch of **Mail Boxes Etc.** in town (Via della Scala 13r; © 055/268-173) does shipping, packing, money grams, and more. Store hours are Monday through Friday 9am to 1pm and 3:30 to 6:30pm. Mail Boxes Etc. franchises are gradually turning into The UPS Store, so don't worry if it's changed by the time you get there.

SHOPPING NEIGHBORHOODS

Tornabuoni   The Via dei Tornabuoni is the main whoop-dee-doo, big-time street for the mainline tourist shopping of the gold coast kind. This is where most of the big-name designers have their shops, and where the cute little specialty stores and leather-goods makers cluster. This is where you'll find everyone from **Gucci** (Via dei Tornabuoni 73r) to **Ferragamo** (Via dei Tornabuoni 16r), but, alas, no Chanel. Who needs Chanel with the Ferragamo museum to keep you busy? If you have only an hour for seeing the best shopping in Florence, perhaps you just want to stroll this street. Although most of the hotsy-totsy names are on Tornabuoni, some are on nearby side streets, especially on **Via della Vigna Nuova.**

The Tornabuoni area begins (or ends) at the Piazza di San Trinita, which is a small *piazza* (plaza) with a very tall, skinny obelisk. The Via dei Tornabuoni itself leads easily into Via della Vigna Nuova, but don't think it ends there. Stay with the street as the numbers climb because **Profumeria Inglese** (no. 97r) is well past the thick of things, but it's a great place for perfumes and beauty supplies (assuming you are not going to France).

Also check out **Via degli Strozzi,** the connector between Tornabuoni and the Piazza della Repubblica. **Emporio Armani** (Piazza Strozzi) is here.

Excelsior/Grand   This neighborhood, home to the Westin Excelsior and Grand hotels backs up to Tornabuoni, where the famed hotels are located. Many good stores are actually on **Piazza Ognissanti;** the rest line **Borgo Ognissanti** until it hits

Piazza Goldini and becomes Via della Vigna Nuova. If all this sounds confusing, don't panic.

The neighborhoods are close to each other and could even be considered one neighborhood, which is why staying at the Westin Excelsior or the Grand Hotel makes good sense if you love shopping, want to walk, and need a luxury property.

The shops in the Excelsior/Grand area are less touristy and more mom-and-pop than the big names in Tornabuoni, but the area does include a big name or two, such as **Bottega Veneta** (Piazza Ognissanti 3).

Grand/Medici You can walk from the luxury hotels at Borgo Ognissanti all the way to the Grand Hotel Villa Medici, another luxury hotel only 2 blocks away. In doing so, you will pass several local resources and a discount shop, as well as two major American car-rental agencies, Avis and Europcar (National).

If you want discount shopping, check out **One Price** (Borgo Ognissanti 74r), where the sweaters come in dreamy colors (all lamb's wool) and sell for about 20€ ($25). If you get lucky, of course—this is how you hit it shopping. I scored on my last trip at **Il Giglio** (Borgo Ognissanti 86r) with a pair of Tod's wannabes (mustardy suede!) for 36€ ($45).

Excelsior/Grand Antiques There are two main antiques areas in Florence, one near the Pitti Palace and the other right beside the Excelsior/Grand area at **Piazza Ognissanti.** If you're facing the Westin Excelsior Hotel (with the Grand Hotel to your rear, the Arno River to your right, and a church to your left) and start walking, you'll pass a small street called Via del Porcellana. From there, look across Borgo Ognissanti to **Fioretto Giampaolo** (no. 43r). Stop in, and then walk a block south toward Tornabuoni until you get to the Piazza Goldini.

At the Piazza Goldini, you'll discover **Via dei Fossi,** which is crammed with antiques dealers. In fact, the area between the two streets and including the **Via del Moro,** which runs next to Via dei Fossi, is host to almost two dozen dealers. Most of these stores sell larger pieces of furniture and medium-to-important antiques; there's not too much junk.

Out-of-Town Touring

If head-for-the-hills is your choice of neighborhood, you've picked a great part of Italy to explore. Yes, you can rent a car and drive; but, if you want someone else to drive you, then you need only call my friend Maria Teresa Berdondini (©/fax 0572/70467; www.tuscanybytuscans.it), who has a private tour service and will arrange anything you want, from olive-oil tastings to private tours to trips to the outlets. Prices are based on whether or not you have an English-speaking escort with you and how far you go. They include departure and return to any hotel in Florence. Here are some samples:

- Half-day shopping tour (4 hr.) to Gucci and Prada outlets with car and English-speaking driver (291€/$364).
- Full-day shopping tour (6 hr.) to Gucci, Prada, and Malo outlets with car and English-speaking driver (478€/$598).
- Half-day walking tour (4 hr.) visiting Florentine artisans in their showrooms with personal shopper (270€/$338).

There are some businesses that are geared to the design trade without being in the antiques business—such as **Riccardo Barthel** (Via dei Forri 11r), which does tiles. One Sunday each fall, (ask your concierge for the exact day because it varies from year to year) all the dealers in the area have open houses.

Arno Alley   The Arno is a river, not a neighborhood; the main street along each bank of the river changes its name every few blocks. On the Duomo side of the river, the portion of street named **Lungarno Amerigo Vespucci,** which becomes **Lungarno Corsini,** is crammed with shops, hotels, and even the famous Harry's Bar.

Some of these shops sell antiques; several of them sell statues and reproductions of major works; some sell shoes, clothes, and/or handbags; and one or two are just fancy TTs.

Note: Several of these shops are open on Sunday.

Duomo Center As in Milan, there is excellent shopping around the Duomo. Naturally, this is an older, more traditional area. Most of these stores are in older buildings. Locals as well as tourists shop here. Because this area has gotten so built up and is filled with an overwhelming number of stores, I now divide it into directions.

There are stores around all four sides of the church (there's even shopping in the church, in a little museum store downstairs) and in the little side streets stretching from the church as well. This is where **Pegna** is located.

Crosstown To me, Crosstown heads from the Duomo to the Arno and over the river (or vice versa). The main shopping street of this part of town is called **Via dei Calzaiuoli,** and it's directly behind the Duomo and runs right smack into the Uffizi. It is closed to street traffic, so pedestrians can wander freely from the Duomo to Piazza della Signoria, another large piazza filled with pigeons, postcards, incredible fountains and statues, tourists and locals, charm and glamour, and everything you think Florence should have. You can't rave about an area too much more than that, can you?

A second main shopping street, **Via Roma,** connects the Duomo and the Ponte Vecchio and runs past Piazza della Repubblica, where many traditional stores are located. This street runs parallel to Via dei Calzaiuoli, and you could mistake it for the main shopping street of town unless you knew better. The Savoy Hotel is on Via Roma.

Just before it reaches the Ponte Vecchio, Via Roma becomes Via por Santa Maria. Don't miss **Luisa Via Roma,** at Via Roma 21r, which is sort of the local version of Barneys.

Deep Town Streets that run from the Duomo in the direction of Santa Croce in the city center are chockablock with cute stores. The best ones are Via del Corso (which becomes Borgo Albizi) and Via Tavolini, which will change its name each block and runs exactly parallel to del Corso. Be sure to take some time to look at the old houses here and to smell the coffee. You'll find the local branch of **LUSH** in this part of town; many of the branches of French stores are here, as are a few discounters.

Aaron's Turn: Nearer My Outlet to Thee

We had a very good shopping trip to Florence and especially enjoyed the **Cascine market (Mercato delle Cascine)**, open Tuesdays only, which was filled with Gola shoes and Diesel jeans at really low prices. We did some market shopping, but were holding out for the outlets, which seems to be the main reason people come to Florence these days.

There is a bus tour you can take, but we signed up for one of Maria Teresa Berdondini's trips with my mom.

Prada   The line outside of the Prada outlet, prior to its morning opening, was what you might expect to see at a Strokes concert in Milan. It was packed with hipsters and euro-trash that were so tragically hip that they probably got sad when they had to take their clothes off each night. Yet their worship was understandable: Inside there were bargains to be found.

Most clothes were 30% off, and some had markings for additional discounts on top of that. You could try the clothes on; the sales help speaks English. I flipped for a Prada suit at 160€ ($200). Didn't fit.

Giorgio Armani, Armani Express, Armani Jeans   The ar-mania of this store is a bit overwhelming. It really is one store divided into three by well-placed curtains. The prices were pretty far from discount, with some short-sleeve shirts at 83€ ($104). The selection was good except for the Armani Jeans division. I mean, for designer jeans, some of the pairs at this store really made me want to hurl (and from the looks of the color combinations, it looked like somebody beat me to it).

There were faded jeans that weren't so much faded as they were tie-dyed, with a yellow or gray undertone. So, for people who are touring with the new incarnation of the Grateful Dead, and want to spend 48€ ($60) on a pair of "discount" jeans, I strongly recommend the Armani outlets. For anyone else, don't bother.

This store is part of an outlet village called The Mall. Jenny enjoyed the rest of the stores for a quick look-see, but most were beyond our budget and not even guy-friendly. Dudes, bring a book.

Dolce & Gabbana   Bad prices and reject clothes. There's not much else to say, this place wasn't worth it on the day we visited.

Some of the 40€ to 48€ ($50–$60) T-shirts made me feel sorry that humanity could have created them. And what kind of person wears this kind of shirt? By far, the worst of the outlet stores in the Florence area.

Pratesi   We went to Pratesi on a different day, because it was a different direction from the other outlets, and we wanted to have plenty of time and not be too wiped, or whipped, by outlet exhaustion.

My mom first met Athos Pratesi when she was pregnant with me, and got her first Pratesi sheets as a baby gift when I was born, so we all go way back with this family. Of course, I had to listen to all kinds of stories about when I was a baby, which is always embarrassing and especially so when you just want to see the prices and hope to afford something good. I know these sheets last forever because my mom's are 25 years old and still going strong.

Jenny and I were also excited to visit the outlet as we have been buying sheets and home goods at Target and Kmart. Because my mom has always bought the Pratesi sheets with little flowers on them, I didn't know they made anything different, so it was pretty cool to see solids and monochromatics, jacquard stripes, and things that weren't too girly.

Jenny really flipped out for the beach line and got shoes (21€/$26) and a tote and all sorts of things at really great prices.

Ponte Vecchio   If you keep walking a few hundred feet from Piazza della Signoria right to the banks of the Arno River, you will see the Ponte Vecchio. You'll zig to the right a few yards, and then walk left to get across the bridge. Or you can connect by continuing straight along Via Roma, which will change its name each block and become the Ponte Vecchio 3 blocks after you pass the Duomo.

By my definition, the Ponte Vecchio neighborhood includes the bridge and the retailers on the Duomo side of the bridge. Once you cross over the bridge, you are in another neighborhood: Pitti.

I consider Ponte Vecchio a distinct area, however, because the entire bridge is populated by jewelry shops. Prices are very high, but looking in windows is free.

Over the Bridge (Pitti & Santo Spirito)   Once you cross over the Ponte Vecchio, you reach a different retailing climate. You are now on the Pitti side of the bridge. The stores are smaller but no less touristy; you get the feeling that real people also shop here. You can wander, discovering your own personal finds; you can stop and get the makings of a picnic or grab a piece of pizza. The shopping goes in two directions: toward the Pitti Palace or uptown along the Arno. (If your back is to the Duomo, turn left along the Arno to head uptown.) See both areas, looking at shops on **Borgo San Jacopo** and on **Via Guicciardini**.

If you are headed to the once-a-month flea market or looking for antiques shops and crafts vendors, the Santo Spirito neighborhood—actually part of Pitti—is where you want to be. Santo Spirito may not be on the tiny freebie maps handed out all over town, but it is truly convenient and easy to find: If you are standing in front of the Pitti with the Pitti behind you, walk straight 1 block.

If you are looking for **Lisa Corti**, it's on Via Bardi, which, if your back is to the bridge, is the street to your left. The store is hidden, so dart into the bridge area from the side to find it.

Santa Croce & Bernini Back Alley   A sneeze behind the Piazza Signoria is the Bernini Palace Hotel and the Borgo dei Greci, which leads to Santa Croce. Shoppers know this area mostly because of the famous Leather School located inside the Santa Croce church (see "Shoes & Leather Goods," later in this chapter). It's nice to wander around this area because it *feels* like it's a little off the beaten track and seems more natural than the parts of town where tourists swarm (yet this is a major tourist area with many, many TTs). Face it—it's all tourist shops. There are also some cafes and pizza eats, more so-called leather factory outlets than you ever care to see in your lifetime, one or two fun antiques-cum-junk stores (the best kind), and a good bit of Sunday retail. If you are lucky enough to catch the Sunday flea market, it's even deeper into this area.

FLORENCE RESOURCES A TO Z

Antiques

As an antiques center, Florence gets pieces from the entire Tuscan area. The problem of fakes, which is so severe in Rome, is not as great here. Anyone can get taken, that's well known, but the chances are less in Florence than in Rome.

- Antiques are available at a flea market at the **Piazza dei Ciompi,** but this is really Grandmother's attic, fun stuff. We're talking garage-sale quality here, but you may uncover a find every now and then (or absolutely nothing). Note that there are two parts to this market, the regulars who are open every day in the center aisles in little huts, and the people who set up on tables in the open air on the last Sunday of each month.

- For more serious stuff, check out any of the following streets: Via Guicciardini, Via Maggio, Via dei Tornabuoni, Via della Vigna Nuova, Via del Porcellana, Borgo Santi Apostoli, Via dei Fossi, Via del Moro, Via di Santo Spirito, or Via della Spada. There's a string of fun shops for everything from old postcards to 1950s jewelry on the Borgo San Jacopo right over the bridge. I happen to like Via dei Fossi for medium-range antiques—possibly affordable.

- Affordable antiques are best bought at flea markets that are regular events, most often held once a month. Better yet, they are best bought at markets that are out of town. Many locals like to go to **Viterbo,** a city about 45 minutes away, because it has a fairly decent Sunday flea market for antiques. Viterbo also gets a less touristy crowd.

- The best flea market in Florence proper is the monthly event held at **Santo Spirito** every second Sunday.
- There's an antiques fair in Pistoia, a half-hour away, on the second Saturday and Sunday of each month; the market is covered, and houses about 150 stalls. There is no market in July and August. Head for the **Via Ciglliegiale.**
- There's a market in Pisa on the second Sunday of each month and the Saturday that precedes it. This market, which also has about 150 dealers, is known for its furniture, which can be bought at a low price and then restored. The market is not held in July and August. It's located on **Via XX Settembre.**
- The town of Siena has a flea market on the third Sunday of each month. There are only about 60 dealers, but the market does get a lot of "smalls" (the trade term for small objets d'art) and locals selling off estate pieces, so buyers can hope to get lucky here. There's no market in August. Head for the **Piazza del Mercato.**
- The biggest (and best) antiques fair in Italy is held in **Arezzo,** about an hour south of Florence by train: It's held the first Sunday of each month and the Saturday that precedes it. There are over 600 dealers at this event, and it does not close in the summer months. Head to the **Piazza Vasari** and work the area to the **Piazza San Francesco.**

Please note that the laws defining what is and is not an antique are different in Italy than in many other countries, so items made from old wood or from older items may be classified as antiques even if they were made yesterday! The craftspeople in the area are gifted at making repros that are so good you can't tell how old they are.

Bath, Beauty & Herbalists

BIZZARRI
Via della Condotta 32r.

This is Logan Bentley's (my Italian correspondent's) secret resource for spices and essences. Some people in town claim it's a hangout for local witches. Call ✆ 055/211-580.

CHIANTI CASHMERE COMPANY
Siena.

Soap made from cashmere goats on a Tuscan farm. Call ✆ 0577/738-080. www.chianticashmere.com.

DE HERBORE
Via del Proconsolo 43r.

Another of the local *erboristerias* (herbalist shops) and source for great looking (and smelling) gift items and cures. This is on the way to Santa Croce. Call ✆ 055/211-706.

ERBORISTERIA PALAZZO VECCHIO
Via Vacchereccia 9r.

This is an herbalist, not a pharmacist—puh-lease! Buy hair tonic, bosom tonics, and much more. It's right in the thick of the shopping in central downtown and the packaging is good and the opportunity for fun gifts is strong. Call ✆ 055/296-055.

LUSH
Via del Corso 23r.

This is the British bath firm that has stores all over Italy and makes a great effort to make the Italian products with local ingredients, so they are different from offerings in other LUSH shops. I am addicted to the *limoncello* soap and shampoo. While prices are hefty (about 4.15€/$5.20 for a bath bomb), this is the only international division of LUSH that custom-makes products from indigenous ingredients. Call ✆ 055/210-265. www.lush.com.

SEPHORA
Via S. Quirico 165.

This is not a large or very well-stocked branch of the French beauty supermarket Sephora. In fact, as far as I am concerned, I just wanted you to know it was here, but feel free to ignore it. For some reason, they do not concentrate on Italian brands and serve instead to service locals with French brands, most of which can be found anywhere. Call © **055/898-60-21.** www.sephora.com.

Books

ART STORE
Piazza del Duomo 50r.

This appears to be a museum shop but has a separate entrance from the museum next door, and offers mostly books. You can find art books as well as guides, children's books, and the usual souvenirs and gifts with an artistic bend. Call © **055/292-559.**

BM BOOK SHOP
Borgo Ognissanti 4r.

This English-language bookshop, right smack in the heart of everything, specializes in American and British books; it's a great place to hang out and ask questions or touch base with the owners. They are located near the Westin Excelsior Hotel in a shopping district you will pass every day. Call © **055/294-575.** bmbookshop@dada.it.

LIBRERIA EDISON
Piazza della Repubblica 27r.

This is sort of the local Barnes & Noble. Although most of the books are in Italian, there are also foreign-language books, which means you will pay 9.60€ ($12) or more for a paperback.

The store is large, continues on the lower and upper levels, and sells everything in book- and communications-related media, from postcards to CDs.

The shop is open on Sunday from 10am to 1:30pm and 3:30pm until 8pm. Other days of the week (including Monday), it's open nonstop from 9am to 8pm. Call © **055/213-110.**

Boutiques

CASINI
Piazza Pitti 30/31r.

This is a two-part store: One part is more leather goods and the other is designer clothes—some of them made especially for the boutique.

The leather goods include shoes, handbags, men's briefcases, and accessories but also the most extraordinary leather clothes for men and women. Prices are quite fair considering the quality and the ability to stitch butter into leather—under 800€ ($1,000) for a reversible jacket. I saw a black leather doctor's bag for 320€ ($400) that was killer chic and surely the same quality as Bottega Veneta.

The owner is American, and therefore, everyone on hand speaks English and understands the American need to blend Italian style with real life. Custom work can be ordered and will be sent to you in the U.S. without duties—it takes about 2 weeks for your order to arrive. Call ✆ 055/210-403. www.casinifirenze.it.

LUISA VIA ROMA
Via Roma 19–21r.

One of the best stores in town—maybe the world—when it comes to fashion, style, whimsy, and the look we crave, but usually can't achieve or afford. Call ✆ 055/217-826.

RASPINI
Via Por Santa Maria 72r.

This firm once owned a ton of boutiques carrying designer brands. Now they have cut back their space but still have some of the world's best-known labels—most are Italian, but there are some international makers also. Rumor has it the space will become another Prada shop. Film at 11. Call ✆ 055/215-796.

Cooking Classes

CUCINA TOSCANA (FAITH HELLER WILLINGER)

Every Wednesday, Faith Willinger, famous for her books and articles and importance in the world of Italian food and wine, gives a private cooking lesson in her home in the heart of town near the Pitti Palace. I do not give the address because, after all, this is Faith's home, and the woman does deserve a little privacy. Once you have booked, you will get directions; her flat is easily reached from all parts of town and is in central Florence.

Technicalities first: The class costs 360€ ($450) for the day but will be discounted to 320€ ($400) per day if you mention Born to Shop when you book. Yes, you get more than $450 worth of fun, and an excellent goody bag to take away with you.

The class begins with a lesson in making the perfect espresso, and then you're off to the market to pick out lunch. The class makes lunch together, gets a few life lessons from Faith, and then eats the lunch ensemble. Sometimes there is a guest chef at lunch. www.faithwillinger.com.

LA CUCINA FIORENTINA

These are group classes (in English) for up to eight participants—you get a trip to market and then kitchen and cooking time, for about 160€ ($200) per person. This is organized through a private eating club and is booked through Tuscany by Tuscans. ©/fax 0572/70467. www.tuscanybytuscans.it.

Costume Jewelry

ANGELA CAPUTI
Borgo San Jacopo 82; Borgo Sant Apostoli 48r.

Caputi is famous for her look—sort of an ethnic big-and-bold statement made with enormous style and affordable prices. She serves up dynamite, creative costume jewelry often made with bright-colored plastics and topped with inventive twists and turns. Prices are amazingly low; 104€ ($130) can buy you a stunning piece of jewelry.

Caputi's original shop is on the Pitti side of the river; the newer shop is on the Trinita side and is right near a cute little hidden courtyard where an olive-oil dealer has a store. The new shop is larger. Call © **055/292-993.**

MARCELLA INNOCENTI
Loggo del Mercato Nuovo 3r.

This small shop, right across from the Straw Market, seems so fancy you may think the jewels in the window are real. But they are faux, and the prices are so low you will giggle. I got gold earrings with scatters "diamonds" for 28€ ($35). In fact, I ended up with three pairs of earrings for a total of just under 80€ ($100). Call © **055/239-85-31.**

Department Stores

COIN
Via dei Calzaiuoli 56r.

A small department store concentrating on ready-to-wear. It features quasi-modern architecture in a multilevel space that exhibits a little of everything for men, women, and children. It's a good place to sniff out next season's fashion direction. Prices aren't at the bargain level, but they are moderate for Italy.

Remember: When the elevator says T you are at street level; S stands for second floor. The biggest news here is that they have totally eliminated makeup and perfume and have only a MAC boutique on the ground floor right at the front door. Call © **055/280-531.**

LA RINASCENTE
Piazza Repubblica.

La Rinascente is right in the heart of town, obviously put there to compete with the lovely Coin. The store is moderately priced, light, modern, fun to shop, and open on Sunday. It is not a great store, so don't be too hurt. Call © **055/219-113.**

Designer Boutiques

For more detail on many of these well-known brand names, check out my "Dictionary of Taste & Design" in chapter 4.

CONTINENTAL BIG NAMES

CARTIER
Via Tornabuoni 40r.

ESCADA
Via degli Strozzi 30–36.

HERMÈS
Piazza degli Antinori 6r.

LACOSTE
Via della Vigna Nuova 33r.

LAUREL
Via della Vigna Nuova 67–69r.

LOUIS VUITTON
Via dei Tornabuoni 2.

YVES SAINT LAURENT
Via dei Tornabuoni 3.

WOLFORD
Via della Vigna Nuova 93–95r.

ITALIAN BIG NAMES

BENETTON
Via por Santa Maria 68r.

BRIONI
Via de Rondinelli 7r.

EMILIO PUCCI
Via dei Tornabouni 22.

EMPORIO ARMANI
Piazza Strozzi.

ERMENEGILDO ZEGNA
Piazza dei Rucellai 4–7r.

FENDI
Via degli Strozzi 21r.

FERRAGAMO
Via dei Tornabuoni 16.

FRETTE
Via Cavour 2.

GIANFRANCO FERRE
Via dei Tosinghi 52r.

GIORGIO ARMANI
Via della Vigna Nuova 51r.

GUCCI
Via dei Tornabuoni 73r; Via Roma 32r.

LORO PIANA
Via della Vigna Nuova 37r.

MARIA RINALDI
Via Panzani 1.

MAX & CO.
Via de Calzaiuoli 89r.

MAX MARA
Via dei Pecori 23r.

MIUMIU
Via Roma 8.

PRADA
Via dei Tornabuoni 7.

PRATESI
Lungarno Corsini 32–34r and 36–38r.

TRUSSARDI
Via dei Tornabuoni 34–36r.

VERSACE
Via dei Tornabuoni 13r.

ZEGNA SPORT
Piazza Rucellai 4–7r.

Foodstuffs

BARONI
Mercato Centrale, Via Galluzzo.

The entire indoor Mercato Centrale is a fabulous source for foods, souvenirs, and memories. Of the many stalls, this is one of the more famous for 30-year-old cheeses that are not exported, designer olive oils, and much, much more. They speak English.

PEGNA
Via dello Studio 8.

Oh, boy, have I got a store for you. Despite the fact that this is a few feet from the Duomo, I needed a local friend to find it for me—it is hidden in plain sight and, if you are a foodie, could very well be the most exciting stop in town. This old-fashioned grocery store sells everything, including English brands of cleaning products. There are foods to take home, foods for picnics, and even gift items in soaps or foodstuffs. Don't miss it. Call © 055/282-701.

TOSCANAMIA
Via Guicciardini 57r.

I do know a TT when I see one but am not above shopping at them, especially one as charming as this one. Although the store sells all sorts of souvenirs, its specialty is food souvenirs—pasta in fashion colors, shrink-wrapped risotto, oil and vinegar sets, excellent quality chocolate (from Stainer), and more. This shop is right near the Pitti. Call © 055/239-92-18.

Home Style

Ditta Luca Della Robbia
Via del Proconsolo 19r.

This place is a little bit off the beaten path (but not enough to count) and is one of the best pottery shops in town. I dare you not to buy. They ship—although it may double the price of your goods. They carry plates, tiles, religious souvenirs, and more. The shop is located between Piazza della Signoria and Santa Croce. Call © 055/283-532.

Galleria Machiavelli
Via por Santa Maria 39/r.

Despite the stupid name for a shop, this is one of the best resources in town for country wares and ceramics. It's located right in the center of downtown, so you can easily pop in. They ship. Call © 055/239-85-86. www.machiavelli.it.

Lisa Corti
Via de' Bardi 58.

Lisa Corti is from Milan and sells in the U.S. through Saks Fifth Avenue. Her shop in Milan is off the beaten path, but wonderful; she is also sold in Positano at Emporio Sirenuese, which is where I discovered this brand.

Corti designs fabrics in bright swirls of color with a southern Italian flair and feel. There's mostly home style, although there are some clothes and even pieces of pottery. Because the goods are printed in India, some locals tend to dismiss this brand, which is silly. Very silly.

The shop in Florence is hard to find, and takes real patience in order to fully explore the merchandise, which is mostly put away. Best buys are table linens that begin around 70€ ($88); last visit, I bought a printed shirt dress for 102€ ($127). Call © 055/264-5600. www.lisacorti.com.

PASSAMANERIA TOSCANA
Piazza San Lorenzo 12r; Via della Vigna Nuova corner of Via dei Federighi.

Maybe you don't plan your travels around your ability to find trim or tassels, but when you luck into a source that makes the best in the world and is affordable, it's time to celebrate.

This firm actually has two shops—both in neighborhoods that you will be visiting anyway. I've been buying my cotton multicolor tassels in Paris for about 4.15€ ($5.20) each (at the flea market, no less)—in Florence, they are 4.70€ ($5.85) each! You'll also find pillowcases, embroideries, brocades, assorted trims, and fabrics. The San Lorenzo shop (© 055/214-670) is larger. Chic, but expensive.

PASSAMANERIA VALMAR
Via Porta Rossa 53r.

This shop is right in the heart of town; just look at your map for easy access to one of the best sources in town for tassels, tie backs, trims, cushions, and more. Call © 055/284-493.

Linens & Lace

BRUNNETO PRATESI
Via Montalbano 41, Pistoia.

See "Beyond Florence," later in this chapter, for how to visit this factory store, which is just a half-hour outside of Florence in the town of Pistoia.

Brunneto Pratesi founded the firm named after him; his grandson was my friend Athos Pratesi, who passed away a few years before my husband. Now the company is run by Athos's son, Frederico. This is one of the last merchant-prince manufacturing Italian families. Call © 0573/526-462.

LORETTA CAPONI
Piazza Antinori 4r.

If you've ever dreamed of being either a Lady Who Lunches or a Lady Who Sleeps Late, this lingerie store is for you. Here you'll find the dreamiest silks in underwear, linen, negligees, and more, as well as some cottons and table linens. This is what having money is all about. Call © **055/213-668.**

PRATESI
Lungarno Corsini 32–34r and 36–38r.

This is a new shop, although old-timers who remember the old store will know this store is nearby. Business has been so great that they expanded into the space next door, hence the two street numbers. Once you waltz inside, you'll know why business is so good and swoon from wanting to touch, or snuggle up, into the gorgeous linens. There's nothing old-fashioned here: The store not only has the full line of Pratesi merchandise but also custom makes whatever you need.

And for the tacky people who want to know the same things I do—yes, there were many (most) prints here that were not at the outlet. While the quality is the same, the selection in the store is larger and broader, and they will make anything you need, in any size, in any print or fabric you select.

There's also a beach line, a baby line, and a cashmere collection. Oh, Athos, you did well, my friend. Call © **055/289-488.** www.pratesi.com.

Makeup & Perfume

If you can help it, don't buy makeup in Florence—it's expensive, and the choices are pretty average. If you're desperate, go to department stores such as Coin or La Rinascente.

The **Profumeria Inglese** (Via dei Tornabuoni 97r) is a temple to good taste, fine goods, and every imaginable brand, right in the heart of the shopping district. There are no bargains here. For beauty cures and treatments, check the pharmacy listings below or the local *erboristas*, listed in "Bath, Beauty & Herbalists," earlier in this chapter.

Markets

MERCATO DELLE CASCINE
Piazzale Vittorio Veneto.

Held once a week (Tues only), this market is famous with locals because it serves them in the same way a department store might. The various vendors are regulars, so everyone gets to know everyone, and some of the vendors even have famous reputations. I found the market fabulous from an academic standpoint but not actually the kind of place where there's much to buy.

Granted, a lot of that depends on luck and taste, but I just didn't need new pots, pans, dishes, tires, or baby clothes. I was wildly interested in the heap of designer handbags that must have been fake; there are handbags beginning at 5.20€ ($6.50). I like the local fabrics, tablecloths, and dish towels; I love the few food vendors. I did work my way through mounds of used clothes and linens in hopes of finding something I had to have.

The market opens at 7am; I got there at 8am, and vendors were still setting up. Even if you arrive by 11am, you should be just fine. To get there, take a bus to the Jolly Hotel or walk along the Arno—it's a bit of a walk from the center of town, considering that once you get to the market you are going to walk even more, but you can do it.

MERCATO DELLE PULCI
Piazza dei Ciompi.

This is the local flea market that sells everything from furniture to pictures, coins, and jewelry; it's great fun especially if the weather is fair. It's held the last Sunday of each month. Meanwhile, every week, Tuesday to Saturday (not at all the same as the once-a-month affair) the regular dealers are open in a small strip of stalls. Possibly not worth the trip.

The Sunday market is an all-day job beginning around 9am; the daily market closes for lunch and follows more traditional business hours. To get there, walk out the back end of the Duomo onto Via dell'Oriuolo, pass the Piazza Salvemini and hit Via

Popolo, which in 1 block takes you to the flea market. It's an easy walk. On Sunday, the nearby Standa is open.

SAN LORENZO
Piazza del Mercato Centrale.

I'm sad to report that a visit to San Lorenzo is much like a trip to Hong Kong. Insiders say that more than 80% of the merchandise for sale comes from Asia.

Nonetheless, the market is a popular shopping venue and if you only go for the ties, well—it's worth the visit. But then, wait, the Central Market is part of the market itself, so you can go for the food too.

The market has a few pushcart dealers, and then several rows of stalls that lead around a bend. The stalls are very well organized; this is a legal fair, and stallholders pay tax to the city. Many of the stalls give you shopping bags with their numbers printed on them. Now, there's class.

With the recent crackdown on phony big-name merchandise, few of the pushcarts have imitations. *A word of caution:* Do not get so excited with the bargains that you don't cast an eagle eye over the goods or, in your haste, think that these are real designer goods. Look for defects; look for details. I have yet to find a faux designer scarf here that really looks good enough to pass as the evil twin sister.

Most stall owners take plastic.

The market is open Tuesday to Saturday from 9am to 7pm. Closed Sunday and Monday.

STRAW MARKET
Via por Santa Maria.

The best thing about the Straw Market is that it doesn't close during lunchtime. It's also within walking distance of the Ponte Vecchio, the Duomo, and all the other parts of Florence you want to see, so you can make your day's itinerary and get it all in. Locals call this market *Porcellino,* in honor of the boar statue that stands here.

This market sells far more junk and much more in the way of souvenirs than the other markets. It also gets more crowded than other markets. Still, it's a marvelous TT and worth a visit, if only to fill a lunch void. The merchandise varies with the season, as it should. It takes a good eye and a steady hand.

The market is open daily, from 9am to 5pm in winter, and 9am to 7pm in summer. Closed tight on Sunday.

SANTA MARIA NOVELLA TRAIN STATION
Piazzale della Stazione.

Technically speaking, the main train station is a train station and not a market. But it functions as a marketplace. There's a McDonald's, stores, and plenty of people and action. There is a mall underneath, with an excellent—although often crowded—Internet cafe. www.firenzesantamarianovella.it

Multiples

OVIESSE
Via Panzani 31.

While Oviesse is one of my favorite Italian brands, and I buy huge amounts from them, my visit to the Florence store was so disappointing that if this was the first Oviesse I ever visited, I might shrug, go on my way, and never even tell you about this large chain of low-cost fashion stores.

There are five stores in Florence and one on the outskirts, but I write about the one that is in the main tourist shopping zone. This store (© 055/239-8963), right near the train station, is so jammed with merchandise and disorganized that it's basically hard to find what's there.

Oviesse makes a great plus-size line as well as men's, women's, and junior clothes. The average linen dress costs 41€ ($51). This branch store has a division of Limoni, a beauty supermarket, attached to the ground floor. Some Oviesse stores have Limoni branches, and others do not.

Note that the suburb store is listed in "Beyond Florence," later in this chapter.

ZARA
Piazza della Repubblica 1.

Zara took its time about opening in Florence, as there were concerns that the local population would not take to the Spanish brand famous for designer looks at midrange prices. The large store is crammed with locals and tourists alike; price tags are marked in various currencies to help you calculate. While Zara has a wide range of products, this store just sells men's and women's clothing. For more product and kids' clothes, go to the suburban store (see "Beyond Florence," later in this chapter). Call © 055/291-745.

Outlets, Discounters & Stock Shops

See the next section for out-of-town factory outlets.

BARBERINO OUTLET MALL
Via della Repubblica.

Now being built and scheduled to open in summer 2006 at the edge of Florence on the western side of town, this mall will be part of the McArthur Glen family of outlet malls, of which there are several already in Italy. www.mcarthurglen.it.

IL GIGLIO
Via Borgo Ognissanti 64.

This is a stock shop, selling whatever they can get their hands on, and, sometimes, it is fabulous. There's usually a mix of shoes and clothes—for men and women. There are some handbags and accessories but not that many. I bought a pair of suede Tod's wannabe driving shoes for 41€ ($51); there were designer sports jackets beginning at 104€ ($130). I thought I'd died and gone to heaven. Call © 055/217-596.

LONGCHAMP
Via Della Scala 12r.

This is an independent store that is marked Longchamp on the outside and sells the French brand at a 20% discount. It's quite close to the S.M.N. Train Station. The largest part of the selection is in the famous nylon totes that Longchamp makes but there are some leather handbags and some accessories such as silk scarves. Call © 055/264-5697.

PIAZZA PITTI
Via della Sprone 13r.

This cashmere outlet with product from their factories is on a street that juts off from the Piazza Pitti. Aside from the usual sweaters and smalls, there are coats and items of clothing for women. Call © 055/283-516.

Outlet Stores near Florence

THE MALL
Via Europa 8.

Take back your Leaning Tower of Pisa and also your pizza pit; in fact leave me alone when it comes to landmarks, museums, and even palaces and pizzas. Give me the bargains. Show me the designer stuff at a real price. Show me The Mall.

Truly named The Mall, this outlet mall is very chic and modern, stark and well designed, up to the standards of any Gucci store. Ignore the busloads of tourists who are pushing about you.

There are many shops—and new ones come on board each year. I have been given permission to list these names: Agnona, Alexander McQueen, Armani, Balenciaga, Bottega Veneta, Emanuel Ungaro, Emilio Pucci, Ermenegildo Zegna, Fendi, Gucci, Hogan, La Perla, Loro Piana, Marni, Salvatore Ferragamo, Sergio Rossi, Stella McCartney, Tod's, Valentino, Yohji Yamamoto, y-3, Yves Saint Laurent.

If that is not enough to get your inner engines revved up, nothing is.

All the stores offer IVA refund materials. The Mall is about a half-hour from the Prada outlet (see the next listing). It is right off the A1 autostrada. Alternatively, it is about a half-hour drive west of Florence, toward the sea. There is a cafe at The Mall. Alas, no hotel.

There are tours to The Mall sold by hotels (about 25€/$33), or you can take a shuttle bus that is free to groups that pre-arrange it.

Open Sunday from 3 to 7pm and closed on major holidays; summer shoppers should note that this includes August 15. Call © 055/865-7775. www.outlet-firenze.com.

SPACE OUTLET/I PELLETTIERI D'ITALIA
Localita Levanella, Montevarchi.

I have listed the official name of this factory, although everyone just calls this "The Prada Outlet." Yes, dear, you heard right.

Montevarchi is an industrial area outside of Arezzo. How far is Arezzo, you ask? Well, about an hour or so by train from Rome and Florence—it's midway between the two, actually, and right on the main train line. It's about a half-hour drive from The Mall.

This situation is a little more formal, and you may feel like you are going to prison. You go behind wire and are given an ID number. The store is large and beautifully arranged and organized. There are other brands here besides Prada and MiuMiu (I found Helmut Lang), and there are shoes as well as sunglasses, clothes, handbags, totes, and so on.

It's hit or miss, but worth the adventure if you are nearby. They now accept credit cards. Open Sunday afternoon from 2:30 to 7:30pm.

Take the A1 south to Valdarno, then follow signs for Montevarchi; look for the parking lot filled with luxury cars. Call © 055/919-6528.

MALO (MAC)
Via di Limite 164.

As soon as I gave away all my cashmeres because they gave me hot flashes, I discovered the Malo outlet where I almost wept with contempt for the insults of middle age. I was forced to buy cashmeres for others, but did get some suede shoes for myself.

Be still my heart—you could faint from the glory of all the colors, let alone the stunningly low prices. Two-ply cashmere sweaters were in the 80€ ($100) price range; four-ply were 120€ ($150). I don't know if I was there for a sale or if this is the regular drill, but you pay half of the price on the tag. Ask!

Note: This outlet has moved to this address rather recently, so there may be a conflict with other guidebooks. The sign outside not only says MAC but also uses the same type face as MAC cosmetics, so it's confusing. Cope. If you are driving and want precise directions, call ✆ 055/894-53-06.

Many Americans are not familiar with the Malo brand because they only have a few stores in the U.S. This is one of the top Italian brands of cashmere, and we are talking about sweaters that would retail from 240€ to 480€ ($300–$600) for a small pittance. I could barely breathe I was having so much fun.

By the way, Malo does make a few other things besides sweaters. Years ago, my late husband bought the world's most chic bathing suit at a Malo store. They had hats and handbags when I was there, fabulous little suede slip-on shoes, and some fashions, a la Donna Karan, in cotton and silk. I was there in winter, so I would guess seasonal stuff turns up toward summer.

Logan's Outlets

BIG BERTHA CASHMERE
Via dell'Industria 19.

Only Logan could come up with a resource with a name like this. It's a catalog company for cashmeres, and better yet, it does *not* close at lunchtime. There's a large selection in terms of sizes and colors. Call ✆ 075/599-75-72.

DESMO
Via Matteotti 22d, S. Donato, Fronzano, Reggello.

Call for specific directions; you will need to hit the Autostrada going toward Reggello, which is outside Florence. No credit cards, but savings of about 30% on Desmo brand handbags. Call © 055/865-2311. www.desmo.it.

ROBERTO CAVALLI
Via Volturno 3, Localita Osmannoro, Sesto Fiorentino.

They are closed on Sundays and closed on Saturdays in winter; otherwise this is the outlet store for the rich, hippie, rock-star designer Roberto Cavalli, who has stepped into the Gianni Versace look since Versace's death. Right off the Autostrada A1. Call © 055/317-754. www.robertocavalli.it.

Paper Goods

Florentine papers are one of Florence's greatest contributions to bookbinding and gift-giving. There are two styles: marbleized and block printed. The marbleized style is readily found in Venice; neither style is handily found in Milan and/or Rome.

In Florence, there are scads of stores selling papered gift items; such items are even sold from souvenir stands, in markets, and at the train station. Prices are generally modest, although they can get up there with larger items.

BOTTEGA ARTIGIANA DEL LIBRO
Lungarno Corsini 38–40r.

This is a small shop, next to the Arno, that has beautiful things and can solve many a gift quandary. Small address books are in the 6.20€ ($7.80) range; pencils are stunning and inexpensive; picture frames range from 4.15€ to 12€ ($5.20–$15), depending on the size. These frames have plastic fronts, not glass. There are photo albums, blank bound books, and all sorts of other items. Note the business cards printed on the back of marbleized paper swatches. Call © 055/289-488.

Cartoleria Parione
Via Parione 10r.

I got a letter from a reader a few years ago, a professional photographer, who was looking for marbleized photo albums that she could use to show her work. She said she could find them in the U.S., but they cost about 80€ ($100) and could I find some in Italy for less. Well, it took me a year, but yes, Virginia, here you go—this store, which sells many of the usual paper goods, also has the photo albums. They come in various sizes, and prices begin at 24€ ($30)! They will ship. The shop is located right in the heart of the Tornabuoni shopping district. Call © 055/215-684.

Giulio Giannini e Figlio
Piazza Pitti 37r.

Historically well known for the marbleized type of Florentine paper, this shop has been in business for centuries. They also make bookplates, calling cards, and items for all other paper needs. I think several paper-wrapped pencils tied with a bow make a great gift; the price obviously depends on how many pencils you buy, but you can put together a beautiful $10 bouquet. There are many good paper shops in Florence, but this is the single most famous. Call © 055/212-621. www.giuliogiannini.it.

Il Papiro
Via Cavour 55r.

This is the most commercially successful of the marbleized-paper stores, with branches (and comparable prices) all over Italy and in the U.S. Call © 055/265-81-03. www.ilpapirofirenze.it.

Pineider
Piazza della Signoria 13r.

Do you love to send handwritten notes in the mail? Thick formal note cards that smell of old money and inseparable style?

At this shop you'll find very conservative, old-time stationery as well as some gift items and the new designs by Rebecca Moses. Prices are steep. This is a serious international status symbol. Call © 055/284-655.

Pharmacies

Not the kind of pharmacy you go to when you need an *aspirina,* these pharmacies seem to be a specialty of Florence—they are old-fashioned, fancy-schmancy places where you can buy creams and goos, local brews, and various homeopathic treatments, as well as European brands or local homemade potions for all sorts of things. There are tons of these places in Florence. One or two will be all you need for great gifts and, possibly, dinner-table conversation.

FARMACEUTICA DI SANTA MARIA NOVELLA
Via della Scala 16r.

Yep. This is the one—the one you've read about in every American and English fashion-and-beauty magazine; the one where you buy the almond cream. At least, that's what I buy here. Go nuts. (Almonds are nuts, so go nuts.) Fabulous gift items, fabulous fun. It's located near the train station and downtown—go out of your way to find it. I had to ask three times just to find it; I was even stumped when I was standing outside the front door. Never mind—walk in! It looks unusual because it's a convent, not a storefront. All the more yummy. Call © 055/216-276. www.smnovella.it.

FARMACIA MOLTENI
Via Calzaiuoli 7r.

Remember this one because it's open every day of the week, 24 hours a day. It's centrally located, and it's where you go in case of a medical emergency of the pharmaceutical kind. It's also gorgeous. Call © 055/215-472.

Shoes & Leather Goods

BONO
Via della Terme 7r.

This is an old-fashioned sandal and boot maker. For sandals, you pick the heel and bottom portion you want and then the uppers and they are custom made—pick them up a few hours later. You can also have bespoke boots or bags. Call © 055/239-6026. giannirillio@virgilio.it.

DESMO
Piazza del Rucellai 10r.

Desmo is one of my best Italian secrets for reasons of pride and pocketbook—excuse the double entendre. They make a top-of-the-line, high-quality, equal-to-the-best-of-them hand-bag at a less than top-of-the-line price. Years ago they made their name as a maker of leather clothing, shoes, and accessories, copying Bottega Veneta creations; now they have their own style and plenty of winners. Colors are always fashionable and up to date; the prices are pretty good—few items in the house top 160€ ($200), and you can get much for considerably less.

Now then, don't let the address throw you; Piazza del Rucellai is a little dip in the Via della Vigna Nuova—you can't miss the shop when you are in the thick of the designer stores. For outlet information, see "Logan's Outlets," above. Call © 055/292-395.

GHERARDINI
Via della Vigna Nuova 57r.

One of the biggest leather-goods names in Italy and Asia but little known otherwise, Gherardini offers a specific look in luggage, shoes for men and women, belts, and accessories. I find their conservative designs drop-dead elegant with old-money style. They also have some tote bags and a printed canvas/vinyl line that is status-y as well as practical. There are two stores in Florence, both in the heart of the central downtown shopping district. Call © **055/215-678**. www.gherardini.it.

HERMINE'S
Via Pietrapiana 72r.

One of the reasons I like this store is that they don't claim to be making Hermès goods—they go out of the way to show you the differences (which aren't obvious). Nonetheless, the quality is high, as are the prices. The store is near the Standa grocery store and off the tourist path, but not far from city center and Santa Croce. Call © **055/241-187**.

LEATHER SCHOOL
Monastery of Santa Croce, Piazza Santa Croce.

If you insist on shopping in one of the many leather factories in Florence, you may as well go to the best—it's actually inside the Santa Croce church and is a leather school with a factory on the premises. The school is open Monday through Saturday year-round, and on Sunday from April 15 to November 15. You enter through the church, except on Sunday, when you enter through the garden. © **055/244-533**. www.leatherschool.com.

LEONCINI
Via della Vigna Nuova 44r.

I stopped here because I saw something I have never seen before or since—an Hermès-style Birkin-like travel tote bag attached to wheels. It was absolutely stunning. Prices began at 520€ ($650) and went up with the size. Regular Birkin-style handbags cost about 338€ ($423). Call © **055/267-0173**.

MADOVA
Via Guicciardini 1.

Gloves are back in style, so stock up. I'll take the yellow, cashmere-lined, butter-soft leather ones . . . or should I think pink? Maybe both? Unlined gloves are about 24€ ($30) and come in about a million colors. There's everything here, from the kind of white kid gloves we used to wear in the 1960s to men's driving gloves to very ornately designed, superbly made, high-button gloves. Call © 055/239-65-26.

MANTELLASSI
Piazza della Repubblica 25r.

If made-to-measure shoes are what you have in mind, step this way with your instep. Men and women can design their own, bring a shoe to be copied, or choose from the many styles displayed. Call © 055/287-275.

SALVATORE FERRAGAMO
Via dei Tornabuoni 16r.

Yes, there are Ferragamo shops all over Italy and all over the world. But none of them come near the parent shop in Florence, which is in a building erected in 1215, complete with vaulted ceilings, stained-glass windows, and enough ambience to bring out your camera. The shop has several connecting antechambers with an incredible selection of shoes, boots, and ready-to-wear . . . as well as a library and a kiddie play room.

Shoes are in American sizes; however, there is a limited selection in big sizes.

Upstairs is the museum, which is *fab-u-lous*. It is not open to the public all day, or open every day, so call to ask for the hours and to make an appointment—they are strict on the appointment stuff. There is also a research library for designers and a small museum gift shop with great merchandise, but very high prices. The postcards cost three times what they should. Save up for shoes, instead.

Each January and July there's a clear-it-all-out sale, but I confess that I left brokenhearted last January. Clothing provided better deals than the shoes. Prices were not as good as the sale at Saks. The sale is held in the basement, which has an entrance at the side door; there are guards and usually lines to get in. Call © 055/292-123.

SERGIO ROSSI
Via Roma 15r.

Even though this brand is part of one of the French luxury conglomerates, it's true Italian style in high heels and luxe leathers. Call © 055/294-873.

TANINO CRISCI
Via dei Tornabuoni 43–45.

Tanino Crisci is a big name in Italian shoes and leather goods with an international reputation, but there are not many stores in the U.S., so Americans may not be familiar with the brand. This is a chain of moderate-to-expensive shoes in sort of sporty, conservative styles. There's something a bit chunky about a lot of the styles, but the look wears forever and looks better every year. Very preppy. The quality is well known; prices range from 112€ to over 160€ ($140–$200). This is a very specific look that is either your style or not. Call © 055/214-692.

They make men's and women's shoes—dress and sports models—and also have belts and small leather goods. Logan, my journalist friend who lives in Rome, found the outlet at Via Garibaldi 9, Casteggio, Pavia.

Beyond Florence

CC I. GIGLI
Via S, Quirico 165, Campo Bisenzio.

Huh? You are probably saying to yourself as you read this, whoooaaa, Suze. But wait, if you have a car you will want to know about this large suburban mall just 5 miles outside, and right off the highway, from Florence toward the sea. There's a branch of every big store you may want to shop, and especially note that there are good branches of **Oviesse** and **Zara**.

CC, by the way, stands for Centro Commericali, which is Italian for mall.

Siena   Siena is not very far from Florence, but it takes some thinking about should you decide to go, unless you have your trusty rent-a-car and are totally free and independent. It's a very pleasant day trip, especially nice for a Monday morning, when most of the stores in Florence are closed, or a Wednesday morning when market is at full throttle. (Beware, it's mobbed.)

There are prepackaged day trips just to Siena or to Siena and medieval San Gimignano, which is not a shopping town but rather one of those incredible hilltop villages. Do note that if you buy a tour you will pay about 40€ ($50) per person for the day trip, whereas if you do it all yourself, it will cost less than 16€ ($20).

The train ride, which is free if you have a railroad pass, is very long (over 2 hr.) and often involves changing trains. It's a better use of your time to pay an additional 12€ ($15) (round-trip) and buy a bus ticket via SITA; you want the *corse rapide* to Siena, which is direct. The bus takes 1 hour and 20 minutes. It drops you on the edge of town, next to market, and within walking distance to everything.

There is a bus basically every hour, although peak travel times have several buses. Best bet is to travel via SITA, on Via Santa Caterina da Siena 15. It's about a block from the S.M.N. Train Station. Round-trip tickets are discounted slightly.

The SITA station has a sign outdoors directing you to where to buy tickets (the *biglietteria*) and an information booth outside of the ticket area. After you buy your tickets, you then must find out which lane your bus will be loading from; there is a large sign high up on the wall near the ticket office.

If you take the bus, it may make local stops as you approach Siena. Don't panic. Your stop is the end of the line, San Domenico Church. When you get off the bus, note the public bathrooms (very clean, pay toilets) and the tourist information office where they sell you a map to the city. If you are standing with your back to the church facing the tourist information office, you'll see that there are two streets to your right. One bears off slightly, and the other turns more dramatically and goes down.

If you are doing this on a Monday morning, most of the stores in downtown Siena will be closed. However, if you take the low road, you'll see many touristy stores that are open, even on Monday. While some open at 9am, many more will open at 11am. In fact, the best time to be in Siena is on a Monday morning between 9 and 11am because you'll have it almost to yourself and you'll still get to go shopping.

The main shopping street is Via Banchi di Sopra, which leads right to the Campo and then goes up the hill as the Via di Citta. Take this to the Duomo (well marked), then follow the signs back down and up the Via della Sapienza, which will bring you back to the bus stop at San Domenico.

Via della Sapienza has a good number of wine (this is Chianti country) and tourist shops, especially close to the bus stop, that remain open during lunchtime, too.

As you approach the Campo, you'll notice various alleys that lead into the square. Some have steps; others are ramps for horses. Each entryway seems to be named for a saint. Many of the alleyways that lead from the shopping street to the Campo are filled with booths or touristy stands. There are more free-standing booths on the Campo itself.

The Campo is surrounded by shops, many of which specialize in pottery, hand-painted in dusty shades and following centuries-old patterns. Some of them are even branches of other stores you will find up the hill, closer to the Duomo.

The best shops are clustered up the Via di Citta, close to the Duomo—you will automatically pass them as you walk around and up.

Pistoia   Okay, okay, so you weren't planning on a side trip to Pistoia. In fact, you've never even heard of it and perhaps think you can survive without it. Wrong.

Pistoia is an adorable little gem worth visiting on its own and doubly worth visiting since it is the home of the **Brunetto Pratesi** factory. The city is about a half-hour from Florence on the train.

You can get a taxi from town to the factory; ask the driver to wait for you. At the Pratesi factory there is a little shop that sells—you guessed it—seconds. If you show your copy of this book, or say you are a friend of the family, you will be allowed to shop there.

Pratesi, as you probably know, is a family business that makes sheets for the royalty of Europe and the movie stars of Hollywood. They are sticklers for perfection: A computer counts the number of stitches in each quilt. If there are five stitches too many, the quilt is a reject! What do they do with this poor, unfortunate, deformed quilt? It will never see the light of day in Beverly Hills, Manhattan, Palm Beach, or even Rome. No, because it has all of five stitches too many, it will be considered a reject, a defect, a second. It will be sold, at a fraction of its *wholesale* price, in the company shop. It's your lucky day.

The store is in the factory, a low-lying modern building, set off the street on your left as you come off the highway, and distinguished only by the discreet signs that say BRUNETTO PRATESI. Not to worry—because it's the most famous factory in the area, everyone knows where it is. Show the printed address to anyone at a nearby gas station or inn, and you will get directions. Don't be intimidated; it's not that hard.

If all this truly makes you nervous, ask your concierge to call ahead and get very specific directions for you: He or she can even arrange a person for you to call in case you get lost. The factory is located at Via Montalbano 41r (✆ 0573/526-462).

Store hours are Monday 2 to 7pm, Tuesday to Friday 9am to noon and 2 to 7pm, Saturday 9am to 1pm, and Sunday 3 to 7pm.

Like all factory outlets, the store sells what it has; you may be lucky or you may not. Last time I was there, the showroom was filled with quilts, nightgowns, and gift items, but low on matched sets. There were blanket covers in various sizes, but you could not put together a whole queen-size bed set. The one total set I priced was no bargain.

Price on an item varies depending on the defect; some items are visibly damaged, some are not. Prices are essentially half of what you would pay at regular retail—a blanket cover that retails for 720€ ($900) costs 320€ ($400) here. If you were expecting giveaway prices, think twice. Then look at the beach totes for 16€ ($20) and faint from their chic and your need to own everything in the line.

Pratesi is one of the leading linen makers in the world, and their goods compete with Porthault as the most sought after by the rich and famous. Considering the quality, these are bargain prices. Do note, however, that Pratesi has sales once a year (in Jan) in their stores in Italy and twice a year in some other cities around the world. In January in Italy, the prices are marked down 30% off retail, and you have the whole store to choose from.

The scenery on the way to Pistoia is not gorgeous, but you drive on a freeway (A11), so you don't need to worry about getting lost on winding country roads.

You can also go by train—get the train at Santa Maria Novella (S.M.N.) in Florence for Pistoia; you can catch a taxi at the station in Pistoia; the factory is some ways out.

Prato Prato is almost a suburb of Florence, it's just on the other side of Pistoia or about a half-hour from Florence. It's not on the tourist bill because it is a mostly industrial town and is the home of many fabric mills and garment makers. For those looking for deals and jobbers, this could be your kinda town.

My basic off-pricer here is **Lo Scorpione,** Viale della Repubblica 278 (© **0574/572-608**), which is a jobber offering designer clothing at 50% regular retail. Yes, big names in sportswear and men's suits. There is another owned by the same company called **Il Giglio,** located at Viale del Serraglio 72.

Forte dei Marmi This is a small beach town, west of Florence on the, uh, coast. It's about an hour away yet a million miles away in that it is a perfect little chic town with wonderful shopping. Stores are open on Sundays; the crowd is old money.

Lucca The good news: Lucca is worth the trouble. The bad news: This is another one of those towns with restricted vehicular traffic, so you have to park outside the walls and walk in. Or rent a bike. Lucca is a small town, so you can easily prowl all over by foot. It's a well-known food town, so you can buy oil and balsamic, but it's also enough of a real-people town that you can enjoy the local Upim.

Deruta This is in Umbria, not Tuscany, and is a bit of a drive (a little over 2 hr. from Florence), but worth it if you are a ceramics freak. The entire town is store after store next to workshop and studio selling nothing but faience, which some locals also call *majolica*.

Among the most famous of the artisans here is Carol LeWitt, an American, who makes large decorative pieces for Fratelli Mari, Via Circonvallazione Nord 1 (© 075/971-0400). Her work is also sold in the U.S. through a firm she owns, called Ceramica, which has six stores.

When you arrive in Deruta, note that there are two shopping parts: the city center, which is a medieval old town, and on the highway approaching town, the lower-city shopping-strip centers. It's easier to walk from place to place in the upper city. Most stores ship. Check out Via Tiberina and Via Mancini for some great shops.

Chapter Seven

....

VENICE

WELCOME TO VENICE

....

Venice and shopping are made for each other; you're going to have the time of your life—even in the crowded high season. In winter, the city can be a little bit chilly or damp, but the town is yours, and you will more than fill your senses—and your shopping bags.

Prices are higher than in other towns; this is not the city for bargains or for fulfilling your dreams of designer clothes. Of course you can find designer clothes, but you will pay dearly for them. Venice is really for the senses, for smells, for gifts, and for whimsy. But still, bargains can be had:

- You can buy what they sell at Bergdorf-Goodman for a fraction of the U.S. price.
- You pay 36€ ($45) in an ordinary shop in Murano for what would cost 10 times that in an ordinary shop in New York.
- You can load up on tourist junk, take it away from Venice, and turn it into great gifts for your loved ones—it won't even look like tourist junk.

Venetian Shopping History

Venice was founded in the 5th century by survivors fleeing from Lombard invaders after the fall of the Roman Empire. She provided a cultural and political link between Eastern and

Western civilizations for many centuries; by the 13th century, the city was a leading (and very wealthy) port of trade.

People have been shopping here ever since.

The absence of cars allows leisurely browsing of the shops, churches, piazzas, and palaces. Every area contains boutiques stocked with the lace, fine glass, paper goods, and leather items for which Venice has become famous. The best thing about shopping in Venice is that you are forced to walk just about everywhere—even if you are just a museum person, you still pass by the shops and can look in the windows.

Conversely, even the most dedicated shopper is going to get an extra surge of excitement just from walking by the churches and museums. In Venice, culture and clutter, of the retailing sort, are all tied into one very attractive bundle.

Most shopkeepers speak English and are quite accustomed to tourists. All shops are anxious for business. Adjustments in price will reflect just how anxious for business shopkeepers are—in season (Carnevale to Oct), when tourists are plentiful, prices are higher, and bargaining is unheard of. In winter, things are sweeter—and cheaper.

GETTING TO VENICE

By Plane

Although the Venice airport is a tad inconvenient, it's not that difficult to use. The airport makes European flight connections a breeze.

Note that if you take a water taxi to/from Marco Polo International Airport and Venice proper, it will cost about 64€ ($80). I take the public water bus for 10€ ($13). It's crowded, but not a problem. Just follow signs from the terminal to the pier.

An ability to handle your luggage will make the difference in whether or not you are in a good mood when you arrive at your hotel. If possible, go with one rolling suitcase.

By Train

To ride the regular express trains, I usually purchase an **Italian Rail Pass** (see chapter 2) or a **Eurailpass**, or I simply buy a ticket from Milan and hop on board the fast train to Venice. There are about 20 trains a day between Venice and Milan. Some go faster than others, but the fastest train is just over 2½ hours.

Sometimes I do second class, but if I'm worried about getting a seat at what might be a peak travel time, I buy a first-class seat and a seat reservation so that I have a specific seat assigned to me. First-class seats on Italian trains are not enormously more expensive than second-class seats and may well be worth the difference.

Do learn how to read an Italian rail schedule, and allow yourself plenty of time for the asking of many, many questions. I once found an intercity train (fast train) on my timetable that appeared perfect—it was outbound from Venice and was stopping in Milan but was marked for Geneva. There was no way I could have known that was my train merely from reading the board in the station. If I'd taken the train marked MILANO, I would have wasted 2 hours.

By Bus

If you are staying in Mestre or Treviso or in the burbs, you can take the bus or train into town. The buses do not run that frequently and can be more confusing than you'd like to think.

By Car

Believe it or not, on my last research trip, I drove to Venice. Or, to be more precise, as close to Venice as one can get in a car.

Because I would be leaving my car—with luggage and shopping trophies—in a parking lot for a few days, I decided to leave my car at the Venice airport rather than in lots in Mestre, as I thought the airport offered more security and easier connections into Venice.

I can't say it was brilliant because it was a tad confusing and time consuming, but it worked fine—patience pays off, I kept telling myself—and a 3-night stay in Venice cost me only 20€ ($25) total in parking. Since it costs 20€ ($25) a day in the lots in Mestre, I thought this was worth the trouble.

There was no shuttle bus from the parking lot to the air terminal or to the pier, so I had to schlep my roller suitcase. Of course, I was able to leave most of my stuff locked in the car, so this was actually easy. The terminal and adjacent lots were undergoing work, so perhaps the situation will be different when you visit.

By Ship

I don't need to tell you that Venice has been a favored cruise destination for, uh, centuries. Some of the most famous shipyards in the world are outside Venice, and many of today's modern ocean liners are built right there. The number of passengers in recent cruise history who have come to Venice by ship has increased enormously in the last 10 years: Some 1 million people a year are expected, just from cruises.

Ships disembark at VTP (Venezia Terminal Passeggeri), which is being renovated to handle the mob scene. The terminal has access for both ferries and cruise ships, and each area is color coordinated so that passengers can easily find the right check-in zones. For details, you can always call ℂ 041/533-4860, or check out www.vtp.it.

ARRIVING IN VENICE

Getting to Town

The most reasonable approach to local transportation is the water bus *(vaporetto)*. The water buses go around town in two different directions: one via the Grand Canal, the other via the Adriatic to San Marco. There are additional routes to various islands and specialty destinations. If you get on (or off) the water

bus at the train station, you are at Ferrovia; the bus station is Piazzale Roma. The lines (and routes) are clearly marked; some lines offer express service with fewer stops. You can get a schedule at the Centro Informazioni ACTV at Piazzale Roma.

Buy the ticket before you board, if possible; it costs slightly more if purchased on board. You can also buy tickets at any shop displaying a sign that says ACTV. Prices have more than doubled in the last 2 years; a single ticket now costs 3.60€ ($4.55).

The water bus may be a little confusing at first, since there are different little floating stations for the different lines—read the destinations listed. Buy your ticket accordingly and give it to the ticket taker when he comes around to ask for it. Sometimes he doesn't ask.

Then walk. Get lost. Enjoy it. Take the vaporetto (*vaporetti* is plural). And yes, take a ride in a gondola at least once in your life.

Bus Savings?

You may be tempted to buy a multiday vaporetto pass thinking this will be easier for you in the long run. I lost a lot of money doing this, as I ended up walking a lot—rarely even using the vaporetto. The 3-day pass may be only 47€ ($59), and yes, it's good for unlimited use, but it's only valuable if you use it a lot.

Porters

The key to smooth sailing, in all senses of the word, is to pack light and know that you can check baggage at the stations—even overnight or over many nights. In these days of international terrorism, it's not easy to find somewhere to leave unaccompanied baggage.

Some hotels will arrange to meet you and will handle luggage for you; many hotels have their own boats to take you back and forth from the airport. Put your Vuitton right here, madame. Fax or e-mail your hotel in advance of your trip to arrange to be met. You'll pay for the service, but it may make your trip a lot more pleasant.

There used to be porters who met the water bus at the train station and then again at San Marco and would help you get to your hotel, but sometimes these guys are nowhere to be seen. This then is another reason to travel in winter; there were tons of them on a recent December trip. My most recent visit was in April, and a porter at San Marco offered to help me. I was headed to the Hotel Luna Baglioni, about 200m (656 ft.) away but was curious about the porter. He would be happy to help me roll my single piece of luggage for a mere 31€ ($39). Thank heavens I knew where my hotel was located!

About Addresses

No city in Italy has a more screwy system for writing addresses; they are virtually impossible to read or to use because there is

Central Venice

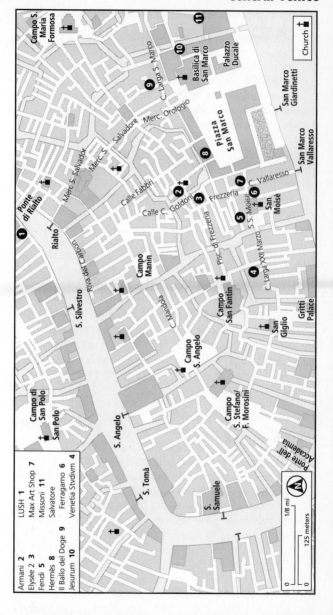

Church ✚

Legend (shops):

Armani **2**
Elysée 2 **3**
Fendi **5**
Hermès **8**
Il Ballo del Doge **9**
Jesurum **10**

LUSH **1**
Max Art Shop **7**
Missoni **11**
Salvatore
Ferragamo **6**
Venetia Stvdivm **4**

Labels on map:

Campo S. Maria Formosa

C. Larga S. Marco
Basilica di San Marco
Palazzo Ducale
San Marco Giardinetti

Merc. Orologio
Piazza San Marco
San Marco Vallaresso

Merc. S. Salvadore
Merc. S. Salvador
Calle Fabbri
C. Vallaresso
Frezzeria
San Moisè
S.S. Moisè

Ponte di Rialto
Rialto
Calle C. Goldoni
Pisc. di Frezzeria
C. Larga XXII Marzo

Riva del Carbon
S. Silvestro
Campo Manin
C. Mandola
Campo San Fantin
San Giglio
Gritti Palace

Campo di San Polo
San Polo
Campo S. Angelo
Campo S. Stefano/ F. Morosini
Ponte dell' Accademia

S. Angelo
S. Tomà
S. Samuele

0   1/8 mi
0   125 meters

Jenny Does Mestre: To Stay or Not to Stay

Just a hop, skip, and confusing bus ride away from beautiful Venice is not-as-beautiful Mestre. Mestre is the equivalent of a suburb that surrounds a cool city; it strives to be cool too, but it's just not quite there. Originally, the town was a haven for tourists who didn't want to pay over-inflated Venice prices for food and lodging, and perhaps it still is during the high season, but that's not what we found. We were there in shoulder season and during a war, so prices in Venice were more flexible. But we didn't know that.

We decided to test Mestre because we thought Venice would be full, and since we had no hotel reservations, did not want to schlep around trying to figure out what to do. Getting off the train in Mestre, we wandered into the hotel information room at the train station to see what the town had to offer.

The "helpful" woman staffing the desk asked how much we wanted to spend on our few nights in her delightful city. After hearing "about 50€ a night," she laughed, almost offensively, and said she didn't think she could find a place that low.

She told us about a "charming" little bed-and-breakfast, La Residenza, for 73€ ($91) per night. One catch, she warned, this charming little B&B provided a bed, but no breakfast. Still, we bit. We were tired.

In order to get to our "bed," we had to go to another hotel, Hotel Vivit in the Piazza Ferretto. The train station woman called and told them we were on our way and told us everything was square, after taking a small deposit.

Then the real fun began. After a 10€ ($12.50) cab ride for only a short distance and then a short walk through the piazza, we found the hotel. The innkeeper informed us that the B&B we had agreed to stay in was full. We would have to stay in the hotel that night (for the same price) and move to the B&B the next morning. We were too weary from traveling to argue.

The room was cute. Small, but not uncomfortable. No frills, but no cockroaches either.

The next morning we packed up our bags and marched them downstairs to the lobby, so we could get our key to our new accommodations. We told the concierge about our situation, to which he replied, "No, mo, you rest here tonight." So, a little confused and apprehensive, we shlepped our bags back upstairs. Considering that we only had 1 day to be in Venice, the waste of all this time was ticking away in our minds.

On checkout day, we went again down to the lobby, a little worried about what would occur as we paid the bill. We were expecting perhaps a different rate, a cheaper rate, as we had not gotten to stay in the "charming" B&B we were hoping for. We thought wrong. Not only did we not get the room for cheaper, even though the man told us, "is cheaper here, you pay same price," but he then informed us they will not accept credit cards, and there is a cash machine just outside in the piazza.

Aaron rushed off to get cash when I noticed something out of the corner of my eye: MasterCard, Visa, and American Express stickers posted on the hotel desk. They did take credit cards. We inquired about it and they quickly told us that yes, they do in fact take credit cards, they just couldn't with us because we were getting "a special price." In other words we were getting screwed.

I think that Mestre has a big business preying on tourists, students, and young people who come to town to save money but then waste time and don't get the best deals. While we were in Venice, we went into a randomly chosen three-star hotel near San Marco. We asked about price, haggled a bit, and were offered a nice room for 52€ ($65), far less than that in Mestre.

The moral of this story? If you are going to Venice, go to Venice. Not Mestre.

---

one address for mail and another for the actual building. My advice? Forget addresses. Walk, enjoy.

If you must get to a specific resource and haven't found it in your general lost-and-found, search-and-shop technique, ask your hotel's concierge to mark it for you on a map. Also take business cards that have maps on them so that you can get back to a specific source.

SLEEPING IN VENICE

My best money-saving trick? Don't sleep in Venice. Come in for a day trip. Padua is only 40km (25 miles) from Venice, an easy commute; Verona is about 90 minutes away (see chapter 10).

For something like Carnevale, where you want to be part of the action and then get out as fast as you can before you have a screaming breakdown (some 250,000 people jam San Marco each day on the Carnevale weekends!), this is an ideal ploy. Even Milan is a responsible place to spend the night during Carnevale.

But since you've probably come to stay for a night or two or three, then just about any hotel will do. Some happen to be a little more magical than others. In Venice, you really pay for location. Since I tend to be there for only a short period of time and every moment is precious to me, I splurge on the hotel. As a repeat customer, I also know my way around from only a handful of hotels; not getting lost is money in the bank of time.

HOTEL BAGLIONI LUNA
San Marco 1243 (ACTV: San Marco).

This is one of my best finds because of the combination of location, luxury, and price. I also did most of the visits on my last trip to Italy by staying in Baglioni hotels, so I was able to do one-stop shopping via reservations.

Right off San Marco, on the fanciest little retail alley in town, the hotel is an old villa transformed into palace hotel. You can fall out the door and into a stream of shoppers or sneak out the side door into a waiting gondola or boat and speed off to a shopping rendezvous by water.

During my stay, I hit one of those unfortunate rain and flood seasons when it was great to be at the hotel because of its location and my ability to run and hide when the rain was too much. It's not inexpensive; expect to pay 240€ ($300) per night, although in winter the rate can be less. This hotel is a member of Leading Hotels of the World (www.lhw.com). ✆ **800/743-8883** or 041/528-9840. www.baglionihotels.com.

Four-Star Finds

HOTEL BISANZIO
Calle della Pietà, Castello 3651 (ACTV: San Zaccaria).

I was just walking along past the Danieli on the way to my girl-friend's restaurant (Al Covo), and on the sidewalk was a sign for this hotel; so I followed it, and lo, a find. It's set back from Riva degli Schiavoni, but it's brilliantly located and charming and real and funky and affordable. It's a Best Western Hotel with only 40 rooms; rates are about 200€ ($250) per night. ✆ **800/528-1234** or 041/42-03-100. www.bisanzio.com.

HOTEL LONDRA PALACE
Riva degli Schiavoni 4171 (ACTV: San Marco).

For years, this hotel was on the shabby chic side—waiting to be kissed and turned into a prince. That miracle has happened; so, if you know this hotel, come back for a visit. If you have never heard of it, wake up and smell the cappuccino. Located on the far side of the Hotel Danieli, the hotel faces the lagoon and is just 2 blocks from San Marco. The style is modern rich luxe in Biedermeier, which allows you to melt into the comforts and leave the real world at Doge's Palace. There are only 50 rooms at this member of the Small Luxury Hotels of the World (✆ **800/525-4800**; www.slh.com). Rates begin at 240€ ($300). ✆ **041/520-0533**. www.hotelondra.it.

Sarah's Three-Star Find

ALA HOTEL
San Marco 2494 (ACTV: San Giglio).

Born to Shop news director Sarah Lahey found this hotel and I was mightily impressed with it. The hotel is a member of the Best Western system and is a few feet away from the Gritti

Palace. The style is less formal but, nonetheless, filled with antiques and beautifully painted walls with high ceilings and Venetian charm. Rooms start at 140€ ($175). Ala be praised, I said with delight. © 041/520-8333. www.hotelala.it.

Snack & Shop

AL COVO
Campiello della Pescaria, Castello (ACTV: Arsenale).

Okay, so this isn't on your ordinary list of legends and landmarks, but it's part of mine because Diane is from Texas and comes to me through my official foodie friends. Also note that this was just named to a list of the 10 best restaurants in Italy.

Diane's husband is the chef, and he is getting increasingly famous and recognized by American authorities, so book now. The restaurant is on the far side of the Danieli, far enough away from the tourists to be pure and family oriented. The food is fabulous (try Diane's walnut cake), and you will get the special treatment you crave from a great team.

On the back of your menu from Al Covo, note that there is an order form for all the products. You take them away with you. These include olive oil, balsamic vinegar, pasta, and polenta. Ask Diane for details when you are there.

If you think I'm the only one on to this place, forget it. It came into my family of journalists because Marcella Hazan brought Faith Heller Willinger here, and Faith brought Patricia Schultz, and she told me, and . . . Note that Al Covo now sells its own products as well. © 041/52-23-812.

CAFFÈ FLORIAN
Piazza San Marco, San Marco (ACTV: San Marco).

So you sit there at sunset on the Piazza San Marco at a little table, drinking a strawberry version of the Bellini because it's strawberry season and Florian won't use canned peaches like they do at Harry's (tsk, tsk).

There's a tiny band shell—they play schmaltzy music— and all you want to do is sing and dance and laugh and cry.

And that's before you see the bill. Just once before you die. No wonder Napoleon said that San Marco was Europe's most elegant drawing room. Ah, yes, they sell the china, the dishes, and their own house brand of coffee and tea and even Asti Spumante. A fabulous gift to bring home for someone who knows Venice.

HARRY'S BAR
Calle Vallaresso, San Marco 1323 (ACTV: San Marco).

There is a Harry's Bar. There is even a Harry (call him Arrigo). And, no, Harry's Bar is not in the Gritti Palace, as many think. It is where Hemingway and the gang liked to hang out and is located halfway between San Marco and the Gritti. This is the home of the famous Bellini.

I have sipped Bellinis at Harry's—it was swell, and, yes, I saw everyone I knew. I have wondered just why Harry's is so famous and later discovered that the thing to do is not sip Bellinis (this is for tourists) but to dine upstairs with a chef whom many consider one of the best in the world. Me? I sit downstairs and nibble on the *croque monsieur,* which is fried to a crisp and makes a super lunch or snack. I also like their *latte macchiato* (milk stained with coffee).

TERRAZZA DANIELI
*Hotel Danieli, Riva degli Schiavoni, San Marco 4196
(ACTV: San Marco).*

The rooftop of the Hotel Danieli has a wonderful restaurant called the Terrace (Terrazza). The view is spectacular, and the food ain't bad. Ian and I always try to book a lunch here while in Venice, but I have also been known to make this my first stop after I arrive, via train, from Milan in the morning. A mere cup of coffee overlooking the Adriatic is enough to make your heart sing. You can afford coffee here, so don't miss it; lunch may strike you as a very expensive splurge. ✆ 041/522-6480.

THE SHOPPING SCENE

Please understand the most basic law of shopping in Venice: Because of transportation, essentially everything is imported to Venice. That means higher prices than anywhere else in Italy. It means you'll pay top dollar for a Coca-Cola, a roll of film, or a pair of Italian-designer shoes. Also, this isn't really a city for designer shopping, although you can buy most everything here.

Your best buys will always be locally made souvenir items, which are quite moderately priced. Also note that the tourist junk here is far more attractive than in any other major Italian city.

There's also more than the usual number of hidden resources, because this is the kind of town where the best stuff is definitely put away. Ask.

The Best Buys in Venice

I have been known to go nuts for glass, handbags, paper goods, and local crafts—all can be best buys in Venice. More important, even if you've seen these items for less money elsewhere, they offer good value as items bought in Venice to be remembered as such and cherished. You don't want to buy your Carnevale mask in Rome just because you might get it cheaper, do you? Marbleized paper items are less in Florence, but only slightly less.

Eyeglass frames   Have your prescription put in back at home, but don't miss the chance to buy chic and/or exotic frames in Venice. Note that there are scads of factories in the Veneto nearby, so you can also go discount shopping for glasses frames if you have a car and the time.

Glass   Murano is the glass capital of Italy, and Venice is the front door to the glass candy store. Even when it's expensive, glass usually costs less here than if bought in the U.S. Also in the glass category are mirrors and chandeliers. Art glass, a sub category, is very expensive but more available than in any other city. If you buy, be sure you spring for shipping and insurance and know what to do if anything goes wrong. You do not want to hand carry a one-of-a-kind glass masterpiece, no matter how stable you think your hands are. As for souvenirs and gift items, the hot style of the moment is a Murano glass ring, which costs about 12€ ($15) and is chic as can be. Find them all over town and the islands too.

Masks   Carnevale has its own rituals—mask-wearing among them. The city now sells scads of masks in every format, from cheap plastic ones to incredibly crafted ones made of leathers or feathers. For the best ones, get to the back streets and alleys and away from the TTs (tourist traps).

Silks   When you see the incredibly pleated teeny-tiny Fortuny silk baggies for jewelry or potpourri for 24€ ($30) at Stadium (Venetia Stvdivm, now expanded to seven branches), you'll know why Marco Polo came home.

The Worst Buys in Venice

If you can help it, don't buy the following:

- **Clothing:** Not a good buy in Venice, unless you need it or hit a sale or bargain.
- **Designer items:** Hermès is more expensive in Venice than in Milan.
- **Film:** Film is expensive everywhere in Europe; it costs about 12€ ($15) a roll in Venice. Besides, if you don't already have a digital camera, you should buy one instead of another pair of shoes.
- **Fake designer handbags:** Give me a break.

The San Marco Rule of Shopping

If you are looking for the best prices on the average tourist items—from souvenirs to snacks—my rule is simple: Avoid San Marco.

San Marco is the center of the tourist universe and, therefore, the center of the highest prices. The farther you go from San Marco, the more the prices drop. Shop on the island where the train station is and you will find the best prices in town.

If you insist on TTs, hit the ones way past San Marco and the Hotel Danieli and on the way to the public gardens. You'll save as much as a euro ($1.25) per item. You'll also avoid the most severe crowds.

The Gondoliers

I don't care how touristy you think it is—riding in a gondola is part of the Venetian experience and something you must do at least once. While you can be hustled by a gondolier, there are fixed prices for their services that vary from season to season. Even if you have to save up for the experience, this is one treat that you shouldn't miss. *Tip:* Take your gondola ride at high tide—at low tide you'll have a view of the scummy exposed sides of the canals.

When there aren't as many rich tourists around, prices drop. The winter price can be 73€ ($91); the spring price for the same service is 78€ ($98), but you can try to bargain. Night service, any time of the year, is 94€ ($118) beginning at 8pm. These are the prices for 50 minutes of sailing time with up to six persons in the boat. For each additional 25-minute period after your first 50 minutes during the day, the flat rate is 38€ ($48); 49€ ($61) at night. You are also expected to tip.

Okay, that was the official line as taught to me by the city. In person, I find that knowing these prices is helpful, as is carrying around a copy of the freebie booklet *Un Ospite di Venezia* that is given away at your hotel and has a section on gondola prices. You can point to the appropriate page when you bargain and try to be tough. You bargain fiercely or find someone you like and forget the money.

Here's where they really get you—it's the time, not the cash. Gondoliers usually do 45 minutes, not 50. They also want far more than the guidelines say they should get; they are especially not friendly when there are lots of tourists around. Their idea of a great fare is a chump who says yes to the quoted price, and then lays a tip on top.

The gondolier will sing to you—it's part of the deal—but if you ask him to stop the boat en route so that you can get

Aaron's Turn: The Gondoliers

It had been my romantic notion to take my girl for a gondola ride once we got to Venice. In fact, one of the reasons we went to Venice was to realize this dream. Ah, well, live and learn.

We quoted a few gondoliers, and the standard price seemed to be 104€ ($130) for a 50- to 60- minute ride. At least that was the standard answer we got, the going rate is supposed to be much cheaper, according to the chart.

One gondolier in particular said that he would give us the short ride (30–40 min.) for 78€ ($98). (How anybody thinks that 40 minutes on a gondola isn't enough for them truly eludes me.) We accepted his offer.

I kept hoping that the guy would start singing to us in Italian, so I kept humming "Volare" under my breath in the hopes that he might subconsciously have the urge to bust into it Dean Martin style. No such luck. He did, however, whistle some cheesy elevator-jazz song for 20 seconds before losing interest in the music and us.

out for a look-see while he waits, or to provide extra services (other than posing in your family snapshot), he will expect more money.

All things are negotiable, but try to have a handle on costs before you get in—nothing spoils the magic more than a fight about money after the fact.

I've seen as many as six people squished into a gondola, so the cost can be amortized into a reasonable expense. You have not seen Venice until you've seen it from a gondola—it is worth the money. If you want an update or an insider fact, call the hot line. © 041/528-5075.

Shopping Hours

High season is March to October, and shops are open from 9am until 12:30 or 1pm and reopen from about 3 or 3:30pm to 7:30pm. If lunchtime closings bore you, remember that the shops on the nearby island of Murano do not close for lunch.

Off season, most Venice shops are closed on Monday until 3pm. During Carnevale weekends, many things are open no matter what day or what time of the day. For Sunday shopping tips, see below.

SUNDAY SHOPPING

Si, si, just about all the stores—including designer shops—are open on Sundays. **Emporio Armani, Trussardi, Versace,** and the like are open on Sunday afternoons. Just about everyone is open on Sundays—but closed on Mondays. They may or may not open Monday later in the afternoon, but Sunday is a day of shopping in Venice.

Sunday is also a good day to visit the islands; shops are open on both Murano and Burano. Check with your concierge for exact opening and closing times, but plan a day trip to Murano as early as you like—the fires are crackling at 9am, and shops are open nonstop until 4 or 5pm. On Burano, Sunday hours tend to be 10am to 1:30pm.

Further note that stores are open in Verona on Sundays. This is a popular Sunday destination for Italians. See chapter 10.

HOLIDAY HOURS

While Venice does have the most liberal of all the holiday hours, stores do close up early on Christmas Eve and New Year's Eve. Some stores are actually open on New Year's Day—but late in the day, after noon. If there are tourists, there are some stores open.

Street Vendors

One of the glories of Venice is the street action—not just the throngs of tourists but the zillions of street vendors who make it possible for you to do very thorough shopping in Venice without ever setting foot inside a store.

The street vendors stay open until the light begins to fade, which in the height of summer can be quite late. There are illegal salespeople hawking wares from blankets all over town—they usually operate during lunch hours and after hours, as there is less chance they will be arrested then. Louis Vuitton anyone? Cartier perhaps?

"This is real Chanel, lady," a vendor tells me with pride. Yeah, sure it is.

Like other retailers, street vendors and cart dealers rig their prices to the needs of the crowd. Therefore, the farther you walk from San Marco, the better the prices at kiosks and carts.

Fairs & Mercatini

San Moisè is the location of many outdoor fairs, from antiques markets to the regular Christmas market. Vendors set up booths and sell from 9am to 8pm.

Buying Venetian Glass

I confess that up until the minute I walked into Bergdorf Goodman one fateful day, I thought that only old ladies liked Venetian glass. Then I took one look at a bowl filled with hand-blown Murano glass in the form of colorful hard candies and flipped out. Such style, such finesse, such color. If this is the passion of little old ladies, sign me up. I've had a sweet tooth ever since. Bergdorf's gets about 12€ ($15) per glass candy. In Venice, you'll pay about 5.20€ ($6.50).

Once you get hooked on glass candies, a whole new world of glass design opens up. Fazzoletto (handkerchief vases) will surely be next. While you may not flip out for pink glass goblets with hand-painted roses and baroque gold doodads, you will gasp when you take in the designs made from the early 1920s right through the 1950s—all highly collectible works of art when they are signed by a big-name glass house. Even post-1950s glass is collectible: What you buy today (if you buy wisely) will be happily inherited by your children.

The colored strings of glass swirled into clear, white, or colored glass are called threads; the value of a piece—aside from the signature—is based on the composition of form, color, and threads or patterns; the way the piece reflects light should also be taken into account, although this is easy to look for in a vase and impossible to consider in a piece of candy. Smoked glass is hot now, as is glass matted with ash, and deco glass. Crizzled glass is crickly-crackled glass with a nice effect, but it won't last over the centuries and makes a bad investment.

The important names to remember are **Venini, Seguso, Brandolini, Poli, Barovier, Toso,** and **Pauly.** A vase from the 1940s went for $125,000 at auction at Christie's in Geneva in 1990; prices continue to rise. New pieces are not inexpensive, as they are considered serious artwork.

Famous designers create styles for glass houses, just as they do for furniture firms. The designer's name associated with a famous glass house can make a piece even more valuable. Do check for signatures, labels, or accompanying materials that uphold the provenance of your piece. If you are buying older pieces of glass—even from the 1950s or so—check the condition carefully.

If you are trading up and browsing for some of the important stuff, here's a quick-fix dictionary to make you sound like a maven:

- *Vetro battute:* Flat beaten glass with a scored surface.
- *Vetro sommerso:* Glass in bubbled, lumpy form is layered over the glass item—the rage in the mid-1930s.
- *Vetro pennelato:* No, it doesn't have pieces of penne pasta in it—this is painted glass with swirly streaks of dancing color that zip across the body of the item inside the glass.
- *Vetro pulegoso:* This is bubbled glass with the tiny bubbles inside the glass—it will never be confused with sommerso when you see the two in person.
- *Vetro inciso:* Flat beaten glass with scored lines all running in the same direction.

- *Vetro pezzato:* Patchwork made of various pieces of colored glass almost in mosaic form; introduced in the early 1950s.
- *Vetro a retorti:* Twisted glass with the threads swirled within the body of the work.
- *Murrina:* Slices of colored glass rods encircled with gold and sold as charms or pendants.

I must take some time here to warn you about the hawkers who offer you free trips to Murano and act as guides. They are dangerous, emotionally and physically, and should be avoided. They not only get a percentage of what you buy but also make their living by preying off tourists and telling half-truths or lies that may convince you to buy something you weren't certain about.

If you want the free boat ride, ask your hotel concierge to book it. If you can afford to get there on your own, do so, and buy only from the houses of good repute. If you ship, be prepared to wait a very, very long time for your package to arrive.

While we are into warnings, I got a note from a reader who asked a glass shop about a specific address in Murano and was wrongly told that the shop had closed and was encouraged to do business where she was asking.

Shipping

Anyone seriously considering glass, or mirrors, or chandeliers is also thinking about shipping. Almost all the stores, even the TTs, will volunteer to ship for you. I am not big on shipping, especially expensive items, but I have noticed that things shipped from Venice do tend to reach their destination—eventually. I have had several nervous letters from readers who have waited many months in a state of panic. My basic advice is simple: Don't fall in love with anything you cannot carry yourself. Always buy from a reputable dealer, and pay with a credit card that has a protection plan on it.

Shopping Neighborhoods

Most of the shops are found in the historical and artistic center, between the **Rialto Bridge (Ponte di Rialto)** and **Piazza San Marco.** A new area of mostly designer shops has been evolving at **San Moisè.**

Looking at a map can be very confusing because of the cobweb of interconnecting streets, bridges, and canals. Finding an address can be equally difficult, as many streets and shops show no numbers, or the numbers are clear, but the street they are on is not clear.

Merceria   One main street will carry you from Piazza San Marco to the Rialto Bridge: Merceria. It hosts hundreds of shops. Many of the shopping streets branch off this one thoroughfare, or are very close. Merceria is not a water bus stop (San Marco is), but if you get yourself to Piazza San Marco and stand at the clock tower with your back to the water, Merceria will be the little street jutting off the arcade right in front of you. If you still can't find it, walk into any shop and ask. You need not speak Italian.

Piazza San Marco   The four rows of arcades that frame Piazza San Marco can be considered a neighborhood unto itself. Three of the arcades create a U shape around the square; the fourth is at a right angle to one of the ends of the U. There are easily a hundred shops here—a few of the shops are showrooms for glass firms and a few sell touristy knickknacks, but most are jewelry or glass shops (or cafes). Although many of these shops have been in business for years, and some of them have extremely famous names, this is the high-rent part of Venice and isn't very funky. I was quite shocked at the high turnover I noticed on my last visit: Many old reliable firms have packed up. One of the newer names to the area is **Michaela Frey,** a Viennese jeweler known for her enamel works who does a fabulous Saint Marks Square–bangle bracelet (with the Venetian lions on it) for those who can handle a pricey, yet very chic, souvenir.

Behind San Marco   Now, here's the tricky part. "Behind San Marco" is my name for the area that includes **San Moisè** and

San Giglio (this way to the Hotel Bauer) and is best represented by the big-time shopping drag called **Via XXII Marzo.** This street comes off of Piazza San Marco from behind and forms an L with the square and Merceria. The farther you get from San Marco, the less commercial.

Frezzeria This is the main shopping street also behind San Marco, but, if your back is to San Marco and you're facing the road to the Hotel Bauer and American Express, it goes off to your right. It's a small alley of a street that twists and turns more than most, and it's packed with small shops, many of which are artisan or crafts shops. There are also some designer stores woven into the texture of the landscape.

Giglio This is a secret part of town tucked back and away from the tourist areas. It's also the home of the **Gritti Palace.** Unless a shop is actually on the piazza, it probably will have a San Moisè address, so you may get confused. Not to worry. Aside from the antiques shops, there's a good paper store and a little market for food for the train or a picnic. It's very civilized and quite divine back here.

Rialto Bridge They might just as well have named it the "Retailo" Bridge—not only are there pushcarts and vendors in the walkway before the bridge, but there are also shops going all the way up and down the bridge itself. The stores are not like the crumbling, charming, old shops that line the Ponte Vecchio in Florence; they are teeny-bopper shops, leather-goods stores, and even sporting-goods stores. Despite the huge number of street vendors from Piazza San Marco to Campo San Zaccaria, street vendors here sell things I've never seen before. Most of it is extremely touristy junk.

Over the Bridge Once across the Rialto, you'll hit a two-pronged trading area. In the arcades behind the street vendors to the left are established shops; in the streets and to your right are green grocers, food vendors, cheese stalls, and, in summer, little men selling little pieces of melon. You can have a walking feast for lunch in any season.

Once you make it past the immediate arcades, bear left and follow the shops and crowds toward **San Polo.** The shops here

Jenny's Turn: From Mestre with Baci

Mestre: So, you have decided to stay in Mestre, but how do you get to Venice? There is a quick bus that will take you there for a mere euro ($1.25). The tickets can be bought at the newsstand; they have to be validated once you are on the bus. Like other European cities, the transportation authority works on the honor system, so don't be surprised if your ticket isn't checked. Just make sure you get on the bus going the right way. We took the bus going in the wrong direction and didn't know until we were at the end of the line. We had to wait an hour for the off-bus and then another 40 minutes to ride the line all the way back to where we started and then to Venice. A trip that should have taken 10 minutes took us about 2½ hours.

Meanwhile, even though your main idea is to visit Venice, you aren't dead, and there are a few places to see in Mestre. If you plan on staying in Mestre, Piazza Ferretto is the place to go for all your young, hip shopping needs. This charming square offers enchanting cafes, and the latest trendy euro-styles. Favorite shops right on the piazza include the following:

- **Caberlotte:** Italian specialty goods and gourmet food market. Great selection of candies, liqueurs, and oils. If the Italian cheeses and wines are too foreign for your distinguished American likes, fear not, they also sell brands like Duncan Hines and Campbell's.
- **Capelletto:** Mostly shoes and handbags, some clothing, all big-name Italian designers (Prada, Gucci, Valentino). Prices on shoes range from 104€ to 624 € ($130–$780).
- **Nara Camice:** Dress shirts and ties for men and women. Very hip, very young. Think rock star at the Grammys. Moderate prices.
- **Reds:** For the trendiest of high-school girls. Very cheap, cute and colorful designs. Prices very low, but quality isn't wonderful.

are a little more of the "real people" nature and a little less expensive. On the other hand, a fair number of them are smaller branches of the big designer shops found on the big island.

Piazzale Roma This is by no means a hot retailing area, but it is where the bus station is and where you will get your vaporetto if you come in from the airport, or if you come by bus. (The train station is not here.) Where there are tourists, there are shops. In the case of Venice, or Venice in summer, where there are tourists, there are scads of street vendors selling everything from T-shirts like the one worn by your favorite gondolier to plates of the Doge's Palace.

Shopping Murano

Two different experiences are to be had here on the island of glassblowers—so watch out, and don't blame me if you hate it. It can be very touristy or very special—it depends on how you organize your time, as well as what season you visit. Go by vaporetto in season, and it can be a zoo. Go by private boat, tour a glass factory, wander town, and then take the vaporetto back: It's easy, it's inexpensive, and it's fun. Depending on the weather, the crowds, and your appetite for colored glass, it can even be glorious.

Sunday on Murano can be heaven. Take no. 5 at San Zaccaria, in front of the Danieli. The visit to Murano can be combined with a trip to Burano (take no. 12), or you can turn around and come back home. It's a long day if you combine both islands.

Murano is also the perfect lunchtime adventure when stores in Venice might be closed. Do not bring small children or strollers with you.

If you want to take a private boat to the island, call one of the glass factories to come get you. Yes, you are obligated to tour the factory, but you aren't obligated to buy. Besides, the tour is fabulous. It's a perfect Sunday adventure; Sunday is a big day on Murano because they cannot close down the furnaces, as the temperature must stay constant, and the workers don't work. Instead, there are demonstrations and tours.

If you go by public transportation, you will arrive in the heart of Murano. When you get off the boat at Murano, you'll know it by the giant signs that say *fornace* (furnace). You have two choices, really: to work the area, or to realize quickly that this is one of the biggest tourist traps known to humankind. Walk briskly toward the museum, and then head for the lighthouse.

By the way, you can also get a free ride to the island by private boat if you go with a hawker, but you *don't* want to do this! He gets 30% of what you spend in a secret kickback, and you get a lot of pressure to buy (see above). If you can take the heat, you will be escorted to the *fornace*. But it may be hell, so beware!

Hawkers will automatically gravitate to you; you need not even look for them. It's better to ask your hotel concierge to contact someone from a proper factory for you.

GLASS WITH CLASS

On Sunday, most showrooms, such as those listed here (and their adjoining shops) are open from 9am to 4pm. TTs open midday.

ARCHIMIDI SEGUSO
Fondamenta Serenella, Murano.

BAROVIER & TOSO
Fondamenta Vetrai 28, Murano.

FOSCARINI
Fondamenta Serenella, Murano.

SENT
Fondamenta Serenella, Murano.

For good, traditional showrooms that have it all, try the resources below. To find these shops, walk from the main drag toward the lighthouse, and you'll wander into a far less touristy world and a hidden street (Viale Garibaldi) of more glassblowers and shops. Once at the lighthouse, round the turn following the water (there's a sidewalk) to find several more glass showrooms, which have boat service and will pick you up at your hotel in town and return you when you are ready to go back.

Colonna Fornace
Fondamenta Vetrai 10–11, Murano.

This is another huge firm that picks you up at your hotel and lets you tour their scads of rooms of stuff. I don't mean to give this place short shrift, as I have enjoyed hours shopping here, but it also sells glass and, at a certain point, can be confused with several others; although this one is the first you come to on some approaches. © 041/739-389.

Vetreria Foscari
Fondamenta dei Battuti 5, Murano.

I asked the concierge at the Bauer Grünwald to pick a source for me, curious to see what he would suggest, and was pleased to find that this was his choice. They sent a boat for me and picked me up at my hotel, then returned me there when I was ready to go home. I even got a Coke along the way. A true delight. I keep going back, even though the source has passed on to another family member, and I don't always stay at the Bauer.

The showroom is made up of a series of salons, organized by category of goods and by price. One room is devoted to chandeliers, other rooms to glassware. You'll also find beads and just about anything else you can imagine.

To get them to pick you up, call at least 1 day in advance. © 041/739-5-40.

Vetreria Gritti
Fondamenta Manin 1, Murano.

The Luna Baglioni concierge chose this glassworks for me; they pick up at the hotel each morning at 9am, so it was easy to get there. They brought me back when I was ready. I asked the concierge to stress that I would not be buying anything, but of course—I ended up buying something.

The showroom was huge with various styles and prices that seemed fair enough. I paid 52€ ($65) for an etched wine carafe. © 041/739-801.

Shopping Burano

Although Murano and Burano sound like twin cities, they are not. But if you visit the two in the same afternoon (get the water bus from the lighthouse on Murano to Burano; it runs hourly, but go there for the exact schedule so that you can plan your time accordingly), you can sightsee and do some shopping at the same time. Many stores in Burano are open on Sunday afternoon, so you can combine the two islands in a fabulous Sunday outing.

As touristy and crass as Murano can be, Burano is totally different—I don't happen to like it as much, but I can see the natural, homespun attraction. Certainly, the colors of the houses are divine. The shopping is awfully touristy. I get the feeling that Murano is in the glass business, and Burano is in the tourist business; there's something in the subtext of the air in Burano that lacks wonder. The lace is rarely handmade; there are few really good shops. But if you like to see, to stroll, and to avoid the throngs of pushing people in San Marco, this is a wonderful side trip. Don't think of it as a shopping adventure; rather, take your artistic eye and just enjoy.

You may want to poke into the fish market, **Fondamenta Pescheria,** held daily in the morning only—not that you're going to buy much, but it's fun and picturesque.

The lace-making school is the **Scuola di Merletti,** Piazza Galuppi (© 041/730-034). The school is closed on Monday, open from 10am to 4pm on Sunday and from 9am to 6pm Tuesday through Saturday.

The boat to Burano from Murano is as big as the ferry that takes you to Nantucket, and you will have the same sense of adventure. Burano is the third stop, so don't have a breakdown wondering when and where to get off (the first stop is Mazzorbo; the second is Torcello). And yes, it's a bit of a schlep, so you'll be on the boat for a while.

When you arrive, you'll see a narrow street lined with shops and think you are in heaven. That's because you haven't been in the shops yet. Pretty soon, you'll think you are in Hong Kong.

Here's the story of the woman in Venice who was buying a lace tablecloth. She had it spread out around her and draped all over—she was oooohing and aaaahing over it, but I knew it was from Hong Kong—like most of the lace in Venice—and I didn't know if I should tell her or not. Well, I didn't say a word because I didn't want to ruin her experience; but readers, you should know the facts.

If you don't like the lace shops, never mind; just take a good look at the colors of the stucco houses and storefronts—they are just fabulous. And the lace school is incredible.

Not all of the shops in the "heart of town" are open on Sunday, but the TTs are. Get the boat schedule before you wander so that you know how long you have—an hour on Burano is probably all you need. Note that when you return to Venice you will probably end up at a vaporetto stop other than San Marco and will have to buy a new ticket and transfer to get back to your hotel.

VENICE RESOURCES A TO Z

Antiques

If you are the type (like me) who likes flea markets and junk and reasonable prices, Venice is not for you (unless you hit it for one of the triannual flea markets—see below). There are also regular real-people flea markets, but they are on the "land" side.

The few antiques shops in Venice are charming and dear and sweet and—should I tell you, or can you guess?—outrageously expensive.

But wait, should you luck into the **Mercatino dell'Antiquariato,** held each April, September, and December, you'll have the giggle of your lifetime. This market is not large, but it's sweet and simple and the kind I like: heaps of stuff on tables lay out in a piazza, the very convenient Campo San Maurizio. The dates are established well in advance and set for each year so that you can call for the exact times (© **041/454-176**). This

3-day event is held on a Friday, Saturday, and Sunday; there is no admission charge.

Bath & Beauty

COIN BEAUTY
Campo S. Luca.

Free-standing store that's trying to be the local version of Sephora; it's also the beauty department of the department store of the same name that is several blocks away and has no other beauty department in the regular store. This is not at all a great store or even a great selection of brands, but if you need something, this is one of the few places to find it. I suffered a nail crisis and turned the town upside down until I found nail polish remover, glue, and nail polish. Call © 041/523-8444.

LUSH
San Polo 89 (Rialto Bridge, San Polo side); Strada Nuova Cannargeio 3822 (Santa Felice).

The British cult fave for deli-style cosmetics, beauty treatments, bath bombs, and more has set up several stores in Venice with more expected. The shop right near Rialto is in the most convenient location for tourists; the goodies are not inexpensive, but they offer high novelty and are currently not available in the U.S. Check it out online; the Italian website gives you insight into the products that are specifically Italian—many differ from what's on hand in other countries. Call © 041/522-1549 for the San Polo location and © 041/241-1200 for the Cannargeio location; www.lush.it.

Beads

GLORIA ASTOLFO
San Marco 1581.

The beads are already made into items of jewelry here, but the style is based on the use of tiny beads and charms and fantasy bijoux. You'll pay about 200€ ($250) for a heavily beaded necklace. Call © **041/520-6827.**

LESLIE ANN GENNINGER DESIGN STUDIO
Calle del Traghetto, Dorsoduro 2793a (Piazza Contarini-Michel, near Ca'Rezzonico Museum).

Talk about living out your best dreams: Leslie is American, lives in Venice, makes beads, and sells them from a fabulous little shop where you can buy ready-made jewelry or individual beads. The beads are made according to medieval (and secret) recipes but are inlaid with silver, which sparkles through.

To get here, take the vaporetto no. 1 to the Ca'Rezzonico stop, turn right, and *voilà*—it's on the corner. Call © **041/522-5565.** www.genningerstudio.com.

Boutiques

ARBOR
Gran Viale Lido 10a.

There are several branches of this boutique on the big island as well as at the Lido beach. Arbor carries the hot names, such as Byblos and Genny. The men's shop sells that stylish Italian look that thin men love to wear. Call © **041/526-1032.**

ELYSEE
Frezzeria, San Marco 1693.

ELYSEE 2
Calle Goldoni, Castello 4485.

This is not one but two very sleek boutiques carrying Mani, Maud Frizon, Mario Valentino, and the Giorgio Armani ready-to-wear collection for men and women. Each shop has its own selection, including some shoes. Call © **041/522-3020** for the Frezzeria location, and © **041/523-6948** for the Calle Goldoni location.

LA COUPOLE
*Via XXII Marzo, San Marco 2366; Frezzeria, San Marco
1674.*

Once again, two boutiques carrying the same big names and
many lines. A few of their makers include Byblos, Alaia, and
the sort-of-local Malo cashmere; shoes from Moschino and earrings from Sharra Pagano of Milan. Both shops are small and
elegant; prices are high. Call © **041/522-4243.**

Crafts

IL BALLO DEL DOGE
San Marco 1823.

Cooperative of 14 artisans.

LA BOTTEGA DEI MASCARERI
Ponte di Rialto, San Polo 80.

Located at the foot of the Rialto, this shop offers unusual papiermâché masks that are a notch above the average fare. Call
© **041/522-3857.**

LA VENEXIANA
Ponte Canonica, Castello 4322.

You'll find masks and other carnival items here as well as some
of the most incredible crafts work I have ever seen. Don't miss
it. Call © **041/523-3558.**

MAX ART SHOP
Frezzeria, San Marco 1232.

This store is right around the corner from the Hotel Bauer and
the San Moisè designer shopping area at the start of Freezia;
it will beckon to you from the velvet-hung windows. Inside,
choose from velvet pillows, clothes, Carnevale-inspired wonder, and Old-World charm. Call © **041/523-3851.**

Designer Boutiques

For more detail on many of these well-known brand names, check out my "Dictionary of Taste & Design" in chapter 4.

ARMANI
Calle Goldin, San Marco 4412.

ARMANI JEANS
Calle Goldoni, San Marco 4485.

BULGARI
Calle Larga XXII Marzo, San Marco 2282.

CARTIER
30124 Venezia, San Marco 606.

DOLCE & GABBANA
San Marco 223–26.

EMILIO PUCCI
San Marco 1318.

ERMENEGILDO ZEGNA
San Marco 1241.

EMPORIO ARMANI
Calle dei Fabbri, San Marco 989.

ETRO
San Marco 1349.

FENDI
Salizzada San Moisè, San Marco 1474.

FOGAL
Calle Merceria dell'Orologio, San Marco 221.

FRETTE
Calle Larga XXII Marzo, San Marco 2070a.

GIANFRANCO FERRÉ
Calle Vallereso 1307.

GIANNI VERSACE
Campo San Moisè, San Marco 1462.

GUCCI
San Marco 1317.

HERMES
Piazza San Marco, San Marco 125.

HOGAN
San Marco 1461.

LA PERLA
Campo San Salvador, San Marco 4828.

LAURA BIAGIOTTI
Via XXII Marzo, San Marco 2400.

LORO PIANA
Ascensione, San Marco 1290–1301.

LOUIS VUITTON
San Marco 1256.

MALO
San Marco 2359.

MARINA RINALDO
San Marco 269a.

MAX & CO.
San Marco 5028.

MAX MARA
Mercerie, San Marco 268.

MISSONI
Calle Vallapresso 1312.

MONT BLANC
San Marco 4610.

PRADA
San Marco 1410.

ROBERTO CAVALLI
Calle Vallaresso 1314.

JUST CAVALLI
San Marco 1814.

SALVATORE FERRAGAMO
Campo San Moisè, San Marco.

SPORT MISSONI
San Marco Mercerie 4918.

TRUSSARDI
Calle Spadaria, 670 and 695.

VALENTINO
Salizzada San Moisè, San Marco 1473.

WOLFORD
Cannaregio 5666.

Eyeglass Frames

I did not list this under "optical" because I feel strongly that you want the optics done where you know what's going on and have a handle on the price. Venice and the nearby Veneto area are the places to buy the frames.

DANILO CARRARO
Calle della Mandola, San Marco 3706.

Local makers of chic and fabulous frames that retail for about 80€ to 120€ ($100–$150) per pair, in all sorts of colors and many types of tortoisey patterns. They also do a hot fashion color for a season and then never do it again. Best of all, they have a website, and you can shop electronically. Call © 041/520-4258. www.otticacarraro.it.

OTTICA URBANI
San Marco 1280.

After I had laser treatment (LASIK) so that I no longer wore eyeglasses, I threw away all my scads of pairs of glasses—except the ones from this store in Venice. While they make myriad styles, the store is most famous for a transparent resin (in fashion colors) in square or round shapes that ensure you look like a cross between a movie star and TS Eliot. You'll also find fabulous reading glasses and even some frames that fold. Call ℂ **041/522-4140**. www.otticaurbani.com.

Fabrics

GAGGIO
San Stefano, San Marco 3441.

Traditional silks, velvets, pleats, block prints, and the to-die-for local look that is part costume and part local treasure. It also has fabrics by the meter, and clothes and styles for the home. Call ℂ **041/522-8574**.

RUBELLI
Campo San Gallo, San Marco 3877.

This Italian house is actually a source to the trade for reproductions of stunningly exquisite silken brocades and formal fabrics of museum quality. They have swatches, and they work with individuals, even if your last name is not Rothschild. Call ℂ **041/523-6110**. www.rubelli.it.

VALLI
San Marco 783.

Valli is a chain of fabric stores with locations in all major cities and factories in Como; this shop in Venice happens to be right along your path, so it's a good place to stop in. The specialty of the house is designer fabrics, straight from the factory as supplied to the design houses, so you can buy the fabric in the same season. It's not cheap, but you can save money. I spent 80€ ($100) on some Gianni Versace silk and made a sarong skirt that I could never afford to buy from Versace ready-made. No phone.

VENETIA STVDIVM
Calle Larga XXII Marco, San Marco 2403; Mercerie, San Marco 723; and others.

Fortuny-style wrinkled fabric (mostly silks) in medieval colors that are pure artistry and, without doubt, the most exciting stores in Venice. They are expanding, so look for stores wherever you wander.

The look is fantasy meets fashion with a fortuny twist—there are long Isadora Duncan–like scarves and little drawstring purses that make the perfect evening bag. Prices begin around 160€ ($200). There are velvets as well as silks, and you should consider bringing your toothbrush so that you can just move in. Heaven on earth.

Note that the main store is near San Moisè, but there are other branches, and each branch promotes a different look. Branch stores in less-touristy parts of town tend to be more home-decor oriented. Call © 041/522-9281 or 041/522-9859.

Foodstuffs

Also consider a stop at Al Cove (see "Snack & Shop," earlier in this chapter), where you can order their products to take away with you.

DROGHERIA MASCARI
San Polo 381.

This is not a drugstore as you may guess from the name but the last remaining spice merchant in Venice. Located in a real-people part of town, you get there by walking over the Rialto Bridge and going on to San Polo. Call © 041/522-9762.

GIACOMO RIZZO
Calle del Aseo 3.

This is a tiny pasta-maker shop with gourmet pasta in assorted strange colors and tastes—great gift items. Closed on Sundays. Yes, they have blueberry pasta. On the other hand, there are plenty that you do want to try—I like artichoke. Right near the Coin department store. Call © **041/522-2824.**

Glass

You'll recognize the difference between quality glass and touristy junk in a matter of seconds. If your eye needs a little training, make a trip to the glass museum on Murano.

L'ISOLA
Campo San Moisé, San Marco 1468.

There are a few branches of this contemporary gallery around town. It is the best source in Venice for the newer names in big glassworks. The store is across from the Bauer. Call © **041/523-1973.**

PAULY & COMPANY
Ponte Consorzi, San Marco 4392.

They don't come much more famous than this house, which was established in 1866. Pauly & Company has worked for most of the royal houses of Europe. They will paint your custom-blown glass to match your china (but not while you wait). They ship. Call © **041/520-9899.**

SEGUSO
San Marco 143.

You'll find bright colors and outstanding contemporary works here. Call © **041/739-048.**

SALVIATI
Campo San Angelo, San Marco 3831.

Among the most famous master glassmakers in Venice. Call © **041/522-7074.** www.salviati.com.

VENINI
Piazzetta dei Leoncini, San Marco 314.

Credited with beginning the second renaissance of glassblowers in Venice (1920–60), Venini is among the best. Buy anything you can afford, and hang on to it for dear life. Call ✆ **041/522-4045.**

ZORA
San Marco 2407.

This is the newer guy in town. The shop is very close to the main branch of Venetia Stvdivm, the best store for silks in town, so you will be here anyway. While Zora makes glass, their specialty is glass picture frames, which are sophisticated and stunning and 320€ ($400) each. There are also tassels, beaded flowers, and golden grape clusters. Even if you buy nothing, don't miss it. You go through a little gate into what looks like a private house, so push on. Call ✆ **041/277-0895.**

Handbags & Leather Goods

FENDI
Salizzada San Moisè, San Marco 1474.

If you have no other chance to shop for Fendi, this store is bigger than the one in Milan, modern, and right in the heart of your stroll across town. It's even near the American Express office, if you run out of cash. They do have sales; prices are about the same all over Italy, so your purchase will not cost less in another city. The store is located behind San Marco on the way to San Giglio, almost across the lane from the Hotel Bauer. Call ✆ **041/520-5733.**

GUCCI
San Marco 258.

Although I find this Gucci small and rather boring, without the flair of shops in other cities, it still offers the same gorgeous merchandise—sometimes on sale. You'll pass it on the way to the Rialto Bridge, so pop in if you have no other chance for Gucci. Call ✆ **041/522-9119.**

Home Style

ANTICHITA E OGGETTI D'ARTE
Frezzeria, San Marco 1691.

Ignore the word *antique* here and concentrate on glam home style, cushions of gilded velvet, velvet devore, painted velvet, and velvet dreams with fringe and beads. Fabrics from centuries past that will make you weep with their glory. Call ℡ 041/523-5666.

MARIO & PEOLA BEVILACQUA
Fondamenta Canonica, San Marco 337B; Campo Santa Maria del Giglio 2520.

These are two different addresses; the San Marco one is the easiest for tourists. The shop is the size of a large closet and is filled with velvets, pillows, tapestries, and tassels. Even if you live in the Sunbelt, you will be tempted to do your home over in dark velvets. Call ℡ 041/528-7581 or 041/241-0662.

RIGATTIERI
San Marco 3532/36.

Located near San Stefano, this shop specializes in faience. It's a two-part shop: One part offers country dishes, and the other more traditional ceramics. A faience plate will cost about 20€ ($25), and they will pack it for travel. Call ℡ 041/523-1081. www.rigattieri-venice.com.

Linen & Lace

JESURUM
Cannaregio 3219.

Yo—they moved. Jesurum has upheld and continued the tradition of Venetian lace–making, which was all but lost in the early 1800s. Just before the art would have died out, two Venetians undertook to restore it. One of the two was Michelangelo Jesurum, who—along with restoring the industry and putting hundreds of lace makers to work—also started a school so that the art would not die.

When you enter the Jesurum lace factory and showrooms, be prepared to flip your wig. The old church has been left with all its beautiful inlaid arches and its vaulted ceiling. Beautiful lace and appliquéd table linens and place mats are displayed on tables throughout the room. Call © **041/524-2540**. www. jesurum.it.

MARIA MAZZARON
Fondamenta dell'Osmarìn, Castello 4970.

This is a private dealer whom you must phone to make an appointment to see her museum-quality treasures. Serious collectors only. Call © **041/522-1392**.

MARTINUZZI
Piazza San Marco, San Marco 67A.

This lace shop is almost as good as Jesurum, and it's located right on the piazza. This is the real thing: embroidered goods, appliquéd linens, very drop-dead fancy Italian bed gear. The atmosphere is more old-lady lace shop than church-goes-retail, but the goods are high quality. Call © **041/522-5068**.

Masks

If you saw the movie or play *Amadeus*, you are familiar with the type of mask worn at Carnevale time in Venice. Carnevale in Venice got so out of hand that it was outlawed in 1797. But it's back again, and with it a renewed interest in masks. One of the most popular styles is a mask covered with bookbinding paper that you can find at a *legatoria*, or paper-goods store (see below). But there also are masks made of leather, papiermâché, fabric, and more. If all this is more than you had in mind, not to worry—there are masks in plastic for 4.70€ ($5.85) that will satisfy your need to participate. After 3 days in Venice, you'll swear you'll die if you see another mask, so make your selection carefully. Many of them seem like trite tourist items.

For a more special item, try any (or all!) of these famous mask makers:

ADRIANO MIANI
Calle Grimani, San Marco 289B.

BRUNO RIZZATO
Ponte dei Barcoli 1831.

LABORATORIO ARTIGIANO MASCHIERE
Piazza San Marco, San Marco 282.

LE MASCHIERE DE DARIO USTINO
Ponte dei Dai 171.

MA BOUTIQUE
Calle Larga San Marco, San Marco 28.

Paper Goods

Legatoria means bookbindery in Italian, and the famous designs are copies of bookbinding papers from hundreds of years ago. The best makers use the same old-fashioned methods that have been in the house for centuries. Many of the shops will make something to order for you, but ask up front whether they will mail it for you; most won't. These papers have become so popular in the U.S. that the paper goods business now is divided between those who are staying old-fashioned and those who are counting the tourist bucks and loving it. When you walk into the various shops, you can feel the difference. There are many 8€ ($10) gift items in these stores. A calendar-diary of the fanciest sort costs 40€ ($50).

Legatoria Piazzesi (Campiella della Feltrina, Santo Stéfano, San Marco) and **Il Papiro** (Calle del Piovan, San Marco 2764), the two most famous paper shops in Venice, are almost across the way from each other, right near Campo San Stéfano at Ponte San Maurizio. Piazzesi also sells old prints. Don't let the street address throw you; just keep walking and you'll see these two beauties. They are past the main tourist shopping but in a gorgeous part of town not far past the Gritti.

There's a relatively new chain of shops around town called **In Folio** that sells paper goods and books and gift items as well as sealing wax and wax seals. When I was a teenager, sealing wax was the rage in America; now it's got a nice medieval bend to it that tourists are scarfing up. There are five or six of these shops scattered around town: San Marco 55; San Marco 739; San Marco 2431; San Marco 4852; and Castello 4615.

Shoes

Check the "Handbags & Leather Goods" listing above for other sources.

BRUNO MAGLI
Calle XXII Marzo 2288; San Marco 1302; Calle Frezzeria 1583/85; San Marco 1583.

As you can tell from the addresses above, Magli has four different shops in Venice, although I swear I saw more. Not only is there a Magli every place you look, but they display different models, forcing you to visit each if only to drool. Call © **041/522-7210** or 041/522-3472.

RENE CAOVILLA
1296 San Marco.

The first shop owned by master shoemaker Caovilla who owns the factories on the mainland where most designer shoes are made. These babies will easily set you back $500, but Cinderella would be so proud.

ROLANDO SEGALIN
Calle dei Fuseri 4365.

An old-fashioned shoemaker who creates everything by hand and made to measure. Unbelievable stuff . . . ranging from the type of creative and crazy things you might expect Elton John to wear (shoes shaped like gondolas) to very simple, elegant court shoes. He'll create or copy anything, although the price is about 400€ ($500) a pair. Closed on Saturday. Call © 041/ 522-2115.

SONNENBLUME
Ponte di Rialto.

Okay, I am going to put this in perspective—I have big feet and can rarely find shoes that fit, and I am on a tight budget. So excuse me if I rant and rave. This source makes old-fashioned espadrilles, sells them from the Rialto Bridge, and makes a fashion statement to boot—you should excuse the expression. Sizes go up to 43. Technically speaking, these are not espadrilles—a French shoe—but a creation made by Italians after World War II when supplies were scarce. The original shoe soles were made from tires. The uppers are made in silk, velvet, and linen in the yummiest fashion colors of the rainbow. You can custom order. Prices are about 32€ ($40) per pair. www.sonnenblume.it.

Weddings

Sure Venice is the most romantic place on earth; you may want to celebrate this fact not by buying glass or gilt but with a lasting memory—a wedding or reaffirmation ceremony, complete with gondola and wedding photos! **Samantha Durell,** an American in Venice, can arrange it all. Call © 041/523-2379.

Chapter Eight

....

MILAN

WELCOME TO MILAN

Milan: the world's most beautiful ugly city.

Sure, you may find it simply ugly as a first-timer, but just wait. Milan grows on you. Milan worms its way into the soul of a shopper and fills you with promise, even if it's just the promise of a new pair of shoes.

If you've been driving across northern Italy visiting factories, being lost in hills, and suffering silently behind some very big trucks—well, friends, Milan is the most beautiful city in the world.

Milan is not a one-night stand. Milan is not the kind of place you fall in love with at a glance (unless you've been driving for days). Milan is not very pretty on the surface. Nonetheless, there's more style per mile than in just about any other city in the world. And the surrounding area is filled with factories and outlets and bargains galore. Did I mention the trucks?

The more I shop Italy, the more I know that Milan is the center of the universe. You can make day trips from Milan, you can rent cars from the Milan airport, and you can catch trains in Milan. You can go in and out of paradise via Milan. You can also buy a lot of shoes.

Milan's real strength is in the inspiration it provides, not only to the fashion world, but to visual and creative types of all sorts. Walk down the streets, pressing your nose to the windows, and you'll get *ideas*. There's no doubt that Milan is the real capital of Italian fashion. It's no secret that international *garmentos* comb the streets and markets to find the goods they will tote to Hong Kong to reproduce in inexpensive copies. A day on the prowl in Milan makes my heart beat faster, my pocketbook grow lighter, and my shoulder grow weary from carrying all those shopping bags.

What you see in Milan today will be in style in America in a year. What you adapt for your own lifestyle will compete with the cutting edge. Even if you can't afford to buy, you will feel invigorated by the city's creative energy just by walking its streets and window-shopping. Milan is not a great tourist town; it's a business city, and one of its businesses just happens to be fashion. So what's not to like? There's surely no business like shoe business. Or fur business. Or ready-to-wear.

ARRIVING & DEPARTING

Because Milan is the hub to the northern Italian area, there are plenty of ways to get in and out of town. But there are a few tricks to learn. There are two big airports, so therein lay the need for discovery. Long-haul flights always have used Malpensa; this bit of news regarding the use of both Malpensa and Linate affects those who are traveling into Milan from another E.U. city.

When I fly to Milan from Paris, I have my choice of airports depending on the airline and flight. It pays to investigate, especially if your time is limited or you are not on an expense account.

Remember: Linate is 15 minutes and 16€ ($20) away from downtown; Malpensa is 1 hour away, and the taxi or limo ride costs about 80€ ($100) or more.

Jenny's Turn: Malpensa To & Fro

So, you've just arrived in Milan. Just can't wait to get out there and see what all the hubbub is surrounding this infamous shopping city? Well, hold on to those traveler's checks, you're going to have to.

When arriving at the Malpensa airport in Milan, you are actually about an hour from the city center (and the shopping). So I should just hop in a cab, you ask? Not unless you want to shell out 78€ to 104€ ($98–$130) for the experience.

Instead, for a mere 10€ ($13), you can take the *Malpensa Bus Express,* a somewhat comfortable coach bus with somewhat relaxing music to transport the weak and weary through the un-picturesque highways to their final destination of Milano Centrale.

You do need to pay in euros, so you have to have changed money. You buy the ticket directly from the driver.

The bus pulls up outside the terminal on the street level, right near the arrivals portion of the airport. It's a little confusing to find, with no real signage, but it's very close to where you pick up your luggage. We knew the bus existed and were determined to take it, but an unenlightened traveler might wimp out.

Once on board, the next 75 minutes is your time to rest up and dream of your Milanese purchases in the not-so-distant future.

By Plane

If you arrive at Malpensa International Airport, you better have a rich sugar daddy, or be prepared to wait for the bus. The bus is easy to find and drops you right at the Centrale train station where you can hop on the metro or get a taxi to your hotel. Of course, you may want to spring for a car and driver, which will cost about 104€ ($130) including the tip.

There is an airport express train for those who can manage their luggage. Naturally, I've never taken it. The train takes 40 minutes travel time; check it out at www.malpensaexpress.it. Remember though that information is in Italian. Aaron and Jenny—my kids and assistants—were assigned to take this train but found it had a change of station that was a huge pain, especially after a 10-hour long-haul flight. They took the bus.

For about 9.60€ ($12), you can indeed take the bus from Malpensa into downtown Milan; the bus runs regularly on the half-hour. Buy your ticket at the marked booth and then line up outside. There are two bus stops outside, so be sure you don't take the employee bus to the parking lot. The bus will deposit you at the Centrale train station in the heart of Milan from which you can take the metro or get a taxi.

Now then, this is a great service, and it's cheap, and it's fine and all that, but hey, you better be able to handle your luggage 'cause *mamma mia*, when they drop you at the train station, they drop you at the side of the building, and the taxi rank is in the *front*. There are no trolleys and no porters and no help whatsoever; go to the front for a trolley.

By Train

If you arrive in Milan by train, you will probably come in to the **Centrale Station** in the heart of downtown. Pay attention as you exit because parts of this station have been changed and (if this is a return trip) the layout may not be as you remember it. Most important, there are no longer any porters. Nor is there an elevator. Oy!

They've also taken out the escalators at the front of the station, so if you have a trolley filled with luggage, you could be calling for your mommy.

Arrivals and departures are now from the front of the Centrale Station. Centrale is connected to the metro if you can manage your luggage and prefer using public transportation rather than a taxi.

There are free trolleys, but they are usually at the entrances to the station: When you pop off the train, it's unlikely that you'll find a trolley when you need one. If you are traveling alone, good luck. You may want to pack your set of airline wheels with you, or invest in the kind of luggage that has rear wheels and a pull cord or handle.

Departure Tips

To get the bus to either airport, take a taxi to the Centrale Station where the bus pickup is. You do not want to enter the main part of the station to catch the bus. The ticket window is to the side, right where you caught the taxi when you arrived. Beware of gypsies and beggars who may annoy you while you wait for the next bus.

Last time I took a taxi to Centrale—to catch a train to Venice, actually—the driver asked me if I wanted the Pullman for the airport or a train, because he will drop you at two different places depending on which you want.

GETTING AROUND

Milan happens to be a good walking city. Once you get yourself to a specific neighborhood, most of the shops, museums, and other attractions are in areas that you can easily navigate by foot. This is why it pays to pick a hotel in the center of the action and near a metro stop.

If you need a taxi, they can be found in stands, hailed in the street, or called. Note that when you call a taxi, the meter starts once the driver heads toward your pickup location. Taxis in Milan are very expensive.

Getting around town on public transportation is not hard. The metro is great, but does not get you everywhere you want to go. However, it gets you to and from your hotel and the best shopping districts. Most of the luxury hotels are within a block of a metro station.

Tram and bus systems are very good. Between these three modes of transport, you'll do just great. Buy tram or bus tickets at a tobacco stand (marked with a T sign out front) before you get on the vehicle. Enter from the rear, and place your ticket in the little box to get it stamped. Keep it; you can use it again if you reboard within 75 minutes.

Metro tickets can be purchased in the station; you will need coins to operate the ticket machines, but there are change machines. Magazine vendors inside stations will not give you change unless you buy something.

Milan's *metropolitana* has three main lines, each color-coded. Tourists will probably find the red line most convenient, as it goes to some of the major shopping areas and also stops at the Duomo. Look for the giant red M that indicates a station. Many guidebooks have a metro map printed inside them.

You can take a regular train to nearby communities, such as Como or Bergamo, or even to Venice, for a day trip. There's a large commuter population that goes to Turin, mostly for business, but you can go there to shop or to see the Shroud.

If you are using a train pass, do not blow a day of travel on a local commuter ticket. The same ticket can get you to Paris or to Como. Save the rail pass for the important stuff. A first-class, round-trip train ticket to Como costs about 16€ ($20).

Metro Milan Area

Milan must be accepted as a total destination. From Milan, you can easily get in and out of Venice and into other northern Italian cities. Milan is less than an hour from Como and not much farther from Turin. From Milan, you can get to Switzerland—or anywhere! Venice is 3 hours away, and Verona . . . well friends . . . Verona is a miracle unto itself (see chapter 10) and just a 2-hour drive.

If you are in a car, you must also learn the various suburbs and cities and highways that serve the great metro area. There are truly thousands of small manufacturers, factories, artisans, and showrooms leading from a spider web of highways. Should you be interested in discovering some of these, create a careful assault plan with a map before you attempt to shop.

Milian

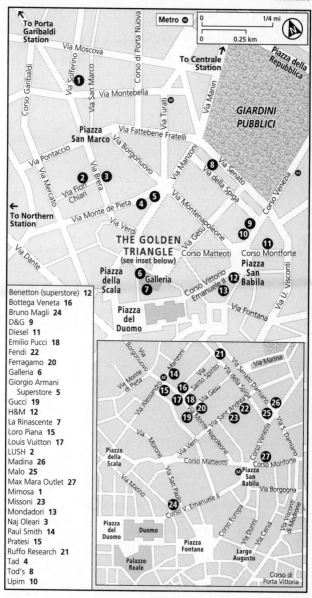

Benetton (superstore) 12
Bottega Veneta 16
Bruno Magli 24
D&G 9
Diesel 11
Emilio Pucci 18
Fendi 22
Ferragamo 20
Galleria 6
Giorgio Armani
    Superstore 5
Gucci 19
H&M 12
La Rinascente 7
Loro Piana 15
Louis Vuitton 17
LUSH 2
Madina 26
Malo 25
Max Mara Outlet 27
Mimosa 1
Missoni 23
Mondadori 13
Naj Oleari 3
Paul Smith 14
Pratesi 15
Ruffo Research 21
Tad 4
Tod's 8
Upim 10

Driving Around

If you want to get to seriously out-of-the-way factory outlets, you'll have to rent a car or hire a car and driver. Hiring a car with driver is not outrageously expensive—about 154€ ($200) a day (this includes the tip) for 150km (93 miles), although there are half-day options.

I have used **Europe Car Service** (✆ 02/942-51-00; fax 02/9424-0140; www.ecs-car.com). If you are going to far-flung outlets, make sure the driver knows where they are. I was very frustrated on one of my outings to be paying by the clock yet to have the driver hopelessly lost.

Another possibility is to hire a taxi driver. I did the Como outlets that way, and it was a positive experience. No, my driver did not speak much English, and I don't speak much Italian, but we had no problem. He drove me all over, waited for me while I shopped, and it cost about 20€ ($25) for a half-day. (I also think that knowing a taxi is waiting—with the meter running—keeps you quick on your toes. I might have spent 3 hr. and 2,400€/$3,000 at **Ratti** if I had stayed longer.)

I have now driven my trusty little Peugeot 306 in and out of Milan and to the nearby outlets. This was made easy by the concierge of my hotel who gave me MapQuest and Michelin printouts. Driving in Milan was not a problem; it's parking that's impossible. Traffic is fierce; highways can be bumper to bumper—make sure you pick an outlet that is worth the trouble.

Some hotels charge you 31€ ($39) for overnight parking. You'll have to figure this into your budget when it comes time to consider a car in the city.

More Milanese Information

There is a local version of the Time Out guide, *Time Out Milano*, but it is in Italian. Buy it at any news kiosk in Milan. The national newspaper *Repubblica* has a Milan section toward the rear of the daily paper that has local listings, weekend happenings, and some flea markets or specialty shopping events.

SLEEPING IN MILAN

In recent years, a number of designers have entered the hotel business—the Versaces in Australia, the Ferragamos in Florence. Now Milan has a new Bulgari hotel (© **02/805-8051**; www. bulgarihotels.com).

Luxury Shopping Hotels

CARLTON HOTEL BAGLIONI
Via Senato 5 (metro: Repubblica).

This is a very small, chic hotel that is a member of Small Luxury Hotels of the World as well as part of the Baglioni chain, which is making huge strides into the luxury market all over Italy. On my most recent research trip to Italy, I did one-stop shopping and booked all Baglioni hotels.

This hotel turned out more perfect than I could imagine—yes, I knew it would be fancy and welcoming, but I didn't know there was a private door leading out the rear of the hotel right onto the Via della Spiga, the private pedestrian shopping street. The hotel is located in the center of all the stores, has a shopping program, and has a concierge who will guide you to various venues.

This is the same concierge who also gave me computer printouts for when I was driving to factories and even to Verona and Venice (which are not hard to find and easy to get to).

The hotel has several styles of decor to suit their fashion-oriented guests—what I call moderne, a style displayed in the new London Baglioni and also in the Florence hotel, that is plush but sleek with emphasis on dark colors and handcrafted built-ins, some rooms that are all Art Deco with original pieces, and then rooms which are in basic, luxury hotel chic. The restaurant is one of the in places in town and good for lunch if you are doing a look-see. A pool is being built into the roof.

Rates are about 240€ ($300) a night, although there are promotions for the off season. You can reserve through Leading

Hotels of the World (www.lhw.com). © **800/745-8883** or 02/77-077. www.baglionihotels.com.

FOUR SEASONS HOTEL
Via del Gesù 8 (metro: Montenapoleone).

What would happen if the fashion angel came to Milan and decided to go into the hotel business? The Four Seasons, of course. You'll find this grand hotel discreetly located in the heart of the Montenapo shopping district. With up-to-date amenities and a posh atmosphere, it has a modern feel without seeming too rococo.

For an extra advantage, hit up the concierge desk for their slick magazine on shopping in Milan. Rooms start at 320€ ($400) per night. © **800/332-3442** or 02/77-088. www.four seasons.com.

GRAND HOTEL ET DE MILAN
Via Manzoni 29 (metro: Montenapoleone).

This is a fancy-schmancy hotel that's romantically small and dark and located on the other side of the luxury shopping district from the Baglioni.

The wonderful decorating style takes you back in time and makes you wonder about this century when the last century had some awfully perfect parts to it. This is the hotel where Verdi stayed and played. History haunts the hallways.

Yet there's a subway stop right alongside the hotel, so you get luxury and real life wrapped up in one. Shuttle service is available to airports and the train station. Expect to pay about 240€ ($300) per night. Reserve with the Leading Hotels of the World (© **800/745-8883**; www.lhw.com/ghmilan). © **02/72-31-41.** Fax 02/8646-0861.

Four-Star Finds

HILTON MILAN
Via Galvani 12 (metro: Centrale).

This Hilton is located near the Centrale train station—it's not glam, but they do have various promotional rates, and the hotel has just been renovated. Watch it, though, the rates are most often per person, which may or may not cost out. Still, a winter promotion of 81€ ($101) per person, which includes breakfast, isn't bad. It's a bit of a schlep to the nearest metro, but you can walk to many places or taxi. © 800-HILTONS or 02/69-831. www.milan.hilton.com.

HOTEL MANIN
Via Manin 7 (metro: Turati).

This is a tiny hotel decorated like an ocean liner from the 1930s. It's right near the gardens and the fashion district and is considered a find by fashion editors and those looking for a good location and an affordable price; it's around 200€ ($250) a night, and can be less out of season. © 02/659-65-11. www. hotelmanin.it.

JOLLY PRESIDENT
Largo Augusto 10 (metro: Duomo).

JOLLY TOURING
Via Tarchetti 2 (metro: Repubblica).

You'll be jolly, too, when you learn about this hotel chain. There are two Jolly hotels in downtown Milan. The President (© 02/77-461) is a business traveler's hotel, with small rooms of modern neo-Italian design. It's a great find because of its location. Largo Augusto is next door to Via Durini, and a block from the Duomo, which can be seen from your window.

The Jolly Touring (© 02/63-35) is located near the Principe and the Palace and shares the same metro with them, but is a block closer to the shopping action. The rooms are much nicer than at the Jolly President. The hotel does cater to groups, but I was quite happy there.

Rates are in the 200 € ($250) per night range with full breakfast buffet. © 800/247-12-77. www.jollyhotels.it.

A Three-Star Gem

HOTEL MANZONI
Via Santo Spirito 20 (metro: Montenapoleone).

I found this hotel by accident—it's small and well priced and in a great location near all the most expensive stores. There's only about 50 rooms, and they rent for between 120€ to 160€ ($150–$200) per night. With breakfast! © 02/7600-5700. www.hotelmanzoni.com.

SNACK & SHOP

CAFFÈ ARMANI
Via Manzoni, Armani Megastore (metro: Montenapoleone).

Because I frequently eat the Caffè Armani in Paris, I thought this would be a good place to test in Milan. It's also almost next door to my hotel, is in the heart of the truly great shopping district, is a few steps from a metro stop, and is part of the Armani superstore. All that said, the food was good and the prices fair, but the portions were so small I wanted to cry. I guess that's how to stay small enough to wear Armani in the first place. © 02/723-186-80.

CAFE GUCCI
Galleria Vittorio Emanuele II.

Yes friends, Gucci has a cafe and its right in the Galleria, so you can't miss it and won't want to even if you just stop for a coffee and a Gucci chocolate. They serve mostly sweets and snacks, but the crowd is to die for and you should plan this as part of your Milan must-do list. Open Sundays 2 to 7pm. © 02/859-79-91.

Cova
Via Montenapoleone 8 (metro: Montenapoleone).

A lot like Sant' Ambroeus (see below), but more formal and touristy because it's on the list of so many out-of-towners. It's a local legend and an "in" place for tea, in between shopping breaks and sweets. Come at 5pm if you want to make the scene. Their chocolates are a status-symbol hostess gift in fall, their jellied fruit squares in summer. Note that there's the old, Russian system for paying if you buy food to go: Make your choice at the counter, pay at the front desk, and return to the counter to pick up your choice. There's a rumor going around town that the real estate that Cova sits on is worth about $25 million, so if they've sold out by the time you get there, well, you can't blame them! © 02/7600-0578.

Peck
Via Spadari 9 (metro: Duomo).

This is possibly the most famous food store in Milan. Use it as your personal headquarters for picnic supplies. They also have a grill. The main food shop is on a side street on the far side of the Duomo, away from the Montenapo area but still convenient enough to be worthwhile. I always buy a picnic to take back on the airplane. Somehow, few airlines are able to provide food like Peck's. © 02/802-31-61. www.peck.it.

Sant' Ambroeus
Corso Matteotti 7 (metro: Babila).

I've fallen in love with this fancy space right off Montenapoleone. They have a bakery and candy shop for take-out orders, or you can stand at the bar or take a table. Sort of the Italian version of tea at the Ritz. They open at 8am if you prefer to breakfast here. I can eat their little *prosciutto crudo* sandwiches all day. © 02/7600-0540. www.santambroeus.org.

THE SHOPPING SCENE

Because Milan is the home of the fashion, fur, and furnishings businesses, you'll quickly find that it's a city that sells style and image. Milan is a city of big business: The souvenir stands are overflowing with an abundance of international magazines, not kitschy plastics. The big toy sold by street vendors? Plastic telephones for kids!

Although Milan was a medieval trading city, in its modern, post–World War II incarnation, Milan has sizzled and made its mark. The city hosts the international furniture salon every other year. There are fashion shows here twice a year, bringing a cadre of fashion reporters from all over the world to tell the fashion mavens just what Italy has to offer. Besides these, there are a zillion fairs and conventions and other business happenings, meaning Milan is always happening. Hmmmm, except in August.

Even if you aren't a fashion editor and don't plan your life around what comes trotting down the catwalk, you'll find that Milan's high-fashion stores offer a peek at what's to come. You'll also find that the markets and real-people shopping reflect the proximity of nearby factories. You'd be amazed at what can fall off a truck.

The best shopping in Milan is at these designer shops and showrooms, or at the discount houses, jobbers, and factory-outlet stores that sell designer clothing, overruns, and samples. If you really care about high fashion at an affordable price, you'll plan to spend January of each year prowling the sales in Milan—not London.

The Best Buys in Milan

Alternative retail   Mavens will give me the evil eye for mentioning this, but Milan is a good place for a bargain. There are good flea markets and street markets, and the buys in Como cannot be underestimated.

It's more than just a resort town; it's heaven for bargain shoppers who want high-quality silks and outlet deals—Armani anyone? Have the words "Factory Store" written over a door ever been more beautiful?

Designer home design Again, maybe not a best buy in terms of price, but a best in terms of selection or unique opportunity. The hottest trend in Milan of late has been that all the big designers are doing home furnishings, from dishes and ashtrays to sheets, and then some. **Versace, Dolce & Gabbana, Missoni,** and **Ferragamo** are all into home design now. It's luxe, it's expensive, and it's gorgeous. Just press your nose to the **D&G Home** store, take one look at dark red silk brocade, leopard prints, and majolica and know that when it works, it works! But wait, I now also shop for home design in the outlet store that **Lisa Corti** has in her workrooms—fabulous stuff and half the price of Saks.

Designer selections While designer merchandise is expensive, the selection and the possibility of a markdown or discovering a small, reasonably priced item is greater. **Etro** isn't a bargain resource and is available in other Italian cities, but it will please you to no end to buy here and to soak up the atmosphere of class, elegance, and northern Italian chic. The Etro outlet, right in town, will also please you to no end.

Young fashions Aaron and Jenny—our 20-something reporters—had a wonderful time exploring shoe, vintage, and fashion shops and found prices often fair. Some items were too high for them but fun to stare at; others were affordable and sensational. There are specific parts of town that cater to the young look and the young wallet (see "Shopping Neighborhoods," later in this chapter). And don't forget my fave: Oviesse (p. 238).

The Worst Buys in Milan

If you can help it, don't buy:

* **Ceramics and faience:** They're hard to find, and therefore expensive.

- **Postcards:** There's a bad selection.
- **Important antiques:** They're prohibitively expensive.
- **Masks, marbleized paper goods, or traditional Italian souvenirs:** These items are best bought where they're made.

Milan Style

In terms of clothing, Milanese style is much more conservative, chic, and sophisticated than the more flamboyant southern Italian style. In Milan, if you don't buy from a trendy designer, you'll actually load up on basics—good cashmere sweaters and shawls, knits, shoes, handbags, and furs. That's right: furs! Northern Italy is one of the few places in the world where it's not only politically correct to wear fur, but part of the fashion scene. In Milan, attitude is part of fashion so you can wear all black and be chic; it need not be expensive or laden with labels—you just need the look and a pair of great sunglasses.

Much of what is for sale in Milan is of the same design school as the English country look; this will interest Europeans far more than Americans looking for hot looks, not tweeds and V necks. Also note that a large influence in Italian fashion these days is the American mail-order catalog look—Levi's, J. Crew, L.L. Bean, and so on. I didn't come to Italy to buy things like this; you probably didn't either, and will someone spare me from Gap wannabes? Still, there's plenty of trendy stuff for the Ferrari in your soul.

Milan is a great place for spotting color trends. Yes, *fashionistas* always dress in black because it's easy, but Italian fashion highlights a few new, key colors each season. Even if you just window-shop, you'll soon see that almost all clothing in any given season, no matter which designer is presenting it, falls into a few color families. Each season will have one or two hot colors that define the season; each season will also have a wide selection of items in black because black is the staple of every Italian (and French) wardrobe. The best thing about these colors is that other designers and even mass retailers in America will pick up these same shades, so what you buy in Italy will carry smoothly into the fashion front for several years.

Another aspect of Milanese style comes in furnishings, home decor, tabletop, and interior design. No matter what size you are or what age you are, you will see things to light your fire in this city of desire.

The Five Best Stores in Milan

In alphabetical order:
10 Corso Como
Corso Como 10 (metro: Garibaldi).

This is one of the best stores in the world because of the way it's bought and the way it constantly changes. It's owned by a woman who is a member of one of the most important fashion families in Italy and sells a little of everything, but all of it seemingly unique. See p. 257. ℂ 02/65-48-31.

Free Shop
Milano Centrale Station (metro: Centrale).

I guess this just reveals the inner down-market part of my soul, but this grocery store sells a little of everything, and most of it is unique and terrific. It's where I buy magic coffee, and notebooks and flavored pastas and all sorts of things. See p. 248. ℂ 02/669-1273.

Lisa Corti
Via Conchetta 6 (tram: 15).

You will spend a lot for a taxi to get here, but to me it's worth it. Corti has shops in other Italian cities, but this is also the showroom and has the best prices. She makes home style and women's clothing in colorful prints; sold for double the price at Saks Fifth Avenue. The showroom is in a courtyard tucked off the street in what might be a private home. For fans, this will be the highlight of your trip to Milan. See p. 249. ℂ 02/5810-0031. www.lisacorti.com.

Max Mara Outlet
Galleria San Carlo 6 (metro: Babila).

The official name of this store is **Diffusione Tessile,** but it is the Max Mara outlet and it's smack dab in the center of everything, easy to get to, and easy to shop. Because Max Mara makes the best wool coats in the world, the store offers better shopping when fall and winter merchandise is in stock. Summer pickings can be slim, although I did get some accessories, some sleeveless silk tops, and other smalls on my last springtime visit. See p. 256. ✆ 02/7600-0829. www.diffusionetessile.it.

Spaccio Etro
Via Spartaco 3 (no nearby metro—ask concierge about bus).

Great prices on quality items—accessories, yard goods, clothes for men and women. You will go mad. See p. 257. ✆ 02/79-81-68.

A Runner-Up

LUSH
Via Fiori Chiari 6 (metro: Duomo).

If you haven't been to a LUSH store in Italy, this is your chance. The store is on the way to the Brera district and offers an Italian version of the famous British bath products (p. 232). I find LUSH expensive and am very over it as a trend—but I am impressed by the Italian branches because of their use of Italian ingredients. This is the usual LUSH with an Italian twist that makes it a must-do. ✆ 02/7201-1442. www.lush.com.

Shopping Hours

The big news in Milan is that shopping hours are not as strict as elsewhere; nor are they as strict as they used to be. Furthermore, Milan now has stores that are open on Sunday!

Lunch hours   Many of the big-name designer shops in Milan are open "nonstop," which means that they do not close for lunch. If you don't want to take a lunch break, shop the Montenapo area.

Dime stores such as **Standa** and **Upim** have always been open nonstop; **La Rinascente**, Milan's most complete department store, has always been open during lunch as well. Of course, most of the **Standa** stores in Milan have become **FNAC** stores, but they are open, too.

Monday hours   Most stores in Milan are closed on Monday through the lunch hour (they open around 3:30 or 4pm). Note that La Rinascente does not open until 1:45pm on Monday. Most of Italy is dead from a retail perspective on Monday morning. But wait!

- Food shops are open.
- Factory stores are frequently open on Monday morning. If you are heading out to a certain factory or two, call ahead. Make no assumptions.
- Como factories are open on Monday morning!

Sunday Shopping

Laws have changed, and all of Italy's big cities have Sunday shopping now; mostly big department stores are open. If you want to shop on a Sunday, try for a flea market. Or go to Venice, which is wide, wide, wide open on Sunday.

Milan is far more dead on Sunday than other communities, but you can get lucky—at certain times of the year, things are popping on Sunday and yes, **La Rina** (the department store, La Rinascente) is open. In fact, you can even have your hair done there on a Sunday—**Aldo Coppola** (© 02/890-597-12) is the only hairdresser in town that's open on Sundays.

During fashion weeks, stores in Montenapo district often open on Sunday; they also have specific Sundays when they open beginning in October going on until Christmas.

Some stores in the Navigli area are also open on Sunday.

The regular Sunday stores are **Corso Como 10** and **Virgin Megastore**. Sunday hours are most often noon to 5pm. **La Rinascente** is open on Sundays from 10am until 8pm.

Outside Milan, in season, Como (only 20 min. away) is wide open on Sunday, although you may want to call ahead to verify that your favorite factory shops will be open on the Sunday that you want to shop them. Some people go to Ancora for Sunday shopping; Verona stores are also open.

Exceptional Shopping Hours

Summer hours   Summer hours begin in the middle of July for some retail businesses; August is a total loss from a shopping point of view because most stores are closed. Sophisticated people wouldn't be caught dead in Milan in August; shoppers beware.

When stores are open in August, they close at lunch on Saturday and do not reopen until 3:30 or 4pm on Monday.

Holiday hours   The period between Christmas and New Year's Day can be tricky. Stores will close early a few days before a major holiday and use any excuse to stay closed during a holiday. Sales begin in the first week of January (usually after Epiphany), but store hours are erratic before then. There are weekend candy markets around the Duomo in the weeks before Lent.

Early January   The first week in January is also slow to slower—all factories are closed until after Epiphany, as are many stores. Others decide to close for inventory.

Night hours   Stores usually close between 7:30 and 8pm. Should you need an all-night pharmacy, there is one at Piazza Duomo and one at the Centrale train station.

Money Matters

American Express's travel office is at the corner of the Via Brera and the Via Dell Orso: It's Via Brera 3. This is in the thick of the shopping district, so you need not go out of your way to get here. If you use traveler's checks, cash them in your hotel—even if they are in euros, they are hard to use in normal stores.

ATMs are easy to find and are your best bet.

Personal Needs

I needed shoelaces in Milan—sounds simple, huh? Forget it! Since **Upim** has gone upscale, it's become harder and harder to find the basics of real life. Upim used to be a lot like Woolworth's. Now it's trying to be more like La Rinascente. It's unlikely you'll find everything you need in real life at an Italian department store, so try Upim as well as any number of pharmacies and grocery stores. P.S.: The shoelaces? **Foot Locker** on Victor Emmanuelle!

Look for a green neon cross if you want a pharmacy. There's a very good pharmacy in the Centrale train station, and they speak English. In fact, the train station has an excellent selection of shops selling basic items you may have left at home: try **Free Shop,** an enormous grocery store that sells everything from food and souvenirs to health and beauty aids—even condoms.

Shopping Neighborhoods

Golden Triangle/Montenapo   All the big designers have gorgeous and prestigious shops here. You can easily explore it in a day or two, or even an hour or two, depending on how much money or how much curiosity you have. Although the main shopping street is **Via Montenapoleone,** sometimes this area is referred to as Montenapo.

This is the chic part of town, where traditional European design flourishes along with Euro-Japanese styles and wild, hot Italian New Wave looks. It includes a couple of little streets that veer off the Via Montenapoleone in a beautiful little web of shopping heaven. This is where you'll find **Gucci, Ferré, Versace, Fendi, Ferragamo,** and **Krizia** boutiques as well as some very tony antiques shops.

There are furniture and fashion showrooms of the trade that are so fancy and secluded that you would never know they were there. There are also some reliable real-people shops, like **Brigatti,** a sporting goods emporium, that you'll enjoy.

The outermost borders of the neighborhood are **Via Manzoni** and **Corso Venezia,** two major commercial streets. Use them mostly for finding your way—although in the past year Corso Venezia has become a hot address for designer bridge lines. Your real shopping streets will be **Via della Spiga, Via Sant' Andrea,** and of course—**Via Montenapoleone.** But don't miss the back streets of this little enclave—streets like Via Gesù, Via Borgospesso, and also Via Manzoni (which is not a back street).

For anyone with limited time in Milan who wants to absorb a lot of the scene in just a few hours, this is the top-priority shopping district for looking around. You may not buy your souvenirs here, but you'll see the stuff that dreams are made of.

Duomo The Duomo is the main landmark of Milan. It's an incredibly detailed and gorgeous cathedral; not a store. It is on the Piazza del Duomo and is happily surrounded by stores. You guessed it, there is even a **Virgin Megastore** to one side and the country's leading department store, **La Rinascente,** to another side.

Via Montenapoleone angles away from Corso Vittorio Emanuele II as you move away from the Duomo, so the Golden Triangle and Duomo neighborhoods sort of back up to each other. This connection makes it very easy to shop these two areas in the same afternoon. When you are finished with them, there are two other shopping neighborhoods, Brera and Jolly Augusto, which you can connect with on the other side of the Duomo. You did come to Milan to shop, didn't you?

Corso Vittorio Emanuele II This neighborhood is filled with big stores, little stores, and half a dozen galleries and minimalls that house even more stores. The most maddening part about this area is that you can hardly find an address. Just wander in and out and around from the Duomo to **Piazza San Babila,** which is only 2 or 3 blocks.

At San Babila, turn left and you'll end up at Via Montenapoleone for entry into the Golden Triangle. Or you can do this in the reverse, of course. But don't forget to check out this intersection. Because the San Babila area is very important, you'll find everything from the new Benetton superstore to Upim to

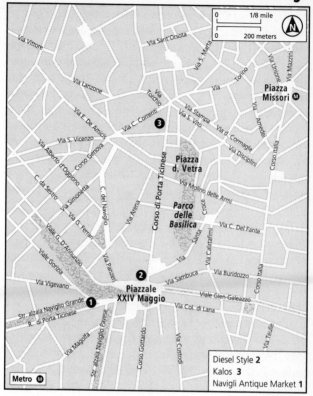

Diesel Style **2**
Kalos **3**
Navigli Antique Market **1**

plastics mongers and fashion mavens. And the Max Mara outlet store is in the mall San Carlo.

At the front end of the Duomo, off the piazza, is a shopping center of historical- and architectural-landmark proportions, the **Galleria**. This is one of the most famous landmarks in Milan, and some tout it as the first mall in Europe. Other galleries in Europe also make the same claim, but who cares? Take one look at the ceiling and you'll marvel. Then visit the **Prada** shop.

The Galleria has a vaulted ceiling and looks like a train station from another, grander, era. Inside there are restaurants and bistros where you can get coffee and sit and watch the parade of passersby. Several big-time shops are here besides **Prada**—don't miss **Rizzoli** for books in English. If you go out the back end, you will be at La Scala. Behind La Scala is the **Brera** area.

If you are at the piazza with the Duomo to your back and have not turned right to enter the Galleria, you can walk straight ahead toward the **Virgin Megastore** and yet more retail. The arcade across from the Duomo is filled with many old names of Milanese retailing and some newer shops, too, including a **Missoni** jeans store that sells their sports line. **Galtruco** is a very famous fabric firm where you can buy every imaginable type of yard goods, including the designer fabrics from local mills.

Brera   Brera is one of the most famous shopping districts of Milan because it has slightly less expensive rents. It's the part of town where young designers can break into retailing and high style, and it has both designer shops and up-and-coming trendsetters.

It's a fair (but not difficult) walk from the Duomo.

The main stretch of Brera is rather commercial, with shops oriented toward teens, and quite a few jeans stores as well as very obvious branches of the famous international retailers, such as **Laura Ashley, Shu Uemura,** and **Naj Oleari.** Behind all this, there are narrow and bewitching back streets, closed to vehicular traffic, that call out to you to explore them. Many of them host the most expensive antiques dealers in the city; some of them are the ateliers of new, hot designers.

There are designer shops in here also, including **Il Bisonte** (Via Madonnina 10) and **Angela Caputi** (Via Madonnina 11). Don't miss **Etro**, Via Pontaccio 17, at the corner of Vicolo Fiori. And while you're in this neck of the woods, don't forget that London's **LUSH**—that adorable deli of bath bombs, face masks, and homemade soaps and suds first created in England—has opened up here at Via Fiori Chiari 6; the store is not identical to the English (or Canadian) versions, and therein lies its charm.

The best way to see it is during the Brera antiques street fair (third Sat of each month), when vendors put out tables in the narrow streets and a well-heeled crowd browses. But any day is a good day. Carry on from Brera to Solferino (the street just changes names) and then over one to Garibaldi.

Largo Augusto/Durini   Another option is to move from the other side of the Duomo to **Corso Vittorio Emanuele II**, and over to **Via Durini**. Via Durini is only a block long, but it's a good-sized block and it's crammed with fabulous stores. It veers off at an angle from San Babila and runs straight to Largo Augusto.

Please note that you can catch a bus to **Il Salvagente**, the discounter, at Largo Augusto, or walk via the **Corso Porta Vittoria,** and be there in 10 minutes. I usually walk because I enjoy window-shopping along the way.

Train Station/Ingrosso   In the area between the Centrale train station and the Repubblica metro station there's a grid system of flat streets that makes up the *garmento* wholesale *(ingrosso)* and discount district of Milan. There are scads of stores here: You can browse and just go in and out—about half of them are closed for lunch, and all of them are closed on

---

Aaron's Turn: Of Course, My Corso

The Corso Buenos Aires is a long street with an amazing number of stores. Unless you are really a die-hard shopper, you might want to break this one up into 2 days. If you can hack it, this street has something for everyone.

My favorites were *JDC* (the "regular" and "urban" stores), *Tanagra,* and *Morgan.*

The JDC urban store is called urban for a reason. The place is exactly like Urban Outfitters from products to store layout and music selection. They had really cool sneakers, with a huge selection of Chuck Taylor's, and great jeans. Also a lot of baseball and made-to-look-vintage T-shirts.

Morgan is one of the few skater shops I've ever seen abroad and is the only store in Italy I found that carried Etnies.

Saturday and Sunday. The area is trying to fashion itself as a fashion destination, calling itself **"CMM"** (**Centro Moda Milano**); it now has a printed brochure of the showrooms and has special hours for holiday shopping and during Fashion Weeks. Get the brochure for free at any showroom. Fax **02/9357-2218.** www.centromodamilano.it.

If your time is limited and you crave high style and multiple marvels, this is not your destination. If you like a bargain and don't mind hit-or-miss shopping, step this way. I had a ball here last time I visited because I got lucky—cashmere twin sets for 200€ ($250) (total price), stores that take credit cards and smile, Tod's boots for 160€ ($200) a pair, lots of brand names, and lots of selection.

For E.U. visitors who specifically come to Milan to beat the high prices in other parts of Europe, this is your cup of tea.

Buenos Aires   Don't cry for me Buenos Aires, I've got my credit cards. This street is more for teens and 'tweens and may not appeal to designer shoppers at all. The street is almost a mile long and features more than 300 shops: It is one of the most concentrated shopping areas in continental Europe. The best stores are located around the Lima station of the metro. Did I mention there is an **Oviesse** store here? In case you haven't been reading that carefully, I am having a love affair with Oviesse and its low-cost fashions.

Avoid shopping on Saturday because it's always mobbed. Remember, this is where the real people shop, so few people will speak English. The clientele is not always chic; the scenery is neither cute nor charming.

Many of the shops have no numbers; often the number by a store represents the block rather than the store address (so many shops may be called "3"), but it's all easy once you're there. Just wander and enjoy—you can't miss the good stuff.

You can get there easily by taking the no. 65 streetcar from the Centrale train station and getting off at Corso Buenos Aires (about three stops). Or take the metro to Loreto and walk toward Venezia or vice versa.

Aaron's Turn: Corso di Porta Ticinese

This whole area feels a lot like SoHo or Williamsburg (Brooklyn) to me: very hip clothing stores, a trendy new *gelateria,* and a charmingly snobbish record store all within a block from each other (just north of the river). The only difference is that much of the culture that was there before it was boutique-ified still remains.

Aside from vintage and outrageously priced denim, the street is home to a large variety of clothing stores. The Diesel clothing company has two stores on the street; **55DSL** and **Diesel Style Lab** are spin-offs from the regular Diesel stores. Just like typical Diesel stores, these shops have hip and trendy clothes and are *really* expensive. Even if you don't buy anything, it's always fun to look.

Porta Ticinese is also the home of a **Stüssy** store and a **Carhartt** store. The Stüssy store was 10 times cooler than any of its stores that I've seen in the U.S. It was the only store in Italy I saw that was hip to the trucker-hat fad, and they had some really fun novelty items. Unfortunately, T-shirts were 41€ ($52) a pop (not outrageous by local standards). The Carhartt store was bigger and had more selection, but was still a bit too pricey.

Magenta   For the opposite type of experience, get to the corso Magenta, a rich residential thoroughfare where the best bakeries, cafes, and shopping brands are located to serve those who live in this area; it's the equal to Paris's 16th or 17th arrondissement. From October to May, do remember to wear your fur.

Navigli   South of the Porta Ticinese is the canal area of Milan. The canals have been mostly built over, so don't spend too much time looking for a lot of water (wait for Venice): There's just the one canal. Yet the Navigli is becoming a funky shopping neighborhood. You can wander around here for an hour or two if you like colorful junk shops, secondhand shops, artist's

Jenny's Turn: My Finds Milanese

CARPE DIEM
Viale Tunisia 1 (metro: Porta Venezia).

Need a frog-shaped toilet bowl or a toaster/CD player and don't know where to go? On Viale Tunisia, just off of the main shopping street of Corso Buenos Aires, lies this cute, kitschy shop where the colors and odd interpretations of normal household items are as vivid and abstract as the imagination will allow. Stop in and pick up those much-needed monkey-shaped lighters or just to look at the marvels of modern non-sensicality. ✆ 02/2951-7833.

KALOS
Corso di Porta Ticinese 50 (metro: Porta Genova).

Walking down Corso di Porta Ticinese, we stumbled upon a funky jewelry shop amongst the vintage clothing stores. I started gazing longingly at the handmade pieces innocently enough, as I often do when walking past a jewelry store. Then I noticed them. The prices. These gorgeous and unique pieces were priced very generously. What an invitation to shop.

I walked away with two necklaces and a pair of earrings for under 40€ ($50), that's my kind of budget. The saleswoman (and jewel designer) was very friendly, although she spoke little English, and gift-wrapped each box uniquely.

The jewelry items make perfect gifts for those at home who want a piece of Italian glamour and at the same time perfect for your wallet. ✆ 02/8940-4329.

studios, and the feeling of getting in on the ground floor of up-and-coming Italian style. Cash only; no one speaks English.

The two streets running along the canal are called **Alzaia Naviglio Grande** and **Ripa di Porta Ticinese.** You can walk down one, cross a bridge, and walk back on the other side. There are some cute restaurants, and you can make an afternoon out of it if this is your kind of thing.

There is an antiques market held on the last Sunday of each month on both sides of the Naviglio Grande. Tell your taxi driver either that you want *"mercatone dell antiquariato"* or the name of the street, Ripa Ticinese, which is one of two streets hosting the market along the canal.

Every Tuesday and Saturday there is a regular street market along the Viale Papiniano. This is a great place for designer clothing that fell off trucks and all sorts of fun fashions and accessories. Plan to be there early—9 to 10am is fine. In addition to two lanes of stalls selling clothing and dry goods, part of the market is fruit and food.

To save money, you can hop on the red line of the metro and get off at San Agostino and be right here.

Porta Vittoria The Corso di Porta Vittoria begins shortly after the Duomo and changes its name to **Corso 22 Marzo**. Just use your feet. I like this walk because it takes you by **Il Salvagente**, the discount designer store, and enables you to see something of middle-class Milan along the way.

The walk along Corso Porta Vittoria takes you through an upper-middle-class neighborhood where you'll find branches of many favorite stores, such as **Max Mara** and **Bassetti**. This is where well-off locals shop, and it's very non-touristy, not unlike the Corso Vercelli. There is a nice branch of **Coin**.

After the street name changes to 22 Marzo, you'll turn left on Via Fratelli Bronzetti to get to **Il Salvagente**. Hail a taxi to take you back to your hotel if you have too much loot.

Aprile & Beyond Not for the average tourist, Aprile stands for the plaza (piazza) of the same name: XXV Aprile. It is an up-and-coming neighborhood that attracts design mavens and fashion editors because of a handful of important shops in the area, including **High Tech** and **Corso Como 10**. The few retailers who have set up shop here are inventive, creative, and exciting, so take a look if you want to be in with the in-crowd. If you are more interested in sightseeing, and don't have much time in Milan, this area may not be for you.

Piazza XXV Aprile is between the Moscova and Garibaldi stops on the green line. After this plaza, Corso Garibaldi changes its name and becomes Corso Como.

MILAN RESOURCES A TO Z

Antiques

Milan's antiques markets are great fun, but don't be afraid to get out of town to explore a few more. In Pavia and Brescia, there are antiques markets on the second Sunday of each month. On the third Sunday, in Carimate (Como), there's a flea market. Begamo Alta also celebrates on the third Sunday, in Piazza Angelini. Many villages have antiques markets on certain Sundays only in April and October: Ask your hotel concierge for details. For markets in Milan proper, see "Flea Markets," later in this chapter.

Antiques stores are mostly located in the Brera area, on or off Via Madonnina, with a few fancier ones in the Montenapo area. The Montenapo shops do not offer affordable items for mere mortals.

Serious dealers include: **Legatoria Conti Borboni** for antique books, at Corso Magenta 31; **Amabile** for carpets, on Via Brera 16; and **Mauro Brucoli** for furniture, on Via della Spiga 46. There's a tiny gallery of about eight or ten shops right near the Sheraton Luxury Hotels—the Palace Hotel and the Principe di Savoia—and the Jolly Touring. Take the Repubblica metro and walk or taxi to **La Piazzetta degli Antiquari** (Via Turati 6).

Bath

LUSH
Via Fiori Chiari 6 (metro: Duomo).

I am assuming that most readers already know the LUSH chain, either from visits in the U.K., U.S., or Canada, or from the press. If you have no idea what I am talking about, this is going to be a must-do experience. For those who already know and may even be bored with the gimmick, snap out of it—what's brilliant here is that the concept has been adapted to local specialties, so you find things such as limoncello shampoo, not sold in stores outside of Italy. While prices are not bargain basement, the novelty factor is high. This street is right off the Via Brera; there are now LUSH stores all over Italy, so if you miss this one, you may still find another in your travels. ✆ 02/7201-1442. www.lush.it.

Mimosa
Via Solferino 12 (metro: Duomo).

This small shop sells bath products from several international brands; what you want are the local brands. I've fallen for a line of mud products called Guam, made by Lacote, which, despite either of these names, is indeed an Italian firm. Many of the products are made with algae; and then there's mud with algae—my fave. There are products for body, face, and for bath. The shop's owner does speak English and will explain products and how to use them. ✆ 02/657-53-03.

Books

There's a small international bookstore upstairs at the Armani Superstore (Via Manzoni 31) and another, larger one upstairs at 10 Corso Como.

Mondadori
Corso Vittorio Emanuele II (metro: Duomo or Babila).

This is a big, modern bookstore with as much crammed downstairs as there is on the street level. They have an enormous selection in every category and a very good travel department. They offer some books in foreign languages, including English, and some gift items. There are now similar bookstores, sort of American-style superstores if you will, in the area and in other parts of Milan. It's a trend. ✆ 02/7600-5832.

RIZZOLI
Galleria Vittorio Emanuele 79 (metro: Duomo).

Large bookstore with books in several languages; travel department toward the front of the store, although they may not have the latest editions of guides. Open evenings and on Sunday. © 02/8646-1071.

Boutiques

FONTANA
Via della Spiga 33 (metro: Montenapoleone).

Modern Italian design of the most expensive and highest order. The interior is swank and very Milan, with lots of marble and sleek woods. The counters are suspended from thin wires and seem to hang in midair. © 02/7600-5372.

GIO MORETTI
Via della Spiga 4 and 6 (metro: Montenapoleone).

There are three different Gio Moretti stores: one for men, one for women, and one for children (across the street). You'll see all the big names here: For women, stock up on Sonia Rykiel, Complice, and those designers who don't have their own free-standing shops. Call © 02/7600-3186.

MICHELE MABELLE/MILANO MONAMOUR
Via della Spiga 36 (metro: Montenapoleone).

The name is enough to make you fall in love. Inside you'll find Norma Kamali, Kansai, and Thierry Mugler, plus wild, sequined T-shirts, a glitzy interior, and piped-in rock music. © 02/79-88-88.

RUFFO RESEARCH
Via Della Spiga 48 (metro: Montenapoleone).

Two different stores, next door to each other, one for men and one for women. It's leather, it's trendy, it's fairly priced considering how cool it is, and you will swoon at how leather can be made to wrap, droop, flow, swing, and dance around the body. The leather is so light and fine that it drapes like fabric. Much of the work is created by Greek designer Sophia Kokosalaki, but the force behind the scenes is the president of the firm, Giacomo Corsi, who insists on innovative style for both the men's and women's lines. Hides come from Tuscany and are worked on by the most famous Italian leather workers in order to get them light enough to meet the requirements of the design technology. The results are downright revolutionary. ✆ 02/78-46-10.

Cashmere

One of the questions I am most frequently asked is about cashmere. Italian cashmere is of the highest quality because of the way it is combed and milled. With so many factories in Northern Italy, there's the chance to buy at outlets or to check out what may have fallen off a truck and is being sold at markets. I saw the best buys at the Tuesday/Saturday markets.

DORIANI
Via Sant' Andrea 2 (metro: Montenapoleone).

More of a men's than women's source, more of an English than a cutting-edge look—but luxe beyond belief. ✆ 02/7600-3030.

LORO PIANA
Via Montenapoleone 27 (metro: Montenapoleone).

A three-story temple to cashmere and luxe, selling not only men's and women's things but also items for the home. There's also interactive displays, such as videos and tests you can perform to see how the fabrics hold up, proving this is an art and a science. ✆ 02/7600-6027.

MALO
Via della Spiga 7 (metro: Montenapoleone).

One of the most famous names in Italian quality cashmere, Malo has opened a shop that sells both men's and women's lines; in summer there are noncashmere items, too. The factory outlet is located outside of Florence (see chapter 6). © 02/7601-6109. www.malo.it.

MANRICO
Via della Spiga 29 (metro: Montenapoleone).

The address says it all—this is a local source for those with money who are in the know. There's also a store in Aspen, so you get the idea. © 02/78-21-55. www.manrico.com.

Costume Jewelry

ANGELA PINTALDI
Piazza Sant Erasmo 9 (metro: Duomo).

This is very serious costume jewelry. Her work is similar to Bulgari, but funkier. For the last decade, Pintaldi has ruled as the "in" creator of creative and expressive jewels, frequently made with semiprecious stones. She also works with ivory and other materials, based on color and texture—pure magic meets pure art. © 02/78-17-78.

Department Stores

COIN
Piazza Giornate 5; Corso Vercelli 30–32; Piazzale Cantore; Piazzale Loreta.

Pronounced "co-*een*," this store is not as convenient or as much fun as La Rinascente. But if you find yourself near one of the stores, by all means check it out. (There are four different locations.) I also find that Coin has more energy than La Rinascente and is more likely to have hot styles and designer copies. In fact, Coin specializes in designer-inspired looks at moderate prices; they have completely re-created themselves in the last 2 years and are far more upscale than ever before. Call © 02/5519-2083 for the Piazza Giornate location.

GIORGIO ARMANI SUPERSTORE
Via Manzoni 31 (metro: Montenapoleone).

I don't know what to call this except a department store, although the word "showroom" comes to mind . . . as does "showcase," as does "ohmigod." I am horrified and delighted with the store and think all students of retail, marketing, and merchandising should rush here for a look-see. Everyone else, well, you are on your own.

The store is almost a city block long in size; it has three levels, some of which bleed through from one to the next to add height and drama. The giant video screen says it all—this is a store for people who don't know how to read (although there is a small bookstore upstairs). There's also a cafe, a branch of Nobu, a florist, and all the Armani lines, many of which have goods that are not sold elsewhere, such as the home furnishings line, which looks like something designed by Terrence Conran. I am partial to the jeans line because the logo is AG, which are my son's initials. To me, the best part of the store is the large makeup bar, because the Armani makeup is great, and relatively hard to find, even in Italy. ✆ **02/7231-8600.** www. armani-viamanzoni31.it.

LA RINASCENTE
Piazza del Duomo (metro: Duomo).

The mother of all Milanese department stores is in the midst of a cultural overhaul—the very culture of its way of selling is indeed being rebuilt by the big gun Vittorio Radice, who is the same man who re-created Selfridge's in London. My best advice: Watch this space.

There's a lot of merchandise in the store, and this is a good place to see a lot and absorb trends and makers quickly. The style of the store is in the American-Anglo model, so don't expect all goods to be Italian or to feel very Italian while shopping here. Although, who knows what to expect once the store has been redone.

Check out the handbag department for a good selection of low-to-moderately priced items. This is one of the few places in Milan where you can get a nice-looking 80€ ($100) bag. Other good departments are children's and active sportswear. The ski clothes are sensational, but expensive. I also like the basement housewares space, especially the small gourmet food market.

The big fashion names are not well represented in women's fashion, but there are lots of "real-people" clothes at fair (for Italy) prices. Here's the latest: The spa (seventh floor) overlooks the spires of the Duomo.

The store does not close for lunch during the week. The hours are extraordinary, especially for Italy: Monday to Saturday 9am to 10pm. The store does have some special Sunday openings now; check the website for details.

Note that this is a full-service department store; along with the cafe, there are hairdresser and beauty facilities, free alterations (except on sale goods), banking facilities with an ATM, customer service, and more. ✆ 02/88-521. www.rinascente.it.

OVIESSE
Corso Buenos Aires 35 (metro: Porta Venezia).

Technically, this might be a lifestyle store, not a department store; it is the antithesis of the Armani Superstore. This is a temple to cheap thrills—the most exciting copies of fashions for the least amount of money you have ever seen—it is the Italian version of H&M and then some. I went nuts here and dream of going to all their other stores. Skirts for 16€ ($20). Knit polo shirts for 12€ ($15). You get my drift. Sizes up to 52, although the sizes run a little small. ✆ 02/2040-4801.

UPIM
Corso Buenos Aires 21 (metro: Porta Venezia), Piazza San Babila5 (metro: Babila), and many others in town.

Bury my heart at the Piazza San Babila, because I will never forgive the Upim powers for what they have done to this store.

Who takes a great dime store and turns it into JCPenney, I ask you?

They don't close for lunch; they may have inexpensive cashmere sweaters (if you come in the winter) and they are worth exploring, but, gosh, I liked the old Upim better. The Buenos Aires store is larger; it also has a grocery store in the basement. The lower level at San Babila has trendy fashion and men's fashion as well as lingerie; on the street level, there's mostly women's fashion with some accessories and makeup. The arrangement is reversed on Corso Buenos Aires. Within Italy, call © 800/ 824-040. www.upim.it.

Designer Boutiques

AMERICAN & CANADIAN BIG NAMES

Obviously you didn't go to Italy to buy American designs. Still, there is an American invasion beginning to take place in many different financial brackets. **Timberland** has three stores in town; **Foot Locker** is everywhere (for convenience's sake, try Corso Vittorio Emanuele II); and **Guess** has opened quite a temple to teens, their second store in Italy, at Piazza San Babila. (The other is in Florence.)

Among the foreign-based arrivals is the makeup guru from Canada, by way of Estée Lauder: **MAC** is now in a very spiffy shop in the Brera district, having already moved off Via Spiga. Also, keep in mind **Laura Ashley** and **Tiffany & Co.**

Continental & U.S. Big Names

Use the Montenapoleone metro for all listings unless otherwise noted. For more detail on many of these well-known brand names, check out my "Dictionary of Taste & Design" in chapter 4.

BURBERRY
Via Pietro Verri 7.

CELINE
Via Montenapoleone 25.

CHANEL
Via Sant' Andrea 10.

CHRISTIAN DIOR
Via Montenapoleone 12.

ESCADA
Corso Matteotti 22 (metro: Babila).

FOGAL
Via Montenapoleone 1.

GAULTIER
Via della Spiga 20.

GIEVES & HAWKES
Via Manzoni 12.

HELMUT LANG
Via Sant' Andrea 15.

HERMES
Via Sant' Andrea 21.

HUGO BOSS
Corso Matteotti 11 (metro: Babila).

KENZO
Via Sant' Andrea 11.

LAURA ASHLEY
Via Brera 4 (metro: Duomo).

LOUIS VUITTON
Via Montenapoleone 14.

PAUL SMITH
Via Manzoni 30.

RENA LANGE
Via della Spiga 7.

SWATCH
Via della Spiga 1.

UNGARO
Via Montenapoleone 27.

VIKTOR & ROLF
Via Sant' Andrea 14.

WOLFORD
Via Manzoni 16b.

YVES SAINT LAURENT (YSL RIVE GAUCHE)
Via Montenapoleone 27.

Italian Big Names

ALBERTA FERRETTI
Via Montenapoleone 20; Philosophy di Alberta Ferretti, Via Montenapoleone 19.

ANTONIO FUSCO
Via Sant' Andrea 11.

BENETTON (SUPERSTORE)
Corso Vittorio Emanuele II (metro: Duomo or Babila).

BLUMARINE (ANNA MOLINARI)
Via della Spiga 42.

BOTTEGA VENETA
Via Montenapoleone 5.

BRIONI
Via Gesù 4.

BYBLOS
Via della Spiga 42.

CERRUTI 1881
Via della Spiga 20.

D & G
Corso Venezia 7.

DOLCE & GABBANA
Via della Spiga 2.

DIESEL
Galleria San Carlo (metro: Babila).

EMILIO PUCCI
Via Montenapoleone 14.

ERMENEGILDO ZEGNA
Via Verri 3.

ETRO
Via Montenapoleone 5.

FENDI
Via Sant' Andrea 16.

FERRAGAMO
Via Montenapoleone 3.

GIANFRANCO FERRÉ
Via Sant' Andrea 15.

GIANNI VERSACE
Via Montenapoleone 11; Atelier Versace, Via Gesù 12;
Versus, Via San Pietro all'Orto 10; Versace Jeans Couture,
Via Carducci 38.

GIORGIO ARMANI
Via Sant' Andrea 9; Armani Superstore, Via Manzoni 31;
Armani Casa, Via Durini 24 (metro: Babila).

GUCCI
Via Montenapoleone 7.

JUST CAVALLI
Via della Spiga 42.

KRIZIA
Via della Spiga 23.

LA PERLA
Via Montenapoleone 1.

LAURA BIAGIOTTI
Via Borgospesso 19.

LES COPAINS
Via Manzoni 21.

MARIELLA BURANI
Via Montenapoleone 3.

MARINA RINALDI
Corso Vittorio Emanuele II at Galleria Passarella 2 (metro: Babila).

MAX & CO.
Via Victor Hugo 1.

MAX MARA
Corso Genova 12.

MISSONI
Via Sant' Andrea 2.

MIU MIU
Corso Venezia 3 (metro: Babila).

MOSCHINO
Via della Spiga 30.

NAJ OLEARI
Via Brera 58 (metro: Duomo).

NAZARENO GABRIELLI
Via Montenapoleone 23.

PRADA
Via Montenapoleone 18.

PRADA (LINGERIE)
Via della Spiga 5.

ROBERTO CAVALLI
Via della Spiga 42.

SAMSONITE
Corso Matteotti 12.

TOD'S
Via della Spiga 22.

Discounters

Also see "Outlets (In Town)," later in this section.

DMAGAZINE
Via Montenapoleone 26 (metro: Montenapoleone).

Considering the address and convenience, this store is a must-do: a discount store selling high-end fashion names right in the heart of the biggest fashion stores in town and not far from a metro stop. Now then, I can't tell you I was knocked out by what I saw, but there were Lagerfeld shoes, Miu Miu clothes, and some Helmut Lang items. The names were in place; I just wasn't tempted, and the store wasn't nearly as much fun as Il Salvagente. Still, when in the neighborhood, take a quick look. © 02/7600-6027.

IL SALVAGENTE
Via Fratelli Bronzetti 16 (no nearby metro).

American and European styles from big-name designers in suits and dresses, even in larger sizes, but you just have to hit it right. Men's clothing is on the second floor. This looks like a prison; you enter through a gate, walk down the drive, and turn into the door where you will be asked to use a locker for your bags and maybe even your handbag. During sales it is mobbed. Il Salvagente is the most famous designer discounter in Italy. This is an operation that makes Loehmann's look classy, but if you are strong enough, you can find stuff here. Attention savvy shoppers.

While the labels are still in the clothes, the merchandise is not well organized, so you must be feeling very strong to go through it all. There's so much here that you have a good chance of finding something worthwhile, but you could strike out.

Clothes are located in several parts of the store and upstairs as well; there are dressing rooms. Not everything is new. Some have been seen on runways or are over a season old; not everything is in perfect condition.

On various visits, however, I've seen Krizia, Gianni Versace, Valentino, Guy Laroche, Trussardi, made-in-Italy Lacroix handbags (for 80€/$100 each!), and more. On my most recent visit, I was truly dizzy from all the choices. I once happened on the January sale when prices at the cash register were 30% less than the lowest ticketed price.

Remember: The atmosphere is drab; the display is zero. This place is for the strong and the hungry. On Wednesday and Saturday, the store does not close for lunch and is open nonstop from 10am till 7pm. ✆ 02/7611-0328.

SALVAGENTE BIMBI
Via Balzaretti 28 (no nearby metro).

This is a separate shop from Il Salvagente, specifically for children's clothing; the layout is similar to the mother shop, but the store is harder to find—take a taxi, of course. It is hard to find a taxi to get you home, so you may want to ask them to call you a cab. "Taxi" in Italian is *taxi*.

Note: I used a car and driver to get here, and my Milanese driver was lost. Still, if you are looking for expensive kids' clothing at affordable prices, this is the place. ✆ 02/2668-0764.

SEVEN GROUP
Via San Gregorio 49 (metro: Centrale).

This was my favorite showroom when I hit the wholesale district near the train station during my last visit; it's a large, open space, not crammed and crowded like many jobbers. They are open to the public, they do take plastic, and they do give tax refunds! They don't speak a lot of English, but who cares? I bought my cashmere twin set here and was tempted by many of the fashions. The bad part is that prices are not clearly marked, and you feel like you're a big pain every time you ask a question. Still, the quality and styling were sublime. ✆ 02/6707-5066.

VESTISTOCK
Viale Romagna 19, Via Boscovich 17, and more (no nearby metro).

A chain of discount shops in various neighborhoods, including the very convenient Buenos Aires for Viale Romagna and the train station district for Via Boscovich. If you hit it lucky, you can choose from labels such as Les Copains, Moschino, Versace, Montana, and more. There are men's, women's, and kids' clothes as well as accessories, so go and have a ball. Take bus 60, 90, or 91 for the Buenos Aires area shop, or call for more specific directions.

If you prefer the store between the train station and many major hotels, it's open nonstop, 9:30am to 6:30pm, Monday to Friday. There were Tod's boots when I visited and plenty of men's clothing in large sizes. ✆ 02/749-0502. www.vestistock.it.

Flea Markets

The following markets sell all manner of old and/or used things—what we Americans consider a flea market. The words the Italians use to describe such a market are *mercato di pulci.* Note that more and more flea markets are opening all over Italy, so ask your hotel concierge if there is a new market, and check the pages of the monthly magazine *Dove* (pronounced "do-*vay*": Italian for "where," not the English "bird") for fairs and flea markets in nearby communities.

BOLLATE ANTIQUE MARKET
Piazza Vittorio Veneto, Bollate.

Take the train or a taxi to this suburb on the north side of Milan, where there is a Sunday *mercato dell'usato,* or antiques market. Unlike most Sunday markets, which are held once a month, this market is held weekly. Most of the 300 dealers sell English antiques, if you can believe that; silver is especially hot, as are old prints. There's not much in the way of bed linens, but there are some old hats and a fair amount of furniture.

Consider renting a car for this day in the country, or hop the bus: take the no. 90 or 91 to the **Piazza della Liberta** in Bollante. Open from 8am to 6pm.

BRERA ANTIQUE MARKET (MERCATONE DELL' ANTIQUARIATO)
Via Brera (metro: Duomo).

This flea market, held on the third Saturday of each month, is a local favorite. Because it takes place right in the heart of downtown Milan (in the shadow of La Scala, in fact), this is a drop-dead chic market to be seen prowling. About 50 antiques dealers set up stalls, and many artists and designers turn out. To find it, just head for Via Brera. Do wear your fur and walk your dog if at all possible.

NAVIGLI ANTIQUE MARKET
Grand Navigli (metro: Porta Genova).

If flea markets are your thing, be in Milan on the last Sunday of the month. Then you can spend the midmorning at this fabulous flea market, which stretches all the way from Porta Ticinese to Porta Genova and the Viale Papiniano. With approximately 400 dealers, some say it is the most stylish flea market in all of Europe.

While the market is open from 8am to 2pm, do remember this is Italy, not New York—things are most lively from 10am to noon. You'll find the usual antiques and wonderful junk, and the crowd is one of Milan's top see-and-be-seen. Take the no. 19 tram to Ripa di Porta Ticinese.

Foodstuffs

ARMANDOLA
Via della Spiga 50 (metro: Montenapoleone).

This is a teeny-weeny, itty-bitty deli with fresh foods, dried mushrooms, tuna in jars, and all sorts of fancy, expensive, and yummy things. I paid 12€ ($15) for a jar of tuna fish; the recipient said it was worth the price. Sometimes I buy a ready-made

picnic here; you can't beat the location for convenience.
© 02/7602-1657.

ENOTECA COTTI
Via Solferino 42 (metro: Doumo).

Considered one of the best wine stores in Milano, they also
have serious olive oil, as is the custom at a good *enoteca*.
© 02/657-29-95.

FREE SHOP
Centrale Station (metro: Centrale).

Don't snicker. I do a lot of my gourmet-food shopping here
because it's convenient. Buy magic coffee here as well as Italian specialty food items for gifts and home use. © 02/669-1273.

Home Style/Showrooms

ARFLEX
Corso Europa 11 (metro: Montenapoleone).

One of the big names in design, Arflex's showroom is filled
with all manner of wild and creative home furnishings. A lip-
stick-red–leather sofa, anyone? © 02/7640-9188. www.arflex.
com.

B&B ITALIA
Via Durini 14 (metro: Babila).

Almost a supermarket of design stuff, this showroom is new
to the area and another in a string of important style shops.
Some smalls and accessories. © 02/76-44-41. www.bebitalia.it.

CASSINA
Via Durini 16 (metro: Babila or Duomo).

One of the long-standing big names in post–World War II
design, Cassina makes mostly office furniture, but all of their

pieces are quite avant-garde. Colors are bright, deep, and vibrant, and the design lines are beyond clean. I popped into this showroom recently to look at the leather chairs designed by Mario Bellini, which are the prototype for the plastic Bellini chairs that my friend Alan makes with Bellini (at a Target store near you). Even though I was just snooping, the people in the showroom could not have been more gracious. ✆ 02/7602-0745. www.cassina.com.

LISA CORTI
Via Conchetta 6 (tram: 15).

I don't even know how to describe this space or shopping situation—it is a showroom, but it's also different. First off, you should know or understand who Lisa Corti is—an artist and magician with color and textiles, whose work is sold at Saks and is best seen in the pages of the Saks home-furnishings catalogs, which always have at least one full page in color with stacks of her things.

Corti is best known for her home design for table and bed and sofa, but also makes clothes for women and children and other accessories, and, at one time, dishes and ceramics. She is an artist and does it all; her work is her signature. Even her postcards are glorious (and free).

The showroom is in the middle of nowhere; if you take a taxi, have the driver wait for you. There is a front door on the street, but I didn't find it and went in through the courtyard. I also called from my mobile phone, as I thought I was lost.

The showroom inside is the real showroom and workroom; the shopping op is sort of like being in the factory outlet. The prices are not low, but are just a fraction of the U.S. price. I paid about 120€ ($150) for a quilt that I had paid 200€ ($250) for in the south of Italy, and that costs 280€ ($350) at Saks. They do de-tax (see chapter 3 for details on getting a tax refund), and someone there does speak English. You might want to call ahead before you make the trek. ✆ 02/5810-0031. www.lisacorti.com.

Linens & Lace

BASSETTI
Corso Vercelli 25; Corso Garibaldi 20; Corso Vittorio Emanuele II 15 (metro: Duomo).

A famous name in linens for years, Bassetti makes the kind of linens that fall between ready-to-wear and couture—they're more affordable than the big-time expensive stuff and far nicer than anything you'd find at the low end. Although they do sell colors, their hot look is paisley fabrics in the Etro vein. There are branch stores in every major Italian city. Within Italy, call ✆ 800/820-129. www.bassetti.com.

FRETTE
Via Montenapoleone 21 (metro: Montenapoleone).

This line has gone so far upscale that they now call it "home couture" with items such as pajamas and robes and leisure clothing, as well as sheets and bedding for sale. Naturally there is a business in custom-created bed linen as well. There is an outlet store near the Jolly Augusto at Largo Augusto. ✆ 02/78-39-50. www.frette.it.

JESURUM
Via Verri 4 (metro: Duomo).

A branch of the Venetian linen house, famous for old lace brocades—really swank stuff, with prices to match. ✆ 02/7601-5045. www.jesurum.it.

PRATESI
Via Montenapoleone 6a (metro: Montenapoleone).

This is a new address and is somewhat hidden in a small arcade, so watch carefully—this is the Milan retail shop for this family-held linen and luxe group. They are most famous for bed linen, but there's also baby- and beachwear, and bathrobes, and quality like you've never seen; prices are 25% to 40% less than in the U.S.

By mentioning this, I am assuming you can't make it to the outlet store (see chapter 6). Sheets sold at regular retail are about 800€ ($1,000) each but will last for well over 25 years. ℂ 02/7601-2755. www.pratesi.com.

Makeup

Don't look now, but there is a color war in Italy, centered in Milan where everyone is suddenly doing makeup. This was probably instigated by the success of the Versace makeup, which was actually launched a few months after the Versace murder and was obviously created before he died. With the success of makeup artist lines in the U.S., several Italian names have jumped into the fray. Most of the names are not familiar to Americans; some of them have pedigrees, however. And then there's Armani.

DIEGO DELLA PALMA
Via Madonnina 15 (metro: Duomo).

This is embarrassing, but here goes: I am forever getting Diego della Palma, a well-known local makeup artist, and Diego della Viale, the creator of Tod's shoes, mixed up. That said, Palma is an artist with connections to the Italian couture houses; he has a small shop that also sells his line, where you can make an appointment for lessons and a makeover. The address is adjacent the Brera district on a great shopping street. ℂ 02/87-68-18.

GIORGIO ARMANI
Via Manzoni 31 (metro: Montenapoleone).

As we go to press, Armani makeup does not have very much distribution in Italy or elsewhere in the world. This could be because the line is so new, and the intent is to keep it very exclusive. Regardless, you can see it all and play with it all at the Armani flagship; the line is also sold in Milan's La Rinascente. I have tested many of the products and adore the pearlized liquid foundation that really does add light to the face. Last time I bought a blush, it was presented to me in its own little Armani canvas tote bag. ℂ 02/7231-8600. www.armani-viamanzoni31.it.

KIKO
Corso Buenos Aires 43 (metro: Loreto).

By the time I got to Kiko, a cute little shop in the best part of the trendy shopping on Buenos Aires, I could no longer tell one brand from the next. I can't quite tell how this line differs from Madina, although it is not as sophisticated in the packaging and marketing. Still, the line is well priced and is getting raves from local fashion editors. ℂ 02/2024-0502.

MAC
Via Fiori Chiari 12 (metro: Duomo).

MAC, the professional color line from Canada, now owned by Estée Lauder, which has gone global and has a freestanding store in Milan in the Brera area. Aside from the products, you can get a makeup lesson or just play with the colors. The professional line is sold; all charitable promotions, such as products whose profits go to good causes, are continued in international stores. ℂ 02/8699-5506.

MADINA MILANO
Corso Venezia 23 (metro: Babila).

With stores in Milan, Tokyo, and New York, Madina is the color story the press is in love with: Madina—sort of the Italian version of France's Terry de Gunzberg—used to do makeup for the opera at La Scala. She is married to the man who owns the most famous luxury cosmetics factory in Europe. The stores are small, but the packaging is very, very slick. Imprinted on the tablets of color are slogans in English, such as "color is seduction" and "color is power."

There are hundreds of shades; the strength of the line is said to be in the intensity of the colors and their staying power. I tested several items, and while I like them, I don't find them any more extraordinary than other brands. Prices are moderate to low—a paint box of 12 shades of cream eye shadow for 12€ ($15) is a steal, and a great gift for anyone. There's also a wide selection of brushes and several styles of makeup bags. There is another store in Milan (Via Meravigli 17), which is on the corner of Corso Magenta, an upscale residential area with nice shopping. ✆ 02/7601-1692. www.madina.it.

Naj Oleari
Via Brera 8 (metro: Duomo).

Because this fabric designer is known for her bright colors, it makes sense that the firm would branch into color cosmetics, which are even sold in most big department stores as well as the flagship boutique. The line is so successful that now spa and treatment products have been added. Don't ask me, I don't make the news, I only report it. ✆ 02/805-6790.

Perlier/Kelemata (Armonia Natural)
Corso Buenos Aires 25 (metro: Loreto).

You may remember Perlier as a French bath line; it was bought by the Italian Klemata family that now has a chain of very spiffy bath and makeup stores all over Italy. There is probably a store coming to a mall near you in no time. This year they joined the color wars and added a color makeup line under the Perlier branding; it is sold only in their stores, which are named Armonia Naturali. There are four other shops dotted around Milan. ✆ 02/2951-8261.

Shu Uemura
Via Brera 2 (metro: Duomo).

Uemura is the king of color, and the man who started it all over 20 years ago in Japan, where he brought professional makeup to the public. His products have a cult following, and he is clearly in a league above all others; so are his prices. ✆ 02/87-53-71.

Markets

To a local, there's a big difference between a market and a flea market. A market sells fruits and vegetables and dry goods, and a flea market sells old junk. See "Flea Markets," earlier in this chapter, for more about the other kind of market.

SAN AGOSTINO MARKET
Viale Papiniano (metro: San Agostino).

First, I must admit that no other guidebook calls this the San Agostino Market. I call it that because San Agostino is the name of the closest metro stop, and it helps me remember where this market is located on the Viale Papiniano.

This is a T-shaped market. The cross of the T is the fruit, food, and vegetable market; the long stroke is the dry-goods market. The dry-goods portion goes on for 2 blocks, so don't quit after the first block. Everything in the world is sold here, including a few designer items that seem to have fallen off the backs of trucks (but are carefully mixed in with less valuable items). For example, one dealer in the dry-goods market seems to specialize in bath articles, but also has a small selection of Missoni bathrobes.

You'll find everything from the latest teen fashions to tapes and CDs, kitchen supplies, car supplies, pet supplies, aprons, and housedresses. There are also socks, towels, batteries, luggage, underwear, sewing thread, running shoes, designer shoes, lace curtains, and fabrics by the bolt. I saw the best cashmeres at the best prices here.

The market is open on Tuesday and Saturday.

Menswear

BOGGI
Piazza San Babila 3 (metro: Babila).

Boggi specializes in the English look, the preppy look; whatever you call it, you'll find cable-knit sweaters and plaid hunting trousers. There are several shops; the main store is near

Via Montenapoleone. It's not cheap here, but the quality is very high. © 02/7600-0366. www.boggi.it.

CASHMERE COTTON AND SILK
Via Madonnina 19 (metro: Duomo).

This is one of those fancy stores on the little side streets of Brera that is worth looking at, if only for its charm. Walk down a rather long corridor until you get into the store, which is modern with an old-fashioned feel. Inside, you'll find Milanese yuppies scurrying around, choosing among the shirts, sweaters, and suits made only of the three fibers in the store's name. Prices are very, very high, but the shopping experience makes you feel like royalty. © 02/805-7426.

DIOR HOMME
Via Montenapoleone 14 (metro: Montenapoleone).

I am not sure which is more gorgeous, the architecture or the slim young things who shop here. All worth staring at in this new store, one of several men's stores created specifically to sell the work of Hedi Slimane. It's very stainless-steel and art-gallery minimal; the dressing rooms have mirrors created by sensors that relay your image onto the wall. © 02/7631-8822. http://fashion.dior.com/homme/.

EDDY MONETTI
Piazza San Babila 4 (metro: Babila).

One of the leading sources for Anglo style in Milan, Monetti deals with rich gentlemen who want to look even richer. They hand-stitch suits and shirts but also sell off the rack. The Monetti customer likes special service and hates to shop; he wants to come here and be pampered and know that he'll walk out looking like a million dollars. © 02/7600-0940.

ERMENEGILDO ZEGNA
Via Pietro Verri 3 (metro: Duomo).

For centuries, the family has excelled in the quality wool business. Until recently, the ready-to-wear was a small sideline, but now, in a smattering of freestanding boutiques, the world's richest men can buy the best suits ready-made in Italy. There's one in Paris, one in Florence, and this shop in Milan, which is the closest to the mill in Biella, and serves as the family flagship store. The shop is large and modern and sells classic tailoring to discriminating men. Although the house is famous for its wools, you can get other items, including cotton or silk dress shirts. © 02/7600-6437. www.zegna.com.

RENCO
Corso Venezia 29 (metro: Babila).

Large sizes for men—business, casual, weekend, sports, shoes, accessories, the works. Note that the phone is toll free within Italy and won't work from the U.S. © 800/95-55-86. www.rencostore.com.

TINCATI
Piazza Oberdan 2 (metro: Montenapoleone), and several other locations.

An old-fashioned men's store, or haberdashery (as they used to be called), with fine woods on the walls and an upper mezzanine filled with stock. Very good old-world reputation. Not for hotshots who want the Euro-Japanese look. Its shirts are famous because they come with a tab that passes between the legs (trust me on this) and an extra collar and two cuffs. © 02/2940-4326. www.tincati.mi.it.

Outlets (In Town)

DIFFUSIONE TESSILE/MAX MARA
Galleria San Carlo 6 (metro: Babila).

I can't stop to sing about this outlet, as I am too busy getting there. It's large, it's clean, it looks like a normal store, it carries all of the Max Mara lines, including the Marina Rinaldi (large size) line; it has two levels; it has coats for 36€ ($45). They take plastic. Note that this location is in a mall. You will easily find the mall but may have trouble finding the actual store, as the mall has alleys. Ask. ✆ 02/7600-0829. www.diffusionetessile.it.

LISA CORTI
Via Conchetta 6 (tram: 15).

See "Home Style/Showrooms," earlier in this chapter.

SPACCIO ETRO
Via Spartaco 3 (no nearby metro).

This began life as an employee store in the firm's offices, but it's open to the public and is the kind of secret that every smart shopper in Milan knows about. Now then, did I have fun? I get sweaty just reminiscing. The tiny shop has two levels; the clothes are downstairs. There are bins of things; I got men's pocket squares for 20€ ($25) each; silk suspenders for 12€ ($15). There is fabric by the meter and everything else. ✆ 02/5502-0216. www.etro.it.

10 CORSO COMO OUTLET STORE
Via Tazzoli 3 (metro: Garibaldi).

With the fashion-forward fashion sold at 10 Corso Como, it's not a surprise that it might not all sell or be too far ahead of its time. When the clothes go off the floor in the main store, they are taken around the corner to the outlet store. Prices range from reasonable to low; in many cases, the marked-down price is what you would have wanted to pay in the first place (240€/$300 instead of 480€/$600) so it doesn't seem like a real bargain. There are some accessories, as well as menswear.

The store is a little hard to find; I was lost and walked a good bit out of my way when, in fact, it's not much more than a block from the 10 Corso Como store. Turn right from the store, then left at the corner, pass the ATA Hotel, and turn onto

Via Tazzoli—which is an oblique left, so pay attention. ✆ 02/2900-2674.

Outlet Malls (Out of Town)

SERRAVALLE
Serravalle Scrivia.

This is the oldest of the American-style outlet malls in Italy, meaning it's about 5 years old. It's closer to Genoa than Milan, although it's only a 90-minute drive from Milan.

Don't try to do this on public transportation from Milan. I spent over an hour with my hotel concierge and his computer trying to route this, and with changing trains and all that stuff, it was a nightmare not worth attempting. ✆ 0143/60-90-00. http://serravalle.mcarthurglen.it/.

Paper Goods

PINEIDER
Corso Europa 13 (metro: Montenapoleone).

Italy's most famous name in paper goods and old-fashioned, heavy-duty, richer-than-thou stationery is Pineider, with stores in every major city. The real news is that this old-time brand has decided to perk itself up as other brands have done. Accordingly, they have hired the American designer Rebecca Moses, who lives in Milan, and have expanded beyond paper goods to gift items that are chic, sublime, and very expensive. There are now a few shops in Milan. ✆ 02/7602-2353. www.pineider.com.

Perfume

For the most part, perfume is expensive in Italy, and you must be smart to catch a bargain, so buy at the airport duty-free or in La Rinascente, where you get a 10% discount at the check-out counter if you show your passport. There are several branches of the enormous German chain, **Douglas,** dotted around the main shopping districts: You may want to ask about their Douglas Card, which you can use in any of their stores worldwide and will bring you extra perks.

If you are a fan of the scent **Acqua di Parma,** note they have their first free-standing store at Via Gesù 3.

If money is no object, pop into **Profumo,** Via Brera 6, where American and English imports are sold at higher prices than you are used to.

Secondhand Fashion

I spent a day touring many of Milan's tony secondhand shops because this form of alternate retail is so important in Paris and New York. I wish I could say this was great, that I bought stuff, or I think you'll want to do it, too. I am listing the best shops, but with the understanding that this kind of shopping is very hit or miss; you are on your own.

L' ARMADIO DI LAURA
Via Voghera 25 (metro: Genova).

This is by far the largest and the best, but it is a bit out of the way, although one saleswoman (who speaks English perfectly) told me that most people come on the metro. The area is industrial; the building is frightening on first approach, but only because everything is unfamiliar. You press the button on the console, enter the gate, cross the courtyard, and enter through a door slightly to your right, at maybe one o'clock on the clock-face system of direction-giving.

The store smells like used clothes; it's the same musty smell all these stores have, but it's not a dirty clothes smell. Designer clothes are packed into racks; there are also some shoes, handbags, and accessories. There are some sizes larger than 46. (Thank God!) In summer the store is open on Monday 10am to 6pm. © 02/836-0606.

MERCATINI MICHELA
Corso Venezia 8 (metro: Babila).

I like this store because it's easy to get to and has very expensive clothes. I've never bought anything, but it's easy to pop up (the store is upstairs in an office building) and check. Sometimes you can find Pucci. They do a big business in wedding gowns. © 02/7600-2521.

Shoes & Leather Goods

Shoe shops obviously abound, with shoes in just about all price ranges. The greatest problem with cheap shoes is that they wear out more quickly than well-made shoes. You can stick to brand-name shoes in Milan, or explore some of the low-cost no-names—it's all here. No-name shoes start at about 24€ ($30) a pair. Better no-name shoes cost 40€ ($50) a pair. Just wander the middle-class neighborhoods where real people shop.

In expensive shoes, there are two completely different schools of thought: English-style, conservative, country classics that you wear for 20 years, and high-fashion fluff bundles that will last only a season or two but will signal the world that you are a major player.

Please note that I have listed several of the big-name leather goods firms under "Italian Big Names," earlier in this chapter, because they are more or less icons in the business and most of them also have clothing lines. The following names are not as famous in the U.S., but they deserve attention while you are studying the scene in Milan.

BOTTEGA VENETA
Via Montenapoleone 5 (metro: Montenapoleone).

BRUNO MAGLI
Corso Vittorio Emmanuele (metro: Duomo).

CASADEI
Via Sant' Andrea 15b (metro: Babila).

COCCINELLE
Via Manzoni ang Via Bigli (metro: Babila).

HOGAN
Via Montenaploeone 23 (metro: Montenapoleone).

VALEXTRA
Piazza San Babila 1 (metro: Babila).

Tabletop & Gifts

HIGH TECH
Piazza XXV Aprile 12 (metro: Garibaldi).

By Milan standards, High Tech is an enormous place. The second floor of this two-story selling space is completely devoted to home furnishings, all with the look we've come to associate with the city of Milan. Begun by Aldo Cibic, formerly of Memphis Milano fame. © 02/624-1101.

LISA CORTI
Via Conchetta 6 (tram: 15).

See "Home Style/Showrooms," earlier in this chapter.

LORENZI
Via Montenapoleone 9 (metro: Montenapoleone).

After you finish with plastics, head to Milan's head cutlery store, where you can also buy pipes and other gifts and gadgets for men. © 02/7602-2848.

MORONIGOMMA
Corso Matteotti 14 (metro: Babila).

This store has plastics from all over the world, so don't buy any of the expensive American products. Instead, get a load of the Italian designer vinyl, the car products, and the household items. With its affordable prices, this may be the only store in Milan where you can go wild and not be sorry the next day.

It's conveniently located at the start of Via Montenapoleone, on the far side of the Piazza San Babila; there are many other wonderful design hangouts in the area. © 02/79-62-20. www. moronigomma.it.

TAD
Via di Croce Rossa 1 (metro: Montenapoleone).

Despite an unfamiliar-sounding address, this is in the heart of the Montenapo area and right near the metro station. (How else would I find it?) Tad is a store filled with ideas, so even if you don't buy anything, stop by and stare. Multilevel shop with candles, gifts, some home furnishings, and so on. © 02/ 869-0110.

Teens & 'Tweens

Teens need no specific addresses; just plop them onto Corso Buenos Aires. Or try these specialty label stops:

DIESEL STORE
Galleria San Carlo (metro: Babila).

All the Diesel products (way beyond jeans) as well as a Style Lab; teen heaven. © 02/7639-0583.

H&M
Corso Vittorio Emanuele II (metro: Babila).

Swedish low-cost retailer has taken space once occupied by Benetton, which shows they are the newest international brand to move in on Italian expertise in low-cost fashion. © 02/7601-7222.

ONYX
Corso Vittorio Emanuele 11 and 24 (metro: Duomo).

Cheap thrills and an amazing scene filled with technology and great clothes at great prices—sort of the local version of H&M

but much younger and less sophisticated than Oviesse. ℂ 02/ 7601-6261.

ZARA

Corso Vittorio Emanuele II (metro: Duomo).

The Spanish retailer has come to town and is making a big dent on Italian fashions, which they somewhat emulate. ℂ 02/ 7639-0606.

BEYOND MILAN

···

Lake Como Area

GETTING THERE

If you have a train pass, don't use it: it's a waste of money to use one of your travel days for the trip to Como. I bought myself a round-trip, first-class ticket for about 12€ ($15). I bought it at the ticket counter in Milan's Centrale Station; the transaction was in Italian, so I didn't get too much of what was happening.

The ticket was marked "via Monza," and I panicked that I would have to make a connection in Monza—I did not. The ride was a simple 20 minutes on a commuter train, nothing to it. On my last trip, I booked a car and driver from Milan for a half-day and 150km (93 miles). The cost was about 160€ ($200), which I thought was okay except the driver kept getting lost. Consider arriving by train and then hiring a local taxi to drive and wait for you.

ARRIVING IN COMO

The train station (Como San Giovanni) is nice: There's a tourist office window to answer questions, a map of the area posted in the hallway, and many free brochures. There's also a newsstand and a bar.

Out front, you'll find a line of taxis and vans with, finally, some English-speaking help. I hired a taxi for the morning to take me around and wait for me. I was told that the flat fare from the train station to the **Ratti** outlet was a mere 6€ ($7.50). You can also get a taxi to drop you at Ratti and come pick you up at the agreed-upon time or when you call. Get your driver's radio number (or Ratti will get you a taxi).

The town proper is located below the train station, within walking distance. However, if you've come on a Monday, most of the town will be closed in the morning, so you might as well head first to your hotel (if you are staying for a while) or the silk outlets.

THE SHOPPING SCENE

The town of Como was the center of the medieval silk industry, although Como no longer has its own worms. For the most part, silk comes from elsewhere but is milled here.

Como lies at the southern end of Lake Como, about 50km (31 miles) north of Milan, and offers all the charm you want in a teeny, old-fashioned village on the edge of a lake surrounded by forest and Switzerland.

The town caters to the wealthy landowners who live in the villas surrounding the lake, as well as to the merely rich and/or fashionable who stop by for the weekend (as Gianni Versace used to do). There are also loads of day-trippers and visitors, many of whom are visiting from Switzerland.

Best buys in the village shops are in clothes, silk scarves, and leather goods. While you'll find lots of antiques, most of them are fakes or reproductions. If you love it, and the price is right, who cares? Remember that U.S. Customs wants an item to be 100 years old or older for you to bring it back into the country duty-free.

If you love fabrics, you owe yourself a visit to **Seterie Moretti** (Via Garibaldi 69), located right on Como's main square, on the corner of Via Galio and Via Garibaldi. The shop was closed on Monday morning when I got there! They do open on Monday afternoon, however.

Seterie Moretti distributes signed fabrics to retail sources such as Galtrucco in Milan and Liberty in London. They retain the screens and rerun them without the designer name and with a slight variation in design. As a result, you get fabrics that look familiar, but are slightly different. There are five rooms of fabrics at Moretti. They speak English and accept credit cards.

Another silk maker is **Mantero,** with a showroom at Via Volta 68. The business was run by eight brothers about 100 years ago—the firm actually produces wool, cotton, and silk. The silk comes from China (as does much Italian silk) but is screened in Italy; it's the ability of the craftspeople who work the screens that makes Italian silk so famous these days. Get a look at Mantero's silk scarves—you will go wild. I have recently begun buying them, about 200€ ($250) each (regular retail, not at the outlet) for the huge shawl size. Rumor has it this firm makes the silk screens for Hermès.

Not only are there house designs (nice botanical prints), but also goods that have been licensed by designers such as Chanel, Ferré, and Saint Laurent. Not bad, eh? I bought Richard a Ferré tie for 36€ ($45) that was so sophisticated, I could have wept: whites and beiges and grays with seashells in a row. There was a scarf, the type I like, for about 160€ ($200) but it wasn't the one I wanted so I gave it up. Later, I found what I wanted for only 40€ ($50) more in a regular retail store. Undoubtedly, this outlet has the most sophisticated merchandise, but the discounts are not huge, so don't panic if they don't have what you want.

These two stores are in the "downtown" Como area and are within walking distance.

The downtown also has cute stores, although no big designer names. I was fond of the local branch of **Standa.**

The star of the area, however, is **Ratti** (Via Cernobbio; © 031/23-32-62). The shop is at the base of the estate of an old villa that is not visible from the road. However, it is on the main road right off the lake, so it's not far at all.

Your taxi driver knows his way here blindfolded. If you are driving yourself, ask for directions—but this is a no-brainer (thank heavens).

You will have no trouble getting in, although because no one here speaks English, having an Italian-speaking driver will make you feel less tense and could be a great morale-builder.

The Ratti outlet store has two rooms jam-packed with the goodies you want to buy—from men's ties and women's silk scarves, to pillows, handbags, blouses, and even bolts of fabric. When I went, there were tons of Etro bathrobes, bolts of Versace fabrics, and enough ties to make you swoon. Now then, about prices: They are cheap, but not dirt-cheap. I paid 32€ ($40) for designer ties. I'm talking big-name designer ties, but, nonetheless, Filene's Basement frequently has the same names for 24€ ($30). I estimate that if you are a keen shopper, you could happily spend a couple of hours here. But you can also do it in 10 minutes. It depends on the stock and your style.

MORE OUTLETS NEAR COMO

EMPORIO DELLA SETTA
Via Canturina 190, Como.

The Emporium of Silk sounds pretty good, huh? Many big designer names are represented in this clearinghouse for silk from the local mills. Discounts are in the 40% range. To add to your savings, there are seasonal sales in January and July. © 031/59-14-20.

MANTERO
Via Volta 68, Como.

Note that this factory is closed Saturday and Sunday. Regular hours are 9:30am to 12:30pm and 2 to 6pm. They do take credit cards, showing just how sophisticated they are. Besides their own distinct line of silks and scarves and ties, there are big-name designer goods as well. You will die and go to heaven; this is the thrill of a lifetime. © 031/27-98-61.

SETERIE MARTINETTI
Via Torriani 41, Como.

By now you surely know that *seterie* means silk maker in Italian. This is rumored to be one of the best silk resources in the area, although there are so many good ones that it is hard to qualify them all. You'll find the usual scarves, ties, robes, and yummy items from the usual cast of international big-name designers. Closed on Monday morning. ☎ 031/26-90-53.

PAST COMO

Not far from Como, you find yourself in Switzerland, headed toward Lugano. But don't panic, you're also on the way to Fox-Town (www.foxtown.ch), which is a 5-minute drive into Switzerland across the Italian border. So what? The good news: FoxTown is an outlet village with 130 stores (200 brands), a casino (for husbands, no doubt), and a cafe. There's quite a large number of big-name designer outlets here, including Yves Saint Laurent, Valentino, Bruno Magli, and Loro Piano.

The bad news? Because you are in Switzerland, prices are not in euros but in Swiss Francs, which are always trading high. Even with a strong euro, you may not want to change money or incur CF charges on your credit cards.

For specific directions, call ☎ 410/848-828-888. They are open 7 days a week, 11am to 7pm nonstop. If you are driving, you want the Mendriso exit, which is 7km (4⅓ miles) from the Swiss-Italian border.

Parabiago

Parabiago is an industrial suburb of Milan, where many of the shoe factories and leather-accessories people have offices. Many consider it within the metro Milano area and not a day trip, however, no public transportation goes here, and when I asked my driving service about getting there, they made it clear they considered it out of town. Whether you take a car,

Remember Armani

For those with cars and a spirit of adventure, head over to the new Armani outlet at the Intai factory, near Bregnano (which is between Milan and Como). Take the Autostrada/A9 to the Como exit, and head for Bregnano; look for the factory at the crossroad of SS35. For more specific directions, call © 031/88-73-73. The shop is closed on Monday; otherwise, the hours are 10am to 1pm and 2 to 7pm. They accept credit cards.

a taxi, or drive yourself, do remember that even factory stores close for lunch.

CLAUDIO MORLACCHI
Via Castelnuovo 24, Parabiago.

While you're in Parabiago, stop by Claudio Morlacchi—the factory looks like a house, but don't be alarmed. Push the large wooden door and enter into a light, airy courtyard. To the right is a room with a small but wonderful display of all the shoes the Morlacchi people make. Among Morlacchi's clients are Lanvin and Guy Laroche. © 0331/55-54-11.

FRATELLI ROSSETTI FACTORY
Via Cantù 24, Parabiago.

There is a Fratelli Rossetti boutique in Milan (Via Montenapoleone 1), but why shop there when you can go to the factory in Parabiago? The Rossetti factory has no ads and no markings; it kind of looks like a prison from the outside. The shop is in a separate building from the factory and houses a large selection of men's and women's shoes and boots in a big open room with blue rubber flooring. The shoes are displayed on L-shaped tables. The help does not speak English, but is very friendly. Men's shoes in traditional styles cost 52€ ($65) a pair; more elaborate slip-ons cost 100€ ($125); boots range from 80€ ($100); high-heel pumps begin at 64€ ($80). © 0331/55-22-26.

Biella

Biella is a mill town in northern Italy, famous because it is the headquarters of the **Zegna** woolen mills. It's also known for the **Fila** outlet store and other nearby outlets. Paola, from the Delta flight, gave me this info.

ERMENEGILDO ZEGNA
Via Roma 99, Centro Zegna, Trivero.

This is the one you've been looking for. This is the really big time of the big time. Of course, price tags—even at discount—can also be big time, but there is no finer or more famous name in Italian wool and cashmere. Trivero is near Biella. They take credit cards, and they are used to tourists and visitors; follow signs to **Centro Zegna**. © 015/75-65-41.

FILA
Via Cesare Battisti 28, Biella.

Here's an exception to factory stores being open on Monday morning—this factory store does open on Monday, but only at 3pm. They close at noon, not 1pm, for lunch daily and reopen at 3pm. Needless to say, Fila is an enormously famous name internationally for sportswear. They are most famous in the U.S. for their tennis gear, but they make clothing and gear for all sports; their ski stuff is sublime. There are bargains for all members of the family, and the store is conveniently located near the cute part of the old city. © 015/34-141.

FRATELLI PIACENZA LANIFICIO
Biella.

This place is a mill for cashmere, wools, and mohair, which is big this year. There are bargains, but you are still looking at price tags over 520€ ($650) for a cashmere coat. Rumor has it that Escada gets its goods here. Call for an appointment and directions. ℰ 015/61-461.

MAGLIFICIO DELLA ARTEMA
Strada Trossi 31, Verrone-Biella.

Located right outside Biella, this is yet another cashmere resource from the famous mills; watch for Artema signs. They sell the Zegna line as well as other Italian labels, including some designer names from the big-name circuit—rotating according to availability, of course. They sell everything from underwear to outerwear. ℰ 015/255-83-82.

Vercelli (Beyond Biella)

Vercelli is actually a province; it includes the city of Biella. It also includes a zillion mills, more known for their wool and cashmere than for silk, but some silken luxuries can be found. Vercelli is about a 2-hour drive (one-way) from Milan, so I didn't go. Let me know how it is if you get there. I did have the concierge call from Milan; he also said that the Loro Piana cashmere factory is nearby, though it has moved recently.

SAMBONET
Via XXVI Aprile 62–64, Vercelli.

When I told Logan the saga of my enthusiasm for the cashmere mill and my reluctance to go on a blind trek, she threw in another nearby resource. From the sublime to the ridiculous, guys, this one sells pots and pans—big-name pots and pans—and stainless, flatware, and silver plate, including seconds from Krupp and the Cordon Bleu lines. ℰ 0161/59-72-19.

Chapter Nine

....

ROMAN DAY TRIPS: NAPLES & THE AMALFI COAST

WELCOME TO NAPLES

Welcome to Naples, where some shopkeepers told me to take off my watches (yes, I do wear two), lest I attract a thief. Welcome to Naples, where the clerks at Ferragamo were not only rude but also refused to redo my tax refund papers when I decided to buy *more*. Welcome to Naples, where I had the best pizza of my life, where I fell madly in love with the scarves at Rubinacci, and where you are less than an hour away from Capri—or Amalfi. It's also a region that's heavily visited by cruise ships or that you can cover in a day trip from Rome. Quick, my *limoncello!*

Getting There

From Rome, you can rent a car for the 2-hour drive to Naples; this gives you a car for driving along the Amalfi coast as well. You can also take the train from Rome. The Naples train station is clean, modern, and not frightening.

If you arrive by cruise ship, the port (the Maritime Center) is next to the heart of town and well situated for your explorations and adventures. Note that the ferries and hydrofoils

Spending the Night in Naples

If you're planning a visit here that will be longer than a day trip, here are a couple of hotels to consider for your stay:

- **Excelsior Hotel:** This ornate hotel (Via Partenope 48; © 081/764-01-11; www.starwoodhotels.com) has a corner location with great views. Cruise passengers enjoy lunch at La Terrazza—you can even see your ship. Each room in the recently remodeled hotel is furnished with antiques.
- **Grand Hotel Vesuvio:** This is the leading hotel of the city (Via Partenope 45; © 081/764-00-44; www.vesuvio.it), located right on the Bay of Naples with a view directly to heaven. There's a fitness center/spa, you can eat on the rooftop, and you are within walking distance from much of the fancy shopping. Do you need more? There are shopping packages as well as a Shopping Fidelity program in which you get a numbered personal card that entitles you to discounts, gifts, and privileges at the city's best shops.

to the islands (Capri, Ischia, and so on) use different piers in other parts of town; there's one alongside the Maritime Center and the other is around the bay, 3.2km (2 miles) away.

Getting Around

For cruisers, you can find taxis at the gates of the Maritime Center; do be clear with drivers about where you are going and be vigilant about the meter; they may attempt to cheat you.

All hotels can get you a taxi; there are taxi stands, usually at big squares, where you can usually find a cab when you are out and about. If the driver is honest and goes by the meter, round up the tab as a tip.

To call a radio taxi, dial © 3296. Remember that traffic is fierce during rush hour and can run up the tab on the taximeter.

There is a metro, with two different lines. But the metro is of better use to residents or sightseers, not shoppers, so I don't

Naples

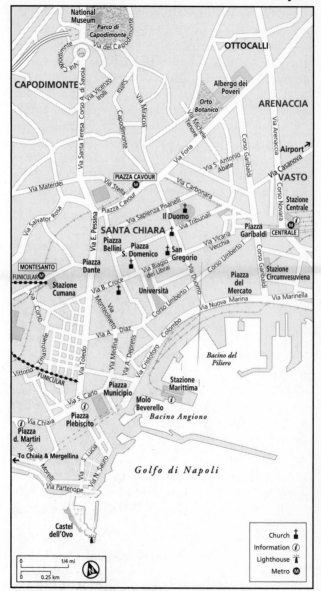

National Museum
Parco di Capodimonte
Via del Capodimonte
CAPODIMONTE
OTTOCALLI
Albergo dei Poveri
ARENACCIA
Orto Botanico
Via Santa Teresa Corso A. di Savoia
Via Vicenzo Irolli
Via Miracoli
Salita Capodimonte
Via Michele Tenore
Via Arenaccia
Airport
Via Casanova
Corso Novara
VASTO
Via Foria
Via S. Antonio Abate
Corso Garibaldi
Stazione Centrale
PIAZZA CAVOUR
Via Materdei
Via Stella
Via Carbonara
Piazza Cavour
Via Salvator Rosa
Via Sapienza Pisanelli
Il Duomo
Via Tribunali
Piazza Garibaldi
CENTRALE
SANTA CHIARA
Via E. Pessina
Piazza Bellini
Piazza S. Domenico
San Gregorio
Via Vicaria Vecchia
Piazza Dante
Via B. Croce
Via Biagio del Librai
Università
Via Duomo
Corso Umberto I
Corso Umberto I
Stazione Circumvesuviana
Via Marinella
MONTESANTO
FUNICULAR
Stazione Cumana
Via Montesiveto
Piazza del Mercato
Via Nuova Marina
Via A. Diaz
Corso Vittorio Emanuele
Via Medina
Via A. Depretis
Via Cristoforo Colombo
Bacino del Piliero
FUNICULAR
Via Toledo
Piazza Municipio
Stazione Marittima
Via S. Carlo
Piazza Plebiscito
Molo Beverello
Bacino Angiono
Via Chiaia
Piazza d. Martiri
To Chiaia & Mergellina
Via Morelli
Via Santa Lucia
Via N. Sauro
Golfo di Napoli
Via Partenope
Castel dell'Ovo

Church	✝	
Information	ⓘ	
Lighthouse	🗼	
Metro	Ⓜ	

0   1/4 mi
0   0.25 km
N

refer you to metro stops in this chapter. Also, when it's hot, you do not want to go into a hole in the ground.

For out-of-town trips, there are several train stations; the main one, Centrale, has trains that will take you to Pompeii and as far as Sorrento. There is a metro station at the main train station. On the waterfront, you'll find ferries that serve the islands, but you cannot get to the waterfront by metro.

You may also want to book a car and driver for the day; your hotel can do this for you. If you rent a car (the concierge can do this for you, or you can get one on arrival at the airport), don't try to drive in town. And remember, when driving the Amalfi Drive: no *limoncello* for you, *cara*.

THE LAY OF THE LAND

Naples is an enormous city. On a day trip, you will probably only want to visit the nice shopping areas, and have a look at the museums, the palm trees, my castle, and the sea. Watch your handbag.

If you think of the Castel dell'Ovo as the heart of the world, then the various areas to visit can be read as you tell time: The castle is at six o'clock, the Maritime Center is at five o'clock, the Via Constantinople and the National Museum are at one o'clock, the historic old town and street of angels are at two o'clock, and the fancy shopping is at ten o'clock.

WARNING

Please be sure to study a map of Naples before you go off on your own; also make sure that the map is to scale. Learn where everything is in relationship to the main icons. The reason I knew I was being cheated by one of my taxi drivers was that he kept heading in the wrong direction, and I *knew* it was the wrong direction.

The Shopping Scene

Walking up and down and around the fancy shopping district in Naples is actually a treat. There are gorgeous antiques stores and great places for an afternoon gelato. It's a nice half-day shopping excursion, after which you can eat, quit, or move to secret sources or even museums (all with good gift shops). Note that it takes more than a weekend to have a custom-made suit made.

Shopping Hours

Stores are normally open from 9 or 9:30am to 1:30pm and 4 or 4:30pm to 8pm. Nothing is open on Sunday. On Monday, remember that you are in Italy, which means that nothing is open in the morning, and some things will open around 4 or 4:30pm.

On Saturday in summer, stores will close for the day at 1:30pm, but in winter they do reopen in the afternoon. If you need a pharmacy on a Sunday or during off hours, there is a listing in the newspaper with the open stores, or your hotel concierge can guide you to an open pharmacy.

Even street markets get going late here, 9am in fine weather. Don't get to a flea market before 9:30am.

Neighborhoods

Maritime Station and Hotel Heaven   Cruise passengers disembark at the clean, modern, safe Maritime Station, right in Naples near the Castel dell'Ovo, a 2,000-year-old fortress that is a monument; a nice touch, adding a little romance to a commercial seaport. There are several shops in the terminal. There's also a bank and a currency exchange office. When a large ship comes to port, street vendors set up outside.

Castel dell'Ovo   Located directly across the street from the Hotel Vesuvio, right near the Maritime Station, the Castel is on a small island, which also houses several adorable alleys for exploring (no shops, sorry) and many restaurants, bars, pizza places, and seafood eateries. It's adorable and great fun. There's a tourist info stand here too.

Luxury shopping   The main upscale shopping district is a few blocks from the strip of luxury hotels on the waterfront. Just walk along the water (with the castle to your rear) until you come to a clump of palm trees that represent the Piazza Vittorio, turn right, and head "up."

Now it gets slightly tricky as this is a district, and you don't want to miss all the parts—you can, and will, miss part of it if you don't look at a map.

The Via Calabritto is one of the main tony shopping streets (Prada at no. 9) with many of the big-name designers (but not all). It stretches from the Piazza Vittorio to the Piazza dei Martiri and the large **Ferragamo** shop. **Versace** is down the street from Ferragamo. You get the drift. There's a chunk of big names in a nugget right here.

There are a few side streets off the Piazza dei Martiri that will make you feel like you're in Italy; there are some antiques shops located down the Via Domenico Morelli.

The area is not without charm, and you can easily segue to the Via dei Mille and Via Gaetano Filangieri, which have the rest of the luxury shops—**Bulgari, Zegna, Hermès, Frette,** and more.

Via Chiaia   This is a real-people shopping street that's between the luxury shopping district and Via Roma. Use it to cross over from one neighborhood to the other or to get to Via dei Mille—it's all an easy walk. Shopping-wise, there's very little to distract you. Italy-wise, it's great fun.

Via Roma   The Via Roma is the commercial heart of town; it is called Via Toledo lower down and becomes Via Roma near Piazza Dante. This street stretches for 3.2km (2 miles) from the Piazza del Plebiscito, right near the Maritime Station, through the center of town, passing the Piazza Carita on its way to the Piazza Dante and then ending near the National Museum.

La Pignasecca   This is foodie-land, just follow Via Pignasecca and Via Portmedina up and down checking out all the tiny specialty shops. This is a central area in the real-people part of town.

Centro Antico   The core of the old town *(centro antico)* includes the famous Via San Gregorio Armend, the street of angels, where all the miniatures and *presepios* (crèches) are made. But don't look for Via San Gregorio Armend on your map, as it's a small area around the church of the same name. Instead you want to find the rectangular area between the Piazza del Gesu and Piazza Dante, reaching over to the Duomo as its other border. The main streets for shopping, gawking, sightseeing, and absorbing the soul of Naples are Via Croce and Via Tribunali. Via Croce will change its name a few times, so fret not. The area is part of a living history, outdoor-museum program that labels the buildings and tells you the path to walk (and shop).

Port Alba Adjacent to the old town, you find the Port Alba, a medieval doorway that leads to a million bookstores. Just beyond this is the Via Constantinopli, filled with antiques shops. Once a month there is an outdoor flea market on the weekend (except in Aug); see the next section, "Antiques & Flea Markets."

Antiques & Flea Markets

Fiera Antiquaria Napoletana
Via Caracciolo.

Getting to this antiques fair is a little tricky, as there is often confusion about the dates; we were sent on the wrong weekend by knowledgeable people, and the listing in *Dove* magazine was equally unclear. Luckily, you can call the market offices directly (✆ 081/62-19-51) and get the dates for the year. A weekend event, the fair is considered the best in southern Italy; it runs from 8am to 2pm.

Mostra Mercato Constantinopoli
Via Constantinopli.

A weekend fair never held on the same weekend as the other fair (Via Caracciolo, see above), this is a more casual event in the street of antiques shops with dealers set up on sidewalks and under tents. Don't bother going if the weather is bad. ✆ 0347/486-37-15. antiquario@tightrope.it.

Local Heroes

MARIANO RUBINACCI
Via Filangieri 26.

This shop is large, sells designer clothes, and offers a sort of Ralph Lauren–local-preppy look, complete with a series of silk scarves that would make Mr. Dumas-Hermès weep with envy. The scarves depict various scenes in Neapolitan history, geography, or iconography and are sold in some hotel and museum gift shops as well. Prices vary depending on the difficulty of the silk screen and range from 120€ to 200€ ($150–$250). The best luxury souvenir in town. © 081/415-793. www. marianorubinacci.it.

MARINELLA'S
Riviera di Chiaia 287.

This itty-bitty tie shop is one of the most famous addresses in Naples. Come holiday season, lines stretch down the street, there are no ties in stock, and shoppers are issued chits, which they gift-wrap to present. The store creates custom ties, as long, short, wide, or thin as you want or need. © 081/764-4214.

MAXI HO
Via Nisco 20; Riviera di Chiaia 95; multiple other locations.

Despite its silly-sounding name, this is one of the best stores in Naples. The various addresses are mostly in the luxury district and are not branches of the same store, but extensions of the store selling different looks. Each store sells a different group of designer brands geared for a certain look or age group. Call © 081/414-721 or 081/247-0072.

UPIM
Via Nisco 11.

Upim is a chain of dime stores, famous throughout Italy. There is a branch right in the heart of the fine shopping area, a

Shoppers Beware

Whether you are on your own or on a ship tour, you may be taken to "factories" to go shopping—be careful, they may or may not offer the real thing, or real deals. They certainly offer kickbacks to your guide.

two-level store with tons of clothes, home fashions, and even underwear. I buy a lot of La Perla copies at Upim and love them. © 081/417-520. www.upim.it.

CAPRI

In Capri, I'm always too busy with the jewelry stores, the sandals, the latest incarnations of Tod's shoes and handbags, the cottons and the cashmeres, and even the lemons to get to the beach or to notice who's not wearing what. Capri is a shopping port. Capri is a shopping day trip. Capri is a spree. This is a town that has streets that are more like alleys, where you stroll in total contentment, remembering Jackie Kennedy, and you happily get lost and found in this maze.

You can research and buy lemon booze from a so-called lemon factory or two, ride in a convertible '57 Chevy stretch (with fins), buy plastic pens with your name on them in Italian, or sink deeply into **Gucci, Prada, Fendi, Hermès,** and all the better names of international and Italian fashion. In between, of course, you eat, sip, stare, and take a nap. The place to hang out? La Piazetta in the center of Capri.

Getting There

You may arrive by cruise ship (and tender ashore) or by hydrofoil from Naples, Amalfi, Sorrento, or another port or resort town. Regardless of how you actually arrive, you'll land near

Secret Source to Capri

If you want a private boat to take you to Capri, contact **Gianni Chervatin** (© 081/837-68-95), former general manager of the Grand Hotel Quisiana in Capri, who arranges jet-set details for the rich and famous. There is a public hydrofoil every half-hour in season.

the funicular that takes you up to Capri proper. Sunglasses, please. If you have luggage, there are porters at the pier. They happen to be very honest, so don't fret.

Although I usually get to Capri via cruise ship, on my last visit I took the hydrofoil from Naples. The trip lasts about 45 minutes, costs about 9.60€ ($12) each way, and is most pleasant if you are on a larger vessel with space around you. There's a ferry or hydrofoil almost every hour; they all arrive at the same place in Capri, but they depart from different stations in Naples, depending on which line you book.

The Lay of the Land

The island of Capri is rather big and has much more to it than just the resort town of Capri. From a serious shopping perspective, you can skip Anacapri, although it's fun visually.

In fact, I think you'll be surprised at the sprawl of downtown Capri. Best yet, a lot of it is hidden in back alleys, so take some time to look at a map. If you follow the main tourist trail, you'll miss the best stuff.

The Shopping Scene

As cruise ports go, Capri ain't bad. There are a lot of stores and a sprinkling of designer shops—small branches of **Prada, Gucci, Fendi, Ferragamo, Malo, Alberta Ferretti, Exte, Tod's, Ferragamo, Hermès,** and so on. As a beach town, Capri has become famous for its sandals, and there are scads of no-name shops selling the latest looks, as well as copies of the latest looks.

There are several *profumeri* (perfume shops). Each one carries several brands on an exclusive basis, but no single shop carries every brand. If you inquire about a brand that a store doesn't carry, the clerk is likely to try to trade you over to the brand they sell, rather than tell you to walk down the street or around the corner. There is also lemon perfume.

The emphasis in Capri is on high-quality goods and cheap sandals; the resort fashions are very body-revealing, in the southern Italian style. Note that the style of goods and the shopping experience is so totally different from Positano (which I discuss later in this chapter) that there is virtually no overlap.

SHOPPING HOURS

Stores open around 9 to 9:30am and close at 1pm, although more and more are staying open during lunch. Those that close will reopen around 3:30pm and stay open until 7pm. Big names tend to be open nonstop.

The tourist traps (TTs) down by the port usually stay open during lunch and are often open until 8pm in the summer.

Stores are open on Sunday.

Note that the season begins March 15 and ends October 15; most stores are closed out of season. It's not unusual for the same owners to have a similar shop in Cortina or another Italian ski resort for the winter season.

THE BEST BUYS IN CAPRI

Cottons and cashmeres   Despite the heat, cashmere is one of the leading lights of Capri. There are several specialty shops that sell premium cashmeres—some of them also sell cottons.

Jewelry   Until I visited Capri and saw its magnificent jewelry, I'd never been one for important (or even real) jewelry. Now I've been converted. There's a good bit of latitude on price. If you have a few thousand dollars, you may be very happy.

Lemons   We're still in southern Italy, so there's lemon vodka galore. I also buy fresh lemons in the market down near the port.

Shoes   Capri has all sorts of shoe stores, from the fancy **Ferragamo** shop and little hole-in-the-wall stores that sell 24€ ($30) pairs of sandals to stores that sell **Tod's** and other designer brands.

SHOPPING NEIGHBORHOODS

Marina Grande   This is where your ship's tender or your ferry or hydrofoil comes to port; on the pier, there's a Customs office and a pushcart vendor selling fresh fruit in newspaper cones and ices. You'll also find several TTs teeming with Blue Grotto souvenirs, a liquor store, a minimart, and the funicular, which takes you up to Capri proper.

Main Street Capri   Capri has two main streets, Via Vittorio Emanuele and Via Camarelle. The former dead-ends to the latter when you hit the **Hotel Quisisana.** If you are facing the hotel from Via Vittorio Emanuele, bear left to explore Via Camarelle.

The island's toniest shops can be found here, selling everything from antiques and jewelry to expensive resort wear and affordable sandals.

Back Street Downtown   Hidden from view, but running parallel to Vittorio Emanuele, is a pedestrian alley—Via Fuorlovado—that is crammed with real-people shops. Don't miss the chance to prowl this street; it's far more charming than the main tourist thoroughfare.

Via Roma   The Via Roma in Capri is what the British call a high street; it's where the bus station is located and where you'll find the main thrust of the town's real-people shopping.

FINDS

ALBERTO & LINA
Via Vittorio Emanuele 18.

This is one of the leading jewelers in town, part of a family that owns several jewelry shops. In case you haven't already guessed, Italian women define themselves and their success in life vis-à-vis their jewelry, which they buy in places like this and wear all of the time. Yes, even to the beach and right into the sea. That's how we all know it's real gold. ✆ 081/837-0643.

CARTHUSIA PROFUMI
Viale Parco Augusto 2.

I am more amused by this store than serious about it, but I have met people who make this a ritual stop when they are in town. Before she had her own perfume line, Liz Taylor was supposed to have been a regular customer. Don't miss the photo op with the tiles on the front of the store. This is a perfumer who makes a local scent that you can only get here; it's very lemony. Cute gifts. ✆ 081/837-0368. www.carthusia.com.

LA CAPANNINA PIÙ
Via Le Botteghe 12bis/14.

This is a very fancy gourmet food store, not at all funky. They sell all sorts of imported foods, so watch out for the English brands—but much to see, touch, and taste. ✆ 081/837-0732. www.capannina-capri.com.

MARCELLO RUBINACCI
Via Camarelle 9.

This is my favorite shop in Capri—I come here first to stare at the colors, touch the cashmeres, sigh about the quality of quality, and then buy a few T-shirts. Because the T-shirts are about 40€ ($50) each, this is my idea of extravagance. Hand-wash your cottons from this store; we had big-time shrinkage when we used the washer/dryer. This brand has expanded and has stores in Naples, Rome, and elsewhere around Italy.

SORRENTO

Most of you will probably arrive by car, train, or tour bus from Naples or Pompeii. A few lucky ones will arrive by cruise ship. However you come, you should stay long enough to see my favorite limoncello.

Of course, Sorrento is more than a chance for a dime store. The little square and the carriages that are pulled by donkeys in fancy dress hats, the narrow alleys crammed with crates heaped with fruits and vegetables, the faience spilling from the stores, the overlook with the view down into the Bay of Naples . . . hmmmm, this is what we saved all that money for. This is what southern Italy is all about.

Sorrento is also the gateway to Positano and the rest of the Amalfi Coast. You can rent a car in Sorrento and drive yourself there. (If you're on a cruise, your ship will even arrange your car rental.) If you're feeling more adventurous, take a bus from the station in Sorrento. Even if Gore Vidal hasn't invited you to the villa for lunch, you're going to want to spend as much time as possible in these gorgeous, adorable, and ever-so-chic hill towns.

Getting There

You can take the train or a bus from Naples, drive, hire a car and driver, or take the hydrofoil from Naples or the ferry from Capri, a mere 8km (5 miles) away.

If you are driving, forget all this hillside nonsense; you'll arrive right at town level and can ignore the port itself. If you're staying only a matter of hours, head right to **Grand Hotel Ambasciatori** (Via Califano 18), which has parking on premises. Or park near the Via Fuonmura, in the heart of town, and then walk. Parking in town is difficult.

The Lay of the Land

Like many Italian resort cities, Sorrento is built on a hill above the harbor. You will come to port at Porto Marina Piccola, and then catch a shuttle bus up into the heart of town, Piazza Tasso. You can walk, but it's pretty far, very steep, and the road is curvy and dangerous.

Cruise passengers can take the ship's shuttle bus. If you miss it, or need instant gratification, a taxi to and from town and the marina costs about 8€ ($10). Like the taxi drivers in Naples, they'll try to run up the meter. (For less than a couple of euros each way, you can take a public bus.) Taxis in town congregate at the **Piazza Tasso,** lining up on the Via Fuonmura.

The Shopping Scene

Sorrento has a lot of charm to it, visually, emotionally, and even from a shopping perspective. There's no serious shopping, but there are several opportunities here that you won't find elsewhere.

While Sorrento has only one or two designer shops (there's an **Emporio Armani**), it does have a branch of **Standa,** one of the best dime stores in Italy, so you can have some serious fun here. Along with a main shopping street, there's a pedestrian back street that's shady and picturesque.

And there are lemons to buy. And where there are lemons, there's *limoncello.* Don't drink *limoncello* and drive, especially when we're talking about the Amalfi Drive!

SHOPPING HOURS

Stores open around 8:30 to 9am and close about 2pm for lunch. They reopen around 4pm. When there are ships in port, hours can be a little more flexible. The major department store in town, **A. Gargiulo & Jannuzzi,** Via Fuonmura, is open (non-stop, mind you) from 8am to 10pm in season.

Banks are open Monday to Friday 9am to 1:30pm and 3 to 4pm. This town is closed on Sunday.

SHOPPING NEIGHBORHOODS

Piazza Tasso   This is the proverbial town square: It's in the middle of everything, and many streets branch off in different directions, with each street offering different shopping opportunities. The donkey carts that you can rent for a trot about town are also here.

Corso Italia   This is the main real-people shopping street. It goes across the city and has two different personalities.

The portion that stretches to your right, if your back is to the sea and the donkeys are in front of you, is the main shopping street, with branches of **Lacoste** (very expensive!), the leather goods and shoe store, **Pollini,** and a few cafes.

Via Fuoro   This is everyone's favorite street because it's a pedestrian alley; no cars, just tourists. There are drug stores, grocery stores, ceramics shops—in sum, everything that's authentically Italian.

Via de Maio   This is the road that leads to the main square from the marina; the 2 blocks before you get to the square are filled with stores—some of which are quite nice. There are also two excellent pharmacies here.

Via Fuonmura   Leading away from town, this street just has a few stores on it and a hotel or two, but it's home to **A. Gargiulo & Jannuzzi** (see below).

FINDS

A. GARGIULO & JANNUZZI
Viale E. Caruso 1.

This is the largest department store in Sorrento, and it was designed for tourists. In business since 1853, it's open from 8am to 10pm nonstop. It's air-conditioned and accustomed to foreign visitors. (They speak English perfectly.) This is not a TT, but rather a sprawling space in several buildings with entire departments devoted to different crafts of the area. The section of the store farthest from the entrance is a ceramics shop. There's a linens department with exquisite work (some of it deservedly very, very expensive), a portion of the store that sells the local inlaid wood marquetry, and some touristy souvenirs near the entrance. © 081/878-1041. www.gargiulo-jannuzzi.it.

LIMONORO
Via San Cesareo 49/53.

This is my favorite limoncello factory; it's pretty—lots of white tile—and has a great selection. There are many different sizes of products, gift packages, and beautiful lemon-laden wrapping paper. © 081/878-5348. www.limonoro.it.

POSITANO

The famed Amalfi Drive begins shortly after you bypass Sorrento and enter the kingdom of the curves, a twisty road that skirts the coast from above and often makes me queasy . . . and very grateful for my regular driver, Franco, who is always booked for me by the Hotel Le Sirenuse.

I never need go farther than Positano, but you can go all the way to Salerno, shopping as you go. Me? Bury my heart in Positano, where it simply can't get much better. And everyone speaks English.

Visitors say Positano; locals say Posi. So, while a day in Sorrento is a pleasant enough way to spend some time, if you're a do-everything kind of person on a cruise or a limited schedule, you can get through the pleasures of Sorrento (pleasurably) in 2 hours, and then be on your way to Posi, via the Amalfi Drive.

Cruise passengers can rent a car for the day, or take a taxi. There's even a public bus from Sorrento for the truly determined (one-way fare is less than 1.60€/$2).

Some of the stores in Posi close for lunch at 1pm and will not reopen until 3 or 3:30pm, so you want to make sure to allow time for shopping before lunch.

Then again, you can avoid the pressure by simply booking yourself into town and staying for a few days. There is water transportation directly from Naples, weather permitting.

The Lay of the Land

Positano is one of the famed hill-clinging towns; it is literally dug into the side of a cliff and terraces itself from the beach to the top of a small mountain. There are some main streets, but most of the shopping is along pedestrian alleys and walkways. What I call "uptown" is the Via Colombo; what I call "downtown" is the Via Mulini. In this city, you are either up or down (or prone). Certainly, the land lies between the black sands and Le Sirenuse; visitors with limited mobility and those who are infirm, short of step or breath, or simply lazy might want to reconsider. The lay of the land is vertical, not horizontal.

The Shopping Scene

If you haven't already learned the International Rule of Inaccessibility, this is a good time to learn it. What makes a city into the kind of haven that the rich and famous like to visit is its inaccessibility to the masses. All the great resort cities of the world, especially in the Mediterranean, are hard to get to.

This being understood, Positano is the center for the rich and famous along the Amalfi Coast. It is adorable, and its stores sell fun things. There are very few tourist traps and no branches of The Gap. On the other hand, the selection gets to look uniform in short order; there are only a handful of stores that sell designer clothes or nonresort items that you might wear in the real world if you don't live in the U.S. sunbelt.

The scene is antithetical to what's happening on Capri. Here it's more laid back, and the look is sort of rich-hippie casual. It's a movie set, and stores display their wares to enchant . . . and sell. Flowers pour out of flowerpots, dishes are piled up on stairwells, cottons fly in the slight breeze, and lemons are dancing everywhere.

Dishes and pottery are big things; many stores sell them, and all stores seem to sell so much of the same thing that you soon get dizzy. There aren't as many jewelry shops as in Capri—the emphasis here is less on the body and more on

comfort or home style. There are bathing-suit and clothing boutiques, but they sell funky fashions and comfortable things, even
comfortably tiny bikinis. Many of the stores specialize in what
I call Mamma Mia fashions: clothes made for short, wide
women with a large bosom. I buy these clothes because they
hide the waist and hips and allow for great comfort and eating space. Pass the pasta, please.

SHOPPING HOURS

Stores open at 9am and close for lunch around 1pm, reopen-
ing at 3, 3:30, or 4pm, and stay open until 7 or 8pm. Many
stores are closed out of season, from mid-October until around
March 15. Stores are open on Sunday and on Monday
morning.

FINDS

CERAMICA ASSUNTA
Via Colombo 97.

Just a few doors downhill and closer to town from Emporio
de Sirenuse, this large shop has a wide selection of local ceramics in assorted styles. Most of the ceramic shops sell more or
less the same wares, but this store is large enough for you to
see everything. They pack and ship and will deliver to your
hotel. ✆ 089/875-008. www.ceramicassunta.it.

EMPORIO DE SIRENUSE
Via Colombo 30 (across the street from Le Sirenuse hotel).

This is where I first discovered my idol, Lisa Corti, and where
I first fell in love with my dear friend Carla, who buys for the
shop and has the eye of a maven, whom I trust with all things
Italian. The tiny shop is a mélange of gorgeous tiles set into
the floors, hand-painted cabinets and armoires, and merchandise in gorgeous colors, all chosen to reflect the energy of
the resort and the passion of the sea.

The Lay of the Clay

Maybe it has something to do with thousands of years of lava and ocean spray and shifting earth and great good luck, but the Amalfi area is home to fabulous clay and is therefore the place to buy dishes. Every other store in Positano sells dishes, but every town in the area has its share. Remember when buying dishes that prices may be low but shipping isn't.

A few years ago there was a hand-painted look that caught on which every store sold. That theme is passé now and solid rustic colors are in style, with a contrast raw border through which you can see some of the baked terra cotta.

For the most fun, head to the Vietri factory in the town of Vietri-sur-Mare, near Salerno. The entire town is filled with factories and stores, but Vietri itself (a popular brand with strong U.S. distribution) allows you into the factory to buy or to design your own wares. ✆ 800/277-5933. www.vietri.com.

Solimene is another firm that does much of the same. ✆ 089/210-243. www.solimene.com.

While perhaps 30% of the merchandise is from Lisa Corti (thank God), the clothes come from Missoni, Etro, and many smaller designers that Americans may not know. Prices are fair, certainly no higher than elsewhere, despite this being a fancy resort. Although I had bought a mound of Corti things in Milan, I ended up with three more tablecloths—different designs I could not live without.

This is one of the best stores in Italy and is worth the trip to Posi if you love color and flair and the art of the unique. There is also a catalog and online business. ✆ 089/812-2026. www.emporiosirenuse.com.

Chapter Ten

....

HIDDEN ITALY

SEEK & YE SHALL FIND

Maybe it's just because I have been writing the Born to Shop series for more than 20 years, or maybe it's because I'm such a sensitive little flower, but on my last research trips to Italy—to do this revision—I had the most fun in the get-away-from-it-all cities, the places I call Hidden Italy. They are hidden in plain sight, of course, and easy to get to by car, train, and even low-cost air flight.

I am not dissing the old faithfuls. I stand to paraphrase that chestnut about London . . . when a man is tired of Venice he is tired of living. But I dream of taking my kids, my tour groups, my beloved ones to Bologna, Parma, Verona, and beyond. What I have seen has awakened new places in my heart and my wanderlust and yes, my suitcase.

While we're talking about my dreams, I think it's only fair to throw in some information about nightmares. I thought that driving around northern Italy and popping into real factories and factory stores would be a dream come true; I thought that Turin, as the host of the 2006 Winter Olympic Games, would be a dream to revisit since I hadn't been there in years. I figured athletic readers would want to shop. I thought it would be fun to return to San Remo and maybe even see what changes are afoot or afloat in Genoa. In my mind, it was all perfect. It wasn't even going to be fattening.

I was very, very wrong on some of those dreams. While Turin may turn out to be brilliant, when I visited for this edition, the work for the Games was in full thrust—the traffic was horrible, many roads were closed, blocked, or diverted, and the most fabulous part of the city was suddenly the industrial suburb of Lingotto where I stayed in a Renzo Piano–designed, luxury Art + Tech Hotel built right into a FIAT factory. I barely even got into downtown Turin, and I never found any Olympic Games T-shirts to sleep in or to hand out as gifts. If Turin is fabulous, it escaped me.

If endless driving behind trucks on a single lane of road is fabulous, that too escaped me.

Be careful what you wish for, you just might get it.

RULES OF THE ROAD

I spent the better part of 2 weeks driving the roads of northern Italy. I did most of it with Dede Parma, a girlhood friend (the only Desdemona in our eighth-grade class in San Antonio, Texas) who you might have already guessed has Italian parents, black hair and blue eyes, and speaks glossy, fluent Italian. In all honesty, you don't want to make this trip without Dede.

Dede has a Blackberry and an office back in Philadelphia where slaves wait on her every call, demand, command, question, and whim. Without that team in the U.S. to look up things online for us and relay information across the sea, we would probably still be out there between the seven hills of Rome and the Swiss border.

This is not to complain—we had a great time. It is to say this is my job; it was not Dede's, and if you are on vacation, you may not want to spend your hard-earned downtime driving behind trucks, being cut off by Italian madmen drivers, and calling outlets in your less-than-flawless Italian to ask if you are near yet.

French country roads are well marked. Italian *highways* are not even moderately well marked, and country roads are so hopeless that Dede, at one point, announced we were on Highway 50 for many hours when, it fact, 50 was the posted speed limit.

There were no restaurants when it was lunchtime or when we wanted to eat. Grocery stores where we thought we could grab picnic supplies may or may not have been open during the lunch break. Factories—or their stores—were often not marked. Directions given in factory outlet guides seemed easy to follow in the bookstore but impossible to match to existing roads. Road conditions were often deplorable, especially on super highways where all lanes, save one, were closed and you had to drive single file behind a convoy of trucks while a madman on a Moto Guzzi motorcycle wove in and out of traffic.

Just keep this in mind: The reason you want to go to northern Italy to drive all around to the factory outlet stores is that the area is filled with factories. So far, so good. But wait. Remember this part: Where there are factories, there are trucks. Why didn't I think of that before I booked this trek?

In my most desperate moments, I prayed that I was in Manhattan with the ability to walk into Bergdorf Goodman and pay full retail price for any desired goods. The notion of a bargain hardly seemed worth the trouble it took for the excursion.

With the same breath, may I say that the driving in the south—actually the middle of Italy—was a pleasure possibly because there were neither as many factories nor as many trucks. Hidden Italy is somewhat hidden from the crazies as well, so I suggest that this chapter might be your guide and your bible if you want to get out there and hit the road, Lorenzo.

If your trip is planned as a romantic getaway or on the basis of relaxation, I'd reconsider an extended driving trip to outlets and outlet malls. If you are doing some of the hidden cities and driving a little in between and hitting a favorite outlet or two, you should be fine. Just remember this last warning: A French driver will tell you are beautiful before he screws you. Not so an Italian driver.

BOLOGNA

Located just about midway between Milan and Florence, Bologna is the most perfect Italian city—not just in Italy, but in the world—because it has the infrastructure to work as a tourist town, but is not so overwhelmed with visitors that the charm has been choked away.

The city has good shopping in terms of all the big brands you may want to buy. It has a good market (Fri–Sat only) and enough well-located luxury hotels to offer choice at a price, as well as delights for those who need them.

Bologna is also a huge university town. As such, there's plenty for teens and 'tweens and those on a low budget. The number of accessible mass-market stores offering low-cost fashion is staggering. There are plenty of stores that sell to plus sizes as well.

Finally, Bologna is one of the most famous food towns in all of Italy. Yes, I'm talking to you. Gelati to die for.

Getting There

This part of Italy is called Emilia-Romagna. Foodies know it as the center of Italian eats. Shoppers know it as the home of various shoe factories and outlet malls. It is pretty much in the center of the country and easy to reach. Bologna is located on the main rail line between Milan and Florence.

- If you can easily connect to the low-cost carriers, the Bologna airport (Marconi) is served by several carriers from either the U.K. or continental Europe.

Bologna

Armonie Naturali **5**
Central Food Market
and Fisherman Street **6**
Market **2**

Oltre **3**
Oviesse **1**
Tzemis **4**

- The drive north from Florence is relatively easy—slightly more than an hour of good highway. Note, however, that this highway becomes one big parking lot on certain travel days or during rush hour. If you plan to drive, do so with much organization.

Booking There

Any good tour operator or smart travel agent will advise you of the fair dates in Bologna. There are many of them and they tend to take all the available hotel space, driving up rates in the process. The fairs are booked years in advance and can be discovered through various ways, including contacting the Bologna Fiere (© **051/282-111**; www.bolognafiere.it).

There's also the CST, Centro Servizi per Turisti (© **800/856-065** in Italy, or 051/648-7607; www.cst.bo.it), which is a tourist organization that helps with dates, hotels, and so on.

Gliterateri Gelateri

One of these gelato locations comes from a famous American food writer, and one of them is my personal find—do a taste test and see for yourself. Hint: Aceto balsamico is a fabulous flavor.

OREFICERIA DEL GELATO
Via degli Orefici 5/f.

GELATERIA STEFINO
Via Galliera 49/b.

Getting Around

The beauty of this town is that you really can walk just about everywhere. The train station is not far from the heart of town.

If you have a car, it is forbidden to drive in the city center, or you must have a pass from your hotel. If you are stopped by a policeman, tell him (or mime) which hotel you are headed to and ask the best directions. Once you arrive at the hotel, have them call the police with your license plate number so that you are not given a ticket. Even if police do not stop you on entering the city center, still ask the hotel desk to give the police your plate numbers.

Should you need a taxi, call © **051/372-727**, which is easy enough to remember. This is a radio taxi service, so you will pay when the driver heads out to fetch you.

If you are out at the fairgrounds or merely in town for a day but with a car, you can park and ride—there is a shuttle bus that will get you into the historical center of town in 8 minutes. The shuttle bus ticket entitles you to free parking in the adjoining lot.

Insider's secret: Bologna is a great city to base yourself for exploration of Italy—you can go to Florence on the train as a day trip and not have to worry about parking, traffic, or hotels. In fact, you are just about equidistant between Florence and Verona (see the section on Verona, later in this chapter, for more about this city).

Sleeping There

ART HOTELS

Hotel Orologio, Via IV Novembre 10.
Hotel Corona d'Oro, Via Oberdan 12.
Hotel Novecento, Piazza Galilei 4/3.
Hotel Commercianti, Via De'Pignattari 11.

I found this small, family-owned hotel chain through Charming Italy (www.charmingitaly.net) and was delighted with the travel site's insider tips. The four hotels in this chain provide parking for guests, which is no small task in this city.

I stayed at the Orologio, the exact three-star hotel we all want to find; the only thing wrong with it was the noisy Americans over at one table at breakfast. The hotel has a small lobby, and then you go upstairs to what is a normal hotel lobby complete with a free e-mail station.

There are 50 rooms; mine had beams and a window with a view out to the main square. Indeed, the hotel is right off the main square and a few steps from one of the central shopping streets. Rates are under 160€ ($200) per night, depending on season and the kind of room. Comparison shoppers may want to note that a suite here costs less than a room at the deluxe Grand Hotel Baglioni.

If you want a fancier hotel, Corono d'Oro is a four-star that is heaven—very luxe—a renovated palace dating back to 1890. Rates here begin at 160€ ($200). Its location is closer to the town's famed towers, on the other side of the square from the Orologio, and also in a key position for shopping. Some of the rooms are more modern, and there are junior suites that are divided with a partition that almost makes an office.

There are two other properties in the family. A short block from Orologio, Hotel Novocento is a four-star with a good location, and is a brand-new, modern, Zen-decor, boutique hotel. The Commercianti is a three-star, and the least charming of the bunch. © 800/908-901 in Italy, or 051/745-7335; www. bolognarthotels.it.

GRAND HOTEL BAGLIONI
Via dell Independenza 8.

The luxury hotel of the city where rock stars, celebrities, business honchos, and diplomats stay. When I was there, the crowd out front was awaiting Bruce Springsteen. The hotel is very grand; you eat breakfast in a charming little glass-enclosed courtyard. The location is smack dab in the middle of the main commercial shopping street and you are not far from the train station or the Friday/Saturday market. While the Grand caters to businessmen, and is always full during fairs, the hotel is the "in" place for all who need or appreciate grand in all senses of the word. Use of computers in the hotel's business center is free, by the way. You can make reservations through Leading Hotels of the World (www.lhw.com) or contact the hotel directly. © 800/745-8883 or 051/225-445; www.baglioni hotels.com.

Snack & Shop

Bologna is an eaters' paradise; you will have no trouble finding cafes with tiny sandwiches, pizza, pasta, and, yes, spaghetti Bolognese.

The Shopping Scene

Take a few centuries worth of history, many universities, throw in a large arena for business fairs, and what do you get? This is a great place to shop with branches of all the big Italian multiples and even a few fancy-schmancy shops such as **Chanel,** which is not even in Florence but is here through a local franchise.

Motown

I am very new to the motorcycle culture, so forgive me if I rant and rave about basics that everyone else knows. However, I find this is important reporting for guys and for women whose husbands might be complaining about a few days out for shopping.

Hey, big spender, sit back and relax—many cars and even more motorcycles are made in the Bologna area—there's shopping, there's riding, there are museums, and there are things to buy and ship. You can even now take your motorcycle on the train with you throughout Italy.

If your dream is to drive a Ferrari (since you figure you'll never own one), Maria Teresa Berdondini has a tour that allows you a few hours to ride. Contact her at **Tuscany by Tuscans** (© 0572/70-467; www.tuscanybytuscans.it). It's expensive, but less than the cost of a new car.

Motorstars (© 059/921-667; www.motorstars.org) is another tour company that offers many formats of tours and rides. The folks here speak English. Their most popular event is an all-day Saturday tour where you tour factories, meet drivers and experts, and shop with an employee discount.

Nearby factories include Ducati, Ferrari, Maserati, and Lamborghini.

Throw into the mix the food markets and stalls, the little mom-and-pop shops, and the chance to get to nearby outlet malls and perhaps you have the very definition of heaven. Oops, I forgot to mention the architecture that is so astonishingly medieval that you will feel like a character in one of Shakespeare's plays. Hmmm, did people in Shakespeare's plays carry shopping bags?

Do not underestimate the number of young people in town as a large influence for retailers. The stores that specialize in well-priced clothing are large, often have many branches through the different parts of town, and are well stocked. You've never seen so much fashion at a price in your life.

As a final note, there is a large market—held on Fridays and Saturdays—that sells a little of everything. Because the shoe-making regions are nearby, the market has especially good deals on shoes. I bought sandals for 12€ ($15) a pair, and I have enormous American feet, so if I can get a fit, anyone can.

The market vendors work on a rotation, so if you are not in town on market day, find out which city has market when you are around. *Insider's tip:* Aim for the market in Modena if at all possible.

Foodie Tours

For a 1-day cooking class in town, contact **Cook Italy** (© 0349/007-8298; www.cookitaly.com). The class takes you to the central food market to shop for ingredients, then you cook your own lunch. The tour lasts 4 or 5 hours and costs 104€ ($130),

If you don't want to cook but do want a guided tour of local food shops and markets, you can book a walking tour that lasts 3 hours and costs 58€ ($72) per person.

La Vecchia Scuola Bolognese (© 051/649-1576; www.la vecchiascuola.com) is the other local cooking school where English is spoken. Their classes specialize in making and cooking pasta.

Shopping Neighborhoods

Main Square   With a large statue of Neptune in the center, the main square (Piazza Maggiore) is not so much a shopping square as it is a directional point from which most things begin or end. The tourist office is on this square and with it an excellent shop for souvenirs.

Via Indipendenza   This is the main commercial drag of town in terms of flagships of the big brands. The street also leads to the market, is home to the Grand Hotel Baglioni, and leads in and out of town and/or toward the train station. There are plenty of cafes, restaurants, outdoor dining, perfumeries, gelati stands, and stores selling cheap thrills. Among some of the finds: **Armonie Naturali** (no. 58/c), which sells the Perlier and Kelemata brand of bath and beauty products; **Tezemis** (no. 34), which sells adorable and low-cost pajamas and underwear for young women; and **Oltre** (nos. 24b/d), a large-sizes brand.

Just off the Via Indipendenza, and impossible to find if you don't know to look for it, is an enormous **Oviesse,** a branch of one of my favorite brands for low-cost Italian fashions. Ask for directions to Via dei Mille 16.

Ugo Bassi   Forgive me, this is confusing and not very funny, but I keep thinking the name of this street is Hugo Boss. It is the main cross street and it intersects Via Indipendzena, forming the two main arteries of town. Ugo Bassi changes its name to Via Rizzoli early on; this too is a main shopping drag.

Via Clavature   This is a small, pedestrian-only shopping street filled with some small branch stores of chains (LUSH) and many mom-and-pop stores offering upscale fashion and style. It leads away from the main square and the more commercial shopping districts.

Fishermen   The street of the old fishermen (Via Pescherie Vecchie) is the heart of the food district. It leads away from the Main Square and is nestled right alongside Via Rizzoli. Aside from the central market, there are scads of food shops and boutiques. Note that this is the core of a neighborhood of several streets, not the only street to see or shop. There are many designer boutiques on this street, including Chanel. Locals call this area the Mercato di Mezzo; it is truly a medieval warren of little alleys. Don't miss **Majani,** on Via Carbonesi, an old-fashioned chocolate maker who is, naturally, closed in the summer.

Ghetto   Like most medieval towns, Bologna has a Jewish ghetto that is still a vibrant part of the commercial zone. While you might not find any designer boutiques, you will find olive oil and food stores. The ghetto is located near the Two Towers and Via Rizzoli.

PARMA & AREA

I was particularly drawn to Parma because of my old friend Dede Parma. When I mentioned to friends that I planned to explore it, they all mentioned either Parma ham or Parmesan cheese. No fools, these friends. Parma isn't where you go if you were born to shop—it's for those who were born to eat, or born to shop for foodstuffs.

I ended up in Parma on a Sunday after a half-day at the nearby Fidenza Village outlet mall. Only the local department store was open, so it was not a day for shoppers, and frankly, it's not a city for shoppers. This is a city for dreamers, for those who worship the miracles that humans make in the name of religion, and for those who want to go to markets, to nearby villages, and to cheese houses. This is a city for those who believe in magic.

Oh, yes, once a year there is a very large antiques fair, an international dealers' affair that is worth coming to visit. Bring business cards.

There are also antiques, markets, stores, and food sources in nearby Modena. I didn't get there this trip but you don't have to make the same mistake. The closest I actually got to Modena was the gas station and Autogrill right outside of town (Nutella sold in a huge glass pitcher, 6.75€/$8.45). I mention Modena now for several reasons. It is not very far from Bologna and is a good market town. Modena also is the far eastern part of northwestern Italy and the easternmost anchor to the shopping one can do on a north-south access between Genoa and Milan or Turin and Como. There are plenty of outlets in the area.

I did buy wonderful shoes from a man who not only works the Modena market but has a shoe store there, so if you're looking for a starting point, try **Le Occasioni di Porta Portese,** Viale della' Cittadella 57 (© **054/214-706;** taccher@tiscali.it). His specialty is designer overstocks for men and women.

ACADEMIA BARILLA
Largo Calamandrei 3/a, Parma.

Foodies please note that while Italy is crawling with designer pasta brands, good old Barilla—king of supermarket pasta—has its own cooking school, offering a range of courses from 1 to 10 days. © **866-77-academia.** www.academiabarilla.com.

AGRINASCENTE
Via S.M. Campagna 22/b, Fidenza.

Forgive me, but I have nicknamed this store The Big Cheese, and I know you will always call it that once you visit and see the trade sign on the road—a giant triangular wedge of cheese. Locals know that any time they see a hexagonal store—looking much like a gunpowder magazine for those of us who remember the tour of Williamsburg—that a cheese house lies within. Most cheese homes sell more than cheese these days.

This particular cheese house is a virtual deli, just lacking the Zabar family and a few dill pickles and onion bagels. They have local wines, oils, vinegars, and, of course, cheese. You can buy the cheese prepacked or ask them to cut it for you. The price is based on the age; the expensive stuff is the oldest and is not exported to the U.S.

Speaking of which, to answer your next question: yes. Yes, it is legal to bring cheese into the U.S. if it has been aged more than 60 days.

If you are attracted to this kind of shopping experience, I am going to assume that you are used to cheese that costs 16€ ($20) a kilo and balsamic vinegar that costs 36€ ($45) for a teeny-weeny bottle. For heaven's sake, don't shell out for the expensive stuff to give as gifts to people who have no idea what it is, how much it costs, or how to use it. Remember, with a lot of these products, a little dab will do ya.

Final tip: Ask for a piece of the special wax paper; once you have taken the plastic off your cheese, it will keep better in the fridge if wrapped in this paper.

This store is open on Sundays until 3pm. © 0524/522-334.
www.agrinascente.it.

FIDENZA VILLAGE
Via San Michele Campagna, Fidenza.

I know I write about stores, not food, but in this part of Italy
it's hard to not think about food. So it's with pleasure that I
report that the best restaurant I have ever enjoyed in an outlet mall is at Fidenza Village. **Barlumeria** bills itself as a cheese
bar, but there's also restaurant service, sandwiches, takeout,
a deli, and even some tastings.

When you plan your shopping trip here, plan the day so
that you can eat lunch here. Also note that Italians tend to think
about lunch around 1pm and eat thereafter. If you go to lunch
around 12:30, the crowds shouldn't be too bad.

Now then, about the mall. The second phase is being built
right now but I had a pretty good time with the mall about a
year after it opened. Created in the style of a fake Italian village populated by Verdi's operas, the mall only lacks blaring
music—say, "Grand March" from *Aida*—and perhaps a herd
of elephants.

The drive from Bologna city center takes 45 minutes on a
Sunday morning—figure an hour during the week. Stay on the
highway (A1) until you exit for Fidenza and then follow signs
for Fashion Village Outlet Shopping—it's well marked. The signs
aren't huge, as you would expect in America, but you aren't
in America, and for Italy, it's a miracle there are signs at all.

I have only visited from Bolonga, but the mall is more or
less equidistant between Milan and Bologna. For my driving
style, I'd say that's an hour from either southern Milan, or once
you are out of town and well onto the road.

There is a shuttle bus between the outlet mall and the
Fidenza railroad station running every half-hour.

Stores there include **Nike; Lagostina,** the Italian kitchen and
cookware brand; **Sapo,** the Italian copycat version of LUSH
with bath bombs and other soaps and bath products; **Elena**

Miro, an Italian firm that makes large-size clothing (the poor man's Marina Rinaldi); and **Samsonite,** where I found a high-quality suitcase for 52€ ($65) to take all my new clothes with me. Among the other 80 stores: **Basetti** (linens), **Campter** (Spanish brand of casual shoes for men and women), **Furla** (Italian handbags), and **Trussardi Jeans.** It's open daily 10am to 8pm. ✆ 0524/335-51. www.fidenzavillage.com.

CASTEL GUELFO

South and east of Bologna you are headed to a totally different factory outlet mall in Castel Guelfo. This is a tiny mall with just about 30 stores that may not be worth the trip, but it is near Locanda Solarola, a starred kitchen and farmhouse hotel, Via Santa Croce 5 (✆ 0542/670-102; www.locandasolarola. com). The farmhouse is open for lunch and for dinner and is open on Sundays, making it the perfect accompaniment for a half-day at this outlet mall. There are also a handful of rooms at the farmhouse, so you may want to simply move in.

CASTEL GUELFO OUTLET
Via del Commerce 20/D.

To get here, take the autostrada A14 from Bologna south toward Rimini and exit at Castel S. Pietro Terme. You'll see the mall. I have already said it was small and want to reiterate that it is small. This may not be worth your time. It's open Sunday from 10am to 8:30pm. ✆ 0542/670-762. www. outletcastelguelfo.it.

VERONA

As I have gotten into a Shakespeare thing with the discovery of my hidden Italy, it will come as no surprise that I am smitten with Verona, home of those Two Gentlemen as well as

Romeo and Juliet. Juliet's house is a major tourist attraction—right off the main shopping street, thank you very much—and is filled with graffiti and love notes. Perhaps there are shopping tips there too.

Getting There

If you consider the boot shape of Italy as a capital letter T, then Verona lies just east of where the T crosses. This means it's just north of Bologna and between Milan and Venice on the east-west axis.

You can get there by train, car, or plane. In fact, the airport is one of the new keys to low-cost Italy and is served by RyanAir.

Getting Around

If you are limiting your visit to beautiful downtown metro Verona, you can walk—driving is to be avoided.

If your travels include other nearby big cities—even places such as Padua—you can also visit on the train. Venice is best reached on the train because of the parking difficulties.

Should you want to strike out for the area rich in factories and, therefore, outlets, or the nearby wine country, you will need a car. In case you aren't that into it, far be it from me to mention that you are in the gorgeous Lake Garda district, that tons of vineyards are all around you, or that the towns stretching from Verona to Venice are filled with factories—you can shop your way right into Marco Polo International Airport outside Venice if you so please. The area specializes in shoes and eyeglasses, but I visited the Bottega Veneta outlet store inside the factory in Vicenza and a Giorgio Armani outlet store in the middle of nowhere but not far at all. Read on.

Please note that I drove to Verona from Venice—an easy and pleasant drive on a good highway—but was lost in Verona for a full hour because of one-way streets, Roman city planning, pedestrian-only thoroughfares, and stern, but handsome,

Verona

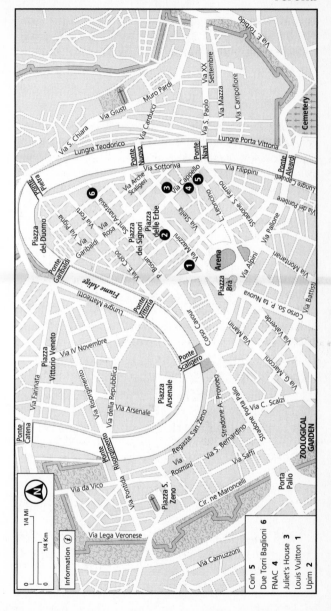

Cemetery

Via E. Torbido

Via XX Settembre

Via Mazza

Via S. Paolo

Via Campofiore

Via S. Chiara

Muro Pardi

Via Giusti

Via Carducci

Lungre Porta Vittoria

Lungre Teodorico

Via Sottoriva

Via Filippini

Ponte Nuovo

Ponte Navi

Ponte Aleardi

Lungre Capuleti

Via Arche Scaligeri

Via Cappello

Sant'Anastasia

Via Stella

Via del Ponière

Ponte Pietra

Piazza del Duomo

Via Pigna

Via Rosa

Via Garibaldi

Piazza delle Erbe

Piazza dei Signori

P. Bosari

Via E. Corso

Via Mazzini

L. Leoncino

Stradone S. Fermo

Via Pallone

Via Montanari

Fiume Adige

Lungre Matteotti

Ponte Garibaldi

Ponte Vittoria

Arena

Piazza Brà

Via Alpini

Corso So. P. ta Nuova

Via Valverde

Via Battisti

Piazza Vittorio Veneto

Via Farinata

Via IV Novembre

Via Risorgimento

Via della Repubblica

Piazza Arsenale

Corso Cavour

Ponte Scaligero

Via Manin

Via G. Marconi

ZOOLOGICAL GARDEN

Ponte Catena

Via Arsenale

Regaste San Zeno

Stradone Porta Palio

Via S. Bernardino

Via C. Scalzi

Ponte Risorgimento

Via Pontida

Via da Vico

Via Rosmini

Piazza S. Zeno

Via Saffi

Porta Palio

Cir. ne Maroncelli

Via Lega Veronese

Via Camuzzoni

1/4 Mi

1/4 Km

Information

Coin **5**

Due Torri Baglioni **6**

FNAC **4**

Juliet's House **3**

Louis Vuitton **1**

Upim **2**

policemen who were quite insistent that the shortest route between two places was not a straight line. "You can't get there from here unless you are on foot" should be written on every T-shirt.

Booking In

Just like Bologna, Verona is a big fair town and hotel rooms simply don't exist when you want them, or just because you want them. If your travel agent doesn't have the fair schedule (which is set up years in advance), call your hotel of choice and ask about fairs before you begin to dream of setting head on pillow.

Fairs tend to be March through May and September through early November; opera season begins in mid-June and ends at the end of August. When it comes to the opera season, many visitors book a year in advance.

Sleeping There

DUE TORRI HOTEL BAGLIONI
Piazza Santa Anastasia 4.

Oh my, I have died and gone to heaven. Oh my, remind me to have my next honeymoon in this hotel. Oh my, don't wake me if I am dreaming. What can you say about a slightly hidden hotel in a slightly hidden city in the middle of heaven? Built into an ancient palazzo, the hotel is furnished in the grand style— my room was small, but draped in velvets and silks and charm, completed with a sleigh bed and view out to, yep, the two towers.

The hotel is on the far side of the town center but easy walking distance to all shopping and is perched at the edge of the Via Santa Anastasia where you can stroll in delight.

Don't forget PamPam pizza across the street or Enoteca (Enoteca Santa Anastasia, Via Massalongo 3b; *℗* 045/801-4448) for wines. *℗* 045/595-044. www.baglionihotels.com.

HOTEL ACCADEMIA
Via Scala 12.

I found this hotel by accident when I was lost downtown; it is in the center of everything and is seemingly the most perfect four-star hotel in town. I didn't get to spend the night because it was sold out. Friends told me that this hotel is a well-known secret address and needs to be booked in advance.

The hotel has rates for three seasons. To understand how prices change, a double room is 180€ ($225) in low season, 219€ ($274) in midseason, and 260€ ($325) in high season. This rate includes tax and breakfast, making Verona look better every minute.

The hotel is in the thick of the shopping district and is a short walk from the Roman arena; it's a palace hotel that has been modernized and does have air-conditioning as well as parking. © 045/596-222. www.accademiavr.it.

The Shopping Scene

We're talking about a medieval town that has a moderate amount of tourists (okay, I was there out of season), the house where Shakespeare's Juliet lived, and a large **Upim** store. This is a great place, and while there aren't nearly as many stores as in Bologna, and the shopping may not be as great as in other towns, what's here is fun and not your average tourist trap (TT). Come to think of it, that market in the center of town is pretty touristy; but hey, the rest is great.

One of the reasons shopping here is so much fun is that the community is wealthy; it attracts well-off shoppers and the city invests time and money in making shopping easy for others. There's even an online shopping guide at www.verona shopping.it.

Also remember that Verona is in northern Italy, not that far from Switzerland (bankers need to shop too) and in a geopolitical area that is influenced by the nearby factories. Fashion and fur talk here. And shoes don't walk, they smile. Believe me; the shoemaker's children do not go barefoot.

Insider's tip: One reason so many locals shop here is that prices, especially on designer goods, are less expensive than in nearby Venice. Venetians shop in Verona, giving you all the more reason to do so as well.

SHOPPING HOURS

Stores in Verona are open on Sundays, making this a popular shopping destination and day out for the upper middle classes from Venice and the Veneto district. You will love the people-watching. Basic Sunday hours are 11am to 7:30pm. Needless to say, Mondays are dead.

Assorted TTs and stores catering to real-people needs are open late during opera season.

SHOPPING NEIGHBORHOODS

Anatasia   This small road (Via Santa Anastasia) leads to and from the Due Torri Hotel Baglioni and the main shopping districts. In its own right, it is all that makes Verona wonderful— an almost alleyway of a street lined with mom-and-pop stores, not a chain to be found. There are antiques stores, food stores, book shops, and more. Oh yes, did I mention all the gelati stands?

Piazza Erbe   If you hadn't known the tourist era was starting by spying the beginning of the designer boutiques (see Lacoste at no. 40), the ricky-ticky-tacky street market set up in the square selling fresh fruit, limoncello, olive oil, chianti, penis-shaped pasta, and Romeo-and-Juliet key chains is a dead giveaway.

Via Mazini   This pedestrian walkway and main shopping thoroughfare is where you find most of the designer stores and fancy boutiques. If the stores aren't from major Italian brands you see everywhere, they may be branches of upmarket Venetian merchants. You will find **Max & Co., Fiorucci, Upim, Penny Black** (a division of Max Mara), **Xanaka** (a low-end clothier from the south of France), **Elena Miro, Mandarina Duck**

(made nearby), and old faithfuls such as **Gucci, Versace, Benetton, Max Mara** and **Marina Rinaldi, Tod's** and Hogan's, Geox, **Loro Piano,** and more. And not to be out done, Louis Vuitton has a huge and impressive store where Via Mazini ends across from the arena.

If you think it's all for rich yuppies, you're wrong—the Fiorucci store is enormous, the Upim is one of the largest and most complete I have ever seen, and there are stores from chains such as **Bershka, Oltre,** and **Xanaka** that specialize in low-cost hot styles. Oltre, by the way, is low-cost high fashion in large sizes. There are also many low-end French chains such as **Pimke** and **Promod.**

This street is luckily filled with banks and ATMs.

Arena   Mazini ends at the Roman theater, which is surrounded by cafes and TTs, as can be expected. Gelati? Did someone say gelati?

Cappello   Quick, what was Juliet's last name? Well, that's the clue (Capulet is the answer) for finding this shopping street as well as Juliet's house. This street is narrow and can be crowded, especially when a tour group falls on Juliet's pad. Stores are mostly Italian chains for mid- to low-end fashion rather than designer brands. But wait, that's not totally true—there's a **Timberland** store here as well as a branch of **Frette,** for linens. There's also **Armani Jeans, Armani Emporio,** and **Sisley.** At the far end of the street is a **FNAC** as well as **Coin** department store. Capulet, oops, Cappello leads away from Piazza Erbe and makes a junction with the beginning of Via Mazini. *Note:* Juliet is, of course, spelled in Italian, making it *Guilietta*.

BEYOND VERONA

The most famous town between Verona and Venice happens to be Padua. But I didn't stop there because I was headed to Vicenza and nearby factories and outlet stores. Despite the scads of outlets in the Veneto, I chose only two simple targets: Bottega Veneta in Vicenza and Giorgio Armani in Trissino, near Vicenza.

Please note that this part of Vincenza is nowhere near the historic city center.

BOTTEGA VENETA FACTORY
Viale della Scienza 15, Vicenza.

Hard to find behind an industrial gate and a handwritten sign, this store is lovely and filled with merchandise. The prices are good, considering that 320€ ($400) for a Bottega Veneta handbag is now a bargain. There are bags, shoes, small leather goods, and clothes. Also, gold, silver, and giftware such as silver-plate picture frames. Nice people. © 0444/396-504.

FACTORY STORE ARMANI
Via Stazione 93, Trissino.

Getting to this store takes a little patience, with roads and access lanes going various directions but seemingly not the way you might need them to go. This outlet is not as large as the Armani outlet in Como (see chapter 8), nor does it have nearly as much stock. Still, it's clean, neat, and easy to shop. My son needed a sports jacket and I found one, half-off of half-off or a mere 120€ ($150) with a coordinating tie for another 26€ ($33). I was thrilled with my good luck. © 0445/492-105.

INDEX

FROMMER'S® COMPLETE TRAVEL GUIDES

Alaska
Alaska Cruises & Ports of Call
American Southwest
Amsterdam
Argentina & Chile
Arizona
Atlanta
Australia
Austria
Bahamas
Barcelona
Beijing
Belgium, Holland & Luxembourg
Bermuda
Boston
Brazil
British Columbia & the Canadian
  Rockies
Brussels & Bruges
Budapest & the Best of Hungary
Calgary
California
Canada
Cancún, Cozumel & the Yucatán
Cape Cod, Nantucket & Martha's
  Vineyard
Caribbean
Caribbean Ports of Call
Carolinas & Georgia
Chicago
China
Colorado
Costa Rica
Cruises & Ports of Call
Cuba
Denmark
Denver, Boulder & Colorado Springs
Edinburgh & Glasgow
England
Europe
Europe by Rail
European Cruises & Ports of Call
Florence, Tuscany & Umbria

Florida
France
Germany
Great Britain
Greece
Greek Islands
Halifax
Hawaii
Hong Kong
Honolulu, Waikiki & Oahu
India
Ireland
Italy
Jamaica
Japan
Kauai
Las Vegas
London
Los Angeles
Madrid
Maine Coast
Maryland & Delaware
Maui
Mexico
Montana & Wyoming
Montréal & Québec City
Munich & the Bavarian Alps
Nashville & Memphis
New England
Newfoundland & Labrador
New Mexico
New Orleans
New York City
New York State
New Zealand
Northern Italy
Norway
Nova Scotia, New Brunswick &
  Prince Edward Island
Oregon
Ottawa
Paris
Peru

Philadelphia & the Amish Country
Portugal
Prague & the Best of the Czech
  Republic
Provence & the Riviera
Puerto Rico
Rome
San Antonio & Austin
San Diego
San Francisco
Santa Fe, Taos & Albuquerque
Scandinavia
Scotland
Seattle
Seville, Granada & the Best of
  Andalusia
Shanghai
Sicily
Singapore & Malaysia
South Africa
South America
South Florida
South Pacific
Southeast Asia
Spain
Sweden
Switzerland
Texas
Thailand
Tokyo
Toronto
Turkey
USA
Utah
Vancouver & Victoria
Vermont, New Hampshire & Maine
Vienna & the Danube Valley
Virgin Islands
Virginia
Walt Disney World® & Orlando
Washington, D.C.
Washington State

FROMMER'S® DOLLAR-A-DAY GUIDES

Australia from $50 a Day
California from $70 a Day
England from $75 a Day
Europe from $85 a Day
Florida from $70 a Day
Hawaii from $80 a Day

Ireland from $80 a Day
Italy from $70 a Day
London from $90 a Day
New York City from $90 a Day
Paris from $90 a Day
San Francisco from $70 a Day

Washington, D.C. from $80 a Day
Portable London from $90 a Day
Portable New York City from $90
  a Day
Portable Paris from $90 a Day

FROMMER'S® PORTABLE GUIDES

Acapulco, Ixtapa & Zihuatanejo
Amsterdam
Aruba
Australia's Great Barrier Reef
Bahamas
Berlin
Big Island of Hawaii
Boston
California Wine Country
Cancún
Cayman Islands
Charleston
Chicago
Disneyland®
Dominican Republic

Dublin
Florence
Frankfurt
Hong Kong
Las Vegas
Las Vegas for Non-Gamblers
London
Los Angeles
Los Cabos & Baja
Maui
Miami
Nantucket & Martha's Vineyard
New Orleans
New York City
Paris

Phoenix & Scottsdale
Portland
Puerto Rico
Puerto Vallarta, Manzanillo &
  Guadalajara
Rio de Janeiro
San Diego
San Francisco
Savannah
Vancouver Island
Venice
Virgin Islands
Washington, D.C.
Whistler

FROMMER'S® NATIONAL PARK GUIDES

Algonquin Provincial Park
Banff & Jasper
Family Vacations in the National
    Parks

Grand Canyon
National Parks of the American West
Rocky Mountain

Yellowstone & Grand Teton
Yosemite & Sequoia/Kings Canyon
Zion & Bryce Canyon

FROMMER'S® MEMORABLE WALKS

Chicago
London

New York
Paris

San Francisco

FROMMER'S® WITH KIDS GUIDES

Chicago
Hawaii
Las Vegas
New York City

Ottawa
San Francisco
Toronto

Vancouver
Walt Disney World® & Orlando
Washington, D.C.

SUZY GERSHMAN'S BORN TO SHOP GUIDES

Born to Shop: France
Born to Shop: Hong Kong, Shanghai
    & Beijing

Born to Shop: Italy
Born to Shop: London

Born to Shop: New York
Born to Shop: Paris

FROMMER'S® IRREVERENT GUIDES

Amsterdam
Boston
Chicago
Las Vegas
London

Los Angeles
Manhattan
New Orleans
Paris
Rome

San Francisco
Seattle & Portland
Vancouver
Walt Disney World®
Washington, D.C.

FROMMER'S® BEST-LOVED DRIVING TOURS

Austria
Britain
California
France

Germany
Ireland
Italy
New England

Northern Italy
Scotland
Spain
Tuscany & Umbria

THE UNOFFICIAL GUIDES®

Beyond Disney
California with Kids
Central Italy
Chicago
Cruises
Disneyland®
England
Florida
Florida with Kids
Inside Disney

Hawaii
Las Vegas
London
Maui
Mexico's Best Beach Resorts
Mini Las Vegas
Mini Mickey
New Orleans
New York City
Paris

San Francisco
Skiing & Snowboarding in the West
South Florida including Miami &
    the Keys
Walt Disney World®
Walt Disney World® for
    Grown-ups
Walt Disney World® with Kids
Washington, D.C.

SPECIAL-INTEREST TITLES

Athens Past & Present
Cities Ranked & Rated
Frommer's Best Day Trips from London
Frommer's Best RV & Tent Campgrounds
    in the U.S.A.
Frommer's Caribbean Hideaways
Frommer's China: The 50 Most Memorable Trips
Frommer's Exploring America by RV
Frommer's Gay & Lesbian Europe

Frommer's NYC Free & Dirt Cheap
Frommer's Road Atlas Europe
Frommer's Road Atlas France
Frommer's Road Atlas Ireland
Frommer's Wonderful Weekends from
    New York City
Retirement Places Rated
Rome Past & Present

Frommer's® Complete Guides

The only guide independent travelers need to make smart choices, avoid rip-offs, get the most for their money, and travel like a pro.

Frommer's®

⊛**WILEY**

Available at bookstores everywhere.

Suzy Gershman's Born to Shop Guides

The Ultimate Guide for People
Who Love Good Value!

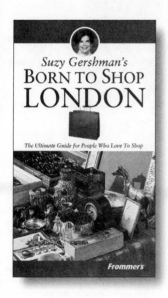

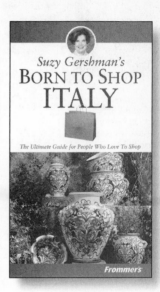

Check out the complete list of Born to Shop Guides:

- France
- Italy
- Hong Kong, Shanghai & Beijing

- London
- New York
- Paris

Frommer's®

Available at bookstores everywhere.

Frommer's® **Portable Guides**

Destinations in a Nutshell

- Frommer's Portable Acapulco, Ixtapa & Zihuatanejo
- Frommer's Portable Amsterdam
- Frommer's Portable Aruba
- Frommer's Portable Australia's Great Barrier Reef
- Frommer's Portable Bahamas
- Frommer's Portable Berlin
- Frommer's Portable Big Island of Hawaii
- Frommer's Portable Boston
- Frommer's Portable California Wine Country
- Frommer's Portable Cancun
- Frommer's Portable Cayman Islands
- Frommer's Portable Charleston
- Frommer's Portable Chicago
- Frommer's Portable Disneyland®
- Frommer's Portable Dominican Republic
- Frommer's Portable Dublin
- Frommer's Portable Florence
- Frommer's Portable Frankfurt
- Frommer's Portable Hong Kong
- Frommer's Portable Houston
- Frommer's Portable Las Vegas
- Frommer's Portable Las Vegas for Non-Gamblers
- Frommer's Portable London
- Frommer's Portable London from $90 a Day
- Frommer's Portable Los Angeles

- Frommer's Portable Los Cabos & Baja
- Frommer's Portable Maine Coast
- Frommer's Portable Maui
- Frommer's Portable Miami
- Frommer's Portable Nantucket & Martha's Vineyard
- Frommer's Portable New Orleans
- Frommer's Portable New York City
- Frommer's Portable New York City from $90 a Day
- Frommer's Portable Paris
- Frommer's Portable Paris from $90 a Day
- Frommer's Portable Phoenix & Scottsdale
- Frommer's Portable Portland
- Frommer's Portable Puerto Rico
- Frommer's Portable Puerto Vallarta, Manzanillo & Guadalajara
- Frommer's Portable Rio de Janeiro
- Frommer's Portable San Diego
- Frommer's Portable San Francisco
- Frommer's Portable Savannah
- Frommer's Portable Seattle
- Frommer's Portable Sydney
- Frommer's Portable Tampa & St. Petersburg
- Frommer's Portable Vancouver
- Frommer's Portable Vancouver Island
- Frommer's Portable Venice
- Frommer's Portable Virgin Islands
- Frommer's Portable Washington, D.C.

Frommer's®

Available at bookstores everywhere.